Car~~e M~~ ~~ew S~~cial Work ~~A Critical Analysis~~

9606834

16.98

LCNA-

A Whiting & Birch Ltd / SCA (Education) Co-Publication

Care Management
and the
New Social Work

A Critical Analysis

Michael Sheppard

Whiting and Birch Ltd
MCMXCV

© Michael Sheppard 1995
All rights reserved. No part of this publication may be
reproduced in any form without permission. Whiting
& Birch Ltd are registered with the Publishers
Licensing Society, London, England and the Copyright
Clearance Centre, Salem Mass. USA.

Published by Whiting & Birch Ltd,
PO Box 872, , London SE23 3HL, England.
USA: Paul & Co, Publishers' Consortium Inc,
PO Box 442, Concord, MA 01742.

British Library Cataloguing in Publication Data.
A CIP catalogue record is available from
the British Library

ISBN 1 871177 77 4 (cased)
ISBN 1 871177 78 2 (limp)

Printed in England by Antony Rowe, Chippenham

Contents

Preface

Care management presents, perhaps, the greatest challenge to social work for at least twenty years. I remember being told once – I cannot recall by whom – that the changes resulting from the National Health Service and Community Care Act would have a greater impact on the provision of social care than the Seebohm Report. Whether or not this is the case, the changes are quite fundamental.

My impression is that much of the response to the development of care management has been a mixture of horror and bemusement. Social workers I have spoken to have been appalled by the apparent bureaucratisation of social care, the deprofessionalisation of many tasks they had formerly undertaken and the sense that care management is just not social work. Many people have expressed concern about the very survival of social work in this new climate of social care. Many academics, as far as I can tell, have simply wandered along behind these changes, not quite sure of what to make of them and without the insights that come from working at the coal face. Others have been hurriedly contacting their publishers to see if they can write the first practice handbook about how social workers can 'do' care management.

For myself, I have had similar feelings. However – and I have been considerably helped in this respect by my wife who is a social worker – I have increasingly felt that there are both elements of continuity and change. It is, I think, wrong to say that care management 'isn't social work'. It is also wrong to think that the provision of social care, and the environment in which social work is practiced, will not change profoundly. They will. How they change is likely to differ as between different local authorities, which will put their own stamp on care management. Nonetheless, elements of care management, it seems to me, are no more than the endorsement of good practice. I cannot see how anyone really interested in providing a good service can protest about systematically undertaken assessments in which, as far as possible, the consumer has considerable influence, and in which what is provided is reviewed and evaluated.

However, there is also a dimension of care management which involves bringing in values and beliefs which are alien to the welfare traditions which have characterised social work practice. I think many practitioners have intuitively grasped this without being absolutely clear about why they should feel this way. Furthermore, this dimension is not to be understood merely by writing a practice handbook: a 'how to do it' text (valuable though this may be for the conduct of practice). This can only be understood by exploring the origins and assumptions underlying care management. This is about the influence of the 'New Right'. It has been practically axiomatic to many in the New Right that the public sector and public sector managers perform more poorly than the private sector; that management is relatively inefficient; that the cost of welfare provision is too high; that professions are frequently a conspiracy against the public; and that the public sector could do with a good dose of the rigours of competition. The New Right's influence may ultimately wane. Their impact on the development of care management, however, cannot be doubted.

This book seeks to answer two questions: what is the impact of care management on social work? and what does social work have distinctively to offer care management? These two questions, it appears to me, are absolutely fundamental if we are to understand the place of social work in the provision of social care. Indeed, it is perhaps upon whether these questions are answered satisfactorily that the survival of social work as a generic activity will depend.

Part One provides the basis for understanding the nature of the relationship between social work and care management. This book seeks first to understand how care management is officially defined through government publications, in order to identify the key areas of care management. It then seeks to understand the 'nature' of social work, in particular with a view to understanding why social work has been 'colonised' by care management, and the extent to which it is a suitable medium for the conduct of care management. Critical analysis of concepts such as social functioning, self realisation and empowerment, reveal them to be insufficient alone as a definition of the purpose of social work. It is social work's position as an arm of social policy and all this entails (discussed in chapter 3) which allows social work to be consistent with care management.

Part Two then brings together social work and care

management within an understanding of developments in social care arising from a 'New Right' ideology. It therefore examines the (agency) context for care management (in the light of the New Managerialism), the conduct of care management (in terms of cost-benefit analysis and expected utility), and its purpose, through a critical analysis of key purposive concepts: empowerment, choice and self determination and Need alleviation. The resulting picture is of a more controlled and accountable practice, heavily underpinned by New Right ideology, with particular meanings attached to empowerment and choice (involving a core of positive notions of self determination) and what I have defined as a 'consensus-objective' notion of need.

Alongside the bureaucratisation of social care, Part Two raises the spectre of deprofessionalisation of practice. Parts Three and Four then seek to examine, in terms of its knowledge base, what social work will have distinctively to offer to care management. This is particularly important where the threat of deprofessionalisation exists, yet there is, as shown in chapter eight a clear problem about the status of applied social science knowledge, derived in part from disagreements about the status of social science knowledge in the first place. The resolution to this problems is presented in terms of the Theory of Emergent Understanding, a novel development, which involves (chapter nine) the development of an approach which I have termed 'reflexive eclecticism' and (chapter 10) 'practice led theory'. 'Practice led theory' involves three key elements, analysed in detail: the 'practice paradigm' of social work knowledge (its assumptive world), the 'principle of convergence' (between theory and practice) and that of 'adequacy of fit'. This 'practice led' approach indicates clearly that our understanding of appropriate knowledge must first be founded on a clear understanding of social work itself. That is what is meant by 'knowledge *for* social work'.

It is argued furthermore that the capacity to assess complex and possibly dangerous situations is a key aspect of social work, and that certain traditional social work approaches lend themselves well to care management. These are interpersonal skills, social systems and social supports and task centred practice. It is argued that social work has a clear place in the professional area of care management and that it is based on their capacity to carry out, with some expertise, these three traditional approaches to practice. The final chapter brings together the main themes of the book and draws conclusions about the extent to which high level education is necessary to provide social work with the professional basis for practice.

The arguments presented in this book are developmental and hence the different sections are closely related to each other. Thus, the constraints of practice, and the knowledge forms identified as appropriate for social work, develop on the basis of arguments developed earlier in the book on the social worker as state functionary, the examination of need, empowerment and choice. At the same time each part may be used discretely. For those who wish to consider the issue of need, for example, the chapter on need will provide a focus for their endeavour.

There has been a recent interest in social work in terms of post modernism. This is, at present, limited, with British publications restricted (as far as I know) to three articles in leading journals, by Howe (in the *British Journal of Social Work*, 1994, 24, 6), Parton and Pardeck et al (in *Social Work and Social Sciences Review*, 1994, 5, 2). This issue is, of course, complex, and one post modernist will not necessarily hold the same views as another. Any comments made will, therefore, be only of a most general nature.

While some aspect of the analysis in this book (e.g. the emphasis on reflexive eclecticism) may appeal to some of this (post-modern) tendency this is not a central concern of the book. This is not to suggest that uncertainty and challenge does not in some respects pervade current social developments. Care management, it seems to me, does not need to be understood in terms of some post-modern fragmentation of areas formerly the occupational domain of social work. Other occupations - psychologists, community psychiatric nurses and so on - clearly have some areas where their skills overlap with those of social work. Care management simply provides the organisational framework in which this becomes rather more open and obvious, as these occupations, like social workers may be care managers. There is, indeed, a clear link (Part 2) between the development of care management and New Right ideology, which does not require reference to some post-modern condition. It is plausible, furthermore, that some areas of work formerly undertaken by social workers simply do not require social work skills and knowledge. If social workers are withdrawn from these areas, this may reflect a better use of resources.

Likewise, a cursory examination of the history of social work and its knowledge base would demonstrate that 'knowledge uncertainty' and dispute in social work has little to do with some newly discovered post modern condition but has been a perennial problem for social work. Its origins lie less in a recently developed scepticism about professional knowledge and authority than in the essentially contested ground of social science epistemology. That much is obvious in chapters four and nine. Social work, furthermore, simply cannot exist in a moral vacuum. The nihilism suggested as a characteristic of some post-modern analysis (e.g. by Parton) simply will not do for social work. Either social work possesses some clear ethical commitment or it is nothing (on this see chapters six and seven). Indeed, the relativism which appears at times to be implicit in some influential social work publications (even CCETSW Paper 30) is, in the end, incompatible with social work. If all morality is relative, we have no ethics at all. In the end it is Kant and not Derrida to whom the sensible and consistent social worker should appeal.

It must be recognised that social work, as an arm of social policy, has always reflected a particular position, or set of positions in relation to those areas of social concern which have been delegated to social workers. Many commentators, have noted an 'in practice' commitment to a consensus ideology and an individualistic approach. These positions have been, and indeed are, contestable. The very existence of State social work, however, is testimony, to a particular commitment, a particular way (or range) of ways of viewing the phenomena which are the concern of social work. It is the link between the influence of New Right ideology on the delivery of welfare services, the state delegated nature of the social worker's role and authority, and the possibilities presented for a distinctive position within care management, that the development of a 'New' social work is considered.

Not everyone will agree with the ideas presented here. I hope, however, that practitioners, students and others in management and higher education, will find these ideas stimulating and helpful. I think if care management has shown us anything, it is that social work is really an arm of social policy, and that some of the more grandiose fantasies presented in the past are not really viable in relation to social work. It is important that social workers, their managers and those involved in social work training hang on to this. I have been greatly helped in writing this book by Norman Jenkins who read an early version of Chapter 10 and by David Stanley, who brought his expertise to his comments on Chapter 9. While I am grateful to them for their comments, I alone am responsible for what follows.

The reader will probably notice that I use the (long established) term 'client' in Part One, but that after this, and particularly after chapter 5, I use the term 'consumer'. This reflects both an awareness of the importance of these labels and my own personal preference for the term client. I think 'client' for all its deficiencies, is a respectful way to term those people with whom social workers work. Terms like 'consumer' and 'customer' create images of popping into Woolworths for some toys. I have always, furthermore, thought that the term 'user' was widely employed as a term of abuse ('Oh that's George. Watch him, he's a bit of a "user"'). Yet, as is demonstrated in this book, these terms have a deep significance. Those who employ the term consumer or customer in the current environment are likely, however unintentionally, to be drawing on the language of the New Right.

Since I began the task of writing this book, my daughter Lauren has been born. She is now (September, 1994, 17 months old) and she has given me an unprecedented opportunity to write deep into the night and early hours of the morning. For this I suppose I should thank her, although I am not sure that I will ever again sleep right through the night. My wife Jo has been unstinting in her support, and has added her own formidable intellect to some of my original ideas. It is to both of them that I dedicate this book.

PART ONE

CARE MANAGEMENT AND SOCIAL WORK

Chapter One

The official definition of care management

Care management has developed as part of a concern about the provision of social and health care and the costs of its provision. The Griffiths Report (1988) on which subsequent developments in care management were founded, identified two core problems to the contemporary provision of social care. The first was the disparate nature of the services responsible for social care which made proper coordination difficult. This had led to a feeling that community care was 'everybody's distant cousin but nobody's baby' (Griffiths, 1988, p iv). The second was a similar problem at the level of individual care: 'a system involving the assignment of a person in need of support to an individual carer so as to become his [sic] responsibility, is rarely made, even where it would be highly applicable' (Griffiths, 1988, p iv). In this respect Griffiths drew attention to earlier reports of the Audit Commission and the Social Services Committee, which in particular criticised the lack of adequate care plans, and designated individuals to ensure they were carried out, for individuals discharged from mental hospital. A third issue, relating specifically to residential care for older people, was the spiralling cost of this care. One major concern was to ensure that care was 'limited to a fixed maximum sum, significantly lower than at present' (Griffiths, 1988, p VII).

Care management was conceived as the means for the effective implementation of community care. The White Paper (1989) *Caring For People*, following Griffiths, stated 'community care means providing the right level of intervention and support to enable people to achieve maximum independence and control over their lives'. In order to achieve this, it was considered, social services should take the leading role in the provision of community

3

care. They would first ensure the needs of individuals within specified groups be identified, packages of care identified and services coordinated and where appropriate a specific care manager, responsible for overseeing the case, be assigned. Second, local authorities should act as purchasers of services in a mixed economy of care, involving voluntary and independent services as well as public provision.

More specifically, Griffiths (1988, p 1) stated that social services departments should, within the available resources:

- Assess the community care needs of their locality, set local priorities and service objectives, and develop local plans in consultation with health authorities in particular.
- Identify and assess individuals' needs, taking full account of personal preferences (and those of informal carers) and design packages of care best suited to enabling the consumer to live as normal a life as possible.
- Arrange the delivery of services to individuals, building first on available contributions of informal carers and neighbouring support, then the provision of domiciliary and day services, or, if appropriate, residential care.
- Act for these purposes as the designers, organisers and purchasers of non health care services, and not primarily direct providers, making maximum use of voluntary and private sector bodies to widen consumer choice, stimulate innovation and encourage efficiency.

Much of this reflects an earlier concern – voiced in the Barclay Report (1982) on the role and task of social workers – with encouraging the development and use of informal caring in the community. It is within this context that, it was conceived the care (originally case) manager should operate. Care management operates within this environment in relation to individual cases: 'Care management is the process of tailoring services to individual needs. Assessment is an integral part of care management but it is only one of several core tasks that make up the whole process'. (Dept of Health, 1991a, p 11). More broadly, the Department of Health (1991e, p 6) has defined care management as the 'method of systematically linking the process of identifying and assessing need with the arrangement, monitoring and review of service provision'.

It has been clear from the start that not all care managers need be social workers. Griffiths (1988) commented on this and in this respect reflected a view in the Barclay Report, that not all social care need be the concern of social workers. The Department of Health has expended considerable energy to defining the role and tasks of the care manager, and this has also been evident in their guides. How, however, has the role of the care manager been operationalised in official documents on care management? What is entailed in practice in care management, and what expectations exist about the way it should be carried out? We may better understand the place of social work in care management when answers have been found to these questions.

NEED

Need is absolutely central to official versions of care management. Care management involves, according to the Department of health (1991b, p 9) a transition from a service led to needs led approach: 'care management emphasise[s] adapting services to need rather than fitting people into existing services'. Need is considered a complex concept which can be defined in a number of different ways. The Practitioners' Guide (Department of Health, 1991a, p 14) defines it as:

> ...the requirements of individuals to enable them to achieve, maintain or restore an acceptable level of social independence or quality of life, as defined by the particular care agency or authority.

Need is considered a 'relative concept' ie we cannot establish an objective notion of needs. It will vary, considers the Department of Health with changes in national legislation, local policy, the availability of resources and the patterns of local demand. Need has to be defined at the local level, it should be explicit, and should distinguish clearly between needs that are a mandatory, legislative responsibility and those that are assumed as a matter of local policy (Department of Health, 1991a p 14).

Need is operationalised, for local authority purposes, into six broad categories: personal/self care; health care; accommodation; finance; education/employment/leisure; transport/access. However, need is also considered a personal concept, and this is significant in view of an emphasis on consumer choice and empowerment. 'Care management seeks to recognise the individuality of need by challenging practitioners to identify the unique characteristics of each individual's needs and develop an

individualised rather than stereotyped response to these needs'
(Dept of Health, 1991a, p 15).

According to Smale et al (1993, p 27) there is a close connection
between the presence of needs and the adequacy of the social
network. This is consistent with the government statement that
'the great bulk of community care is provided by friends, family
and neighbours' (White Paper, 1989, 1.9). Social problems arise,
Smale et al, argue, because of the malfunctioning of a network of
people. The assessment of the dependency needs of a person is
inseparable from the dependability of others. We cannot, therefore,
assume that the user is the only consumer of services. An emphasis
must be placed not only on the needs of the user, but on the needs
of the carer also. The network is both, potentially, part of the
overall evaluation of consumer need, but also a significant element
of social care provision. Hence a considerable amount of the care
manager's work may involve supporting families and dealing with
conflicts in relationships (an aspect of need). The social network is
also part of two dimensions of care provision, the other being the
formal providers of social care purchased in the care management
process (such as residential or day care).

The social network, however, does not simply have to be already
existing family and friends. Miller et al (1991) identify four types
of partnership that care managers will have with support schemes:
working with community groups; working with secondary
volunteers (from another organisation); working with existing
voluntary organisations; and setting up and working with newly
formed voluntary agencies.

EMPOWERMENT AND CONSUMER CHOICE

The rationalisation for this reorganisation, and needs led
approach, according to official guides, is the empowerment of
users and carers. One sense in which this is used is empowering
people to live as independent a life as possible. Indeed, it is the
absence of, or limits to independence, that defines a state of need.
Independence can mean independence from formal intervention.
Smale et al (1993) draw attention to extensive research results
which show a large proportion of older people in residential care
would rather not be there (Sinclair et al, 1990; Neill et al 1988) and
that many could have been maintained in their own homes with
relatively little support. They comment also (p 24) that 'it is clear
that people are normally cared for in our community by their

relatives and friends or neighbours'. A focus on the supportive capacities of the social network, while recognising the consequent burden, can facilitate in this respect consumer choice.

There is also a second sense in which empowerment is used. Instead of users and carers being subordinate to the wishes of service providers, the roles should be progressively adjusted (Dept of Health, 1991a, p 11). Empowerment, then, in this sense, clearly means giving users and carers greater power and control, relative to service providers, than was previously the case. The central issue for care management, therefore is the extent to which care managers can 'carry out assessments and deliver, or make sure somebody else delivers, a service so that customers exercise real choice' (Smale et al, 1993, p 5). Anything less than this 'runs the risk of maintaining or even increasing people's powerlessness'.

Smale et al identify a particular model underlying this emphasis on consumer choice, which they call the exchange model. Here the professional concentrates on an exchange of information between themselves, users and carers. They seek to engage all others in identifying their perceptions of the situation, its problems, availability of resources and the need for others; a definition of the problem and its resolution are arrived at as much through the consumers' initiative as the professionals'; and the professional will not, typically, lead the dialogue, as they have limited knowledge of the situation. 'People are, and always will be, the expert on themselves' (Smale et al, 1993, p 13) indicates the egalitarian dimension to the care management relationship.

Practitioners are expected to encourage participation by all users and carers to the limits of their capacity. Apart from the ethical commitment to this position, two pragmatic reasons are given: that a more passive role will only reinforce a sense of dependence and the greater the user/carer participation the more they will be committed to act on the outcome of the assessment (Dept of Health, 1991b). There may be occasions where the user is unable to represent their own interests satisfactorily, because, for example, they suffer learning difficulties. Under these circumstances, a friend, relative or carer may help them in expressing their views. Alternatively, local authorities are urged to encourage the establishment of representation and advocacy schemes where some independent person may assist the user in presenting their wishes and choices.

However, there are limits to consumer choice. Multiple need perspectives, it is recognised may exist, with differences between users, carers and other agencies involved. The care manager is urged to aim for a degree of consensus while giving the user's views the most weight. However, where there remains disagreement and 'having weighed the views of all the parties, the assessing practitioner is responsible for defining the user's needs' (Dept of Health, 1991b, p 53). Hence there is a point where power reverts back into the care manager's hands.

A second limit lies with social control. Care management, as is clear from the Practitioners' Guide involves at times social control. Practitioners need be aware of the distinction between social support and social control, where 'the former offers choices to the consumer while the latter imposes solutions'. However, this social control constitutes a major part of the social work task as care management, and we need question the relationship between claims to empowerment and the reality of social control. Obvious examples include some mental health or child protection referrals. In these circumstances, Smale et al argue (1993, p 18) 'assessment is a process in which users and carers are or are not 'empowered' to make informed choices and participate in the control of the arrangements that can be made for their care in the community'. However, this social control dimension inevitably seriously affects consumer choice, a matter which will be considered in more detail in chapter six.

THE MIXED ECONOMY OF CARE

There are two key organisational elements to care management: the split between purchasers and providers, and the mixed economy of care. The purchaser/ provider split is a shorthand for two distinct areas of work (a) the assessment of individuals' needs, the arrangements and purchase of services to meet them (care management) and (b) direct service provision (care provision). It is the former which is the focus of this book. The mixed economy of care involves the large scale extension of independent provision of social care in addition to (and frequently as a replacement for) existing publicly provided social care. This involves an alliance of 'market forces' with the 'planned economy' of social care, in which, while much care provision will be independently provided, this provision is considerably influenced by the local authority's purchasing power. Hence while social care should overall be carefully planned, the mixed economy of care seeks 'to obtain the benefits of efficiency from increased competition' (Dept of Health, 1991e, p 6).

The influence of a private market philosophy, and the extent to which this is enthusiastically embraced by some apparently unlikely sources, such as the National Institute for Social Work, is evident in the supermarket metaphor given by Smale et al (1993). They refer explicitly to the 'social services supermarket' (p 4).

> On entering the shop to acquire your package of goods...this person explains that their job is to work with you to identify your needs and to form an opinion as to what kind of package of goods you need and what resources can be called upon to obtain them. The shopping manager also explains that this supermarket no longer provides many 'goods' themselves, but the manager will contract with a supplier who does.

There is, then, a clear connection between the marketisation of social care provision and the purchaser-provider split. These, in turn, in official thinking, are prerequisites for the proper exercise of consumer choice. The care manager can act as 'agent' for the users and carers, with no personal or professional interest in one rather than another form of care except that which, in discussion with the consumers, it is in their interests to receive.

A further element lies in the capacity to develop services which will become more responsive both individually and organisationally to consumer need. This is at the local level, a service planning task. Hence in order to encourage a range of resources, through which consumer choice is encouraged, care management has to be backed by a commitment to service planning and development. The major responsibility for this should rest with staff other than care managers, either located in a separate unit, or with middle managers in the organisation. Economies of scale may dictate the need for some 'block' service contracting, but as care managers assume greater responsibility for financial management they will increasingly have flexibility to negotiate individual service contracts.

A third element is its encouragement of needs led rather than service led thinking: 'It is easy to slip out of thinking 'what does this person need?' into 'what have we got that he/she could have' (Dept of Health, 1991b, p 14). Where both the care management and provision tasks are undertaken by the same organisation or professional, then the identification, unintentional though it may be, of practitioners with existing resources, can lead to considerably less flexibility in responding to needs. This thinking, it is intended should be imaginative: 'within resource constraints, practitioners should be given full rein to their creativity in devising ways of meeting needs...clearly those who have some or all of the budget delegated to them will have greater scope to create alternatives' (Dept of Health, 1991b, p 63).

While purchasing and providing staff are to be managed and monitored separately, and at the organisational level this appears, in principle, fairly straightforward, it leads to the development of some pretty fine distinctions at the level of practice. Hence while it is recognised that there is an important counselling component to assessment in care management, and this may be carried over into the subsequent monitoring and reviewing phases, where it 'shades into a therapeutic intervention in its own right' (Dept of Health, 1991a, p 35) it should be regarded as a service to be provided by a different practitioner. How far such a distinction is sustainable in the real world of practice is another matter, and this will be considered further in chapter eleven.

Nonetheless, there is some recognition of the dangers of a complete split between purchaser and provider functions. According to the Managers' Guide (Dept of Health, 1991a, p 22):

> ...the inherent danger of assessment becoming divorced from the realities of service provision will have to be countered. Agencies may introduce safeguards, such as [1] rotating staff between assessment and service providing functions, or [2] providing opportunities for practitioners to undertake both functions but in respect of different users.

At the very least, it is considered, agencies will want to maximise the extent to which assessors and service providers are able to influence each other's practice.

It is quite clear, however, that with the purchaser-provider split, the mixed economy of care is envisaged to produce a variety of competing care providers, where competition will lead to efficiency and care management will provide some direction to this resource development. However, the structure of social care may as easily produce a duopoly of non competing service providers alongside the purchasing service. Furthermore, moving a vulnerable person from one inappropriate or inadequate resource to another may not be as easy as transferring your custom from Sainsbury's to Tescos.

COSTING: MATCHING NEEDS TO RESOURCES

Needs may be central to care management, but so too is the issue of costing. Efficiency in service provision is quite consistent with the marketisation of social care (with an implicit assumption that previous approaches were less efficient). Agencies should 'strive to improve their cost effectiveness' (Dept of Health, 1991b, p 63). The common aim of all care management is to produce a quality service as cost effectively as possible within an agreed timescale. To achieve this aim practitioners are expected to be firm in setting standards, costs and deadlines and rigorous in holding service providers to account (Dept of Health, 1991b, p 73).

Although not in any sense explicit in this respect, care management is committed to the maximisation of consumer utility ie that consumers should experience maximum need satisfaction within the constraints of a particular budget. Hence practitioners are expected to establish users' wishes and the costs of the selected options of social care provision. The costs are expected to be reconciled with existing resource provision (the available budget). There is a concern with equity in this respect. It is expected that agencies issue guidelines to care managers on the level of expenditure appropriate to different needs in order to ensure consistency of resource allocation.

The care management process, therefore requires costing of the care plan. This should at the very least involve indicative costing to aid in improving agency cost effectiveness. Where practitioners have budget authority it is 'vital' that practitioners provide an accurate costing of the care plan. Additionally some assessment of financial means of the user will be required. Local authorities, within their discretion, are encouraged to levy on services other than care management and assessment, subject to the users' ability to pay (Dept of Health, 1991d). As a point of good practice, therefore, it is considered that no user should agree to a care plan until they have been advised in writing of any charges involved.

PERSONNEL AND PROCESS ISSUES

The Griffiths Report (1988) emphasised that care management should not be equated with social work as it, at the time, existed. Not all care managers would be social workers, and the purchaser provider split, it was thought meant that some, at least, of the traditional social work role would be divided up. Much of the organisation of care management has involved attempts to delineate different levels of assessment, and a concomitant distinction between personnel levels involved in the care management process.

Care management seeks to develop a system whereby the service outcome is not presupposed in the initial assessment response. In pursuit of this a range of vocationally and professionally qualified staff are required by social services in order to assess needs of differing levels of severity and complexity. Beyond this there should be defined access to a range of specialist staff or to assessment staff in other agencies. This is intended to reflect the wide range and severity of needs confronted by social services. Local authorities it is stated, should seek to identify triggers whereby likely needs other than those stated in the referral might be identified. These might include, for example, a history of mental illness or addiction to alcohol or drugs. These could be used to indicate where a more complex assessment than might initially be indicated would be needed. It is possible, from the Department of Health classification to identify three occupational levels for care management.

- The first level of response is Administrative or Receptionist. This is appropriate when assessments are simple, needs are simple and defined and service provision is straightforward (eg disabled car badge).
- The second level is that of vocationally qualified or specialist ancillary staff. Vocationally qualified staff may be involved in limited or multiple assessment. The needs would be, respectively, either limited, defined and low risk, or a range of limited, defined and low risk needs. The kind of service outcome could involve low level domiciliary support, assistance with meals, chiropody and basic nursing. Simple specialist assessment would involve defined, specialist and low risk needs, and the service outcome might, for example, be simple disability equipment.
- The third level is that of professional assessment. This falls into three categories. The first, complex specialist assessment, relates to ill defined, complex and high risk needs and a service outcome might be, for example, home adaptation. The second is complex assessment. Here there are ill defined, interrelated, complex, volatile and high risk needs, and the service outcome might be speech therapy. The third is comprehensive assessment. Here needs are ill defined, multiple, interrelated, high risk and severe. The service

outcome might be family therapy, substitute care, intensive and domiciliary support.

It should be emphasised that even at the level of professional assessment, not all care management is likely to be undertaken by social workers. This is quite evident when it is noted that some service outcomes include home adaptation or speech therapy, which involve the assessment of needs which other professionals are better qualified to identify. It should be apparent, therefore, that care management cannot be regarded as a social work activity *per se*, and that social work therefore has to justify its place amongst other groups performing care managerial roles. Why, for example, can tasks not be performed by less qualified individuals (at the vocational level)? even at the professional level, what does social work have to offer that is distinctive from other professionals? Social work no longer can count on a pre-eminent role in social care, and this has been reflected in the employment and use of individuals who are not social workers, in roles which were formally undertaken by social workers. Social work clearly has to justify its place amongst other groups performing care managerial roles.

There are, however, two associated developments which relate closely to personnel issues and professional authority. Care management seeks to devolve authority to the lowest possible level while at the same time ensuring accountability. Hence care managers are encouraged to 'have a more entrepreneurial approach and to have the confidence to innovate' (Dept of Health, 1991a, p 36). Such devolution, if it is to be meaningful, should include some measure of financial authority, including holding individual budgets. Devolution may go all the way down to the care manager, but it may also rest with, or be shared with the care manager's immediate superior. Where responsibility is shared between practitioners and their first line manager on a team basis, it is envisaged that this will provide mutual support for the development of new skills and the testing out of new ways of working.

Along with increased responsibility, however, goes increased accountability. Accountability, it is expected will be in two directions: to the consumer and to the employing agency. There are two ways in which accountability to the consumer is achieved. The first is through an open and available complaints procedure which a consumer may use where they are dissatisfied with the service they have received. The second is an involvement at all stages of the care management process in the process of decision making and evaluation of the services received. Hence, for example, consumers 'should be given encouragement to play an active part in the [monitoring] process' (Dept of Health, 1991b, p 77). This relates both to their individual case and also to the corporate monitoring of services through, for example, user/carer consultative groups.

Accountability to the agency occurs through the formal means of line management and organisational systems developed to monitor the quality of services provided (Dept of Health 1991a). Hence practitioners are expected to be held to account for outcomes achieved with users (rather than the process involved in obtaining that result). The whole process of care management is self consciously designed to encourage systematic professional activities. It is expected that skills should be developed in specifying outcomes and monitoring their achievement through the care management process. Greater importance is expected to be attached to the systematic recording by practitioners of their activities. Furthermore, computers may be used to monitor widely and systematically the achievements of action plans.

QUALITY ASSURANCE, SKILLS
AND THE PROCESS OF CARE MANAGEMENT

Care management is a process which does not simply seek to separate assessment from service provision, but which seeks to systemise the assessment, review and evaluation of the social care provided. There are seven stages identified: publishing information, determining the level of assessment, assessing need, care planning, implementing the care plan, monitoring and reviewing. It is clear from this list that care management is considered a step by step process which is envisaged as a technical activity: one in which the technique of conducting care management is of considerable importance. The 'technicalisation' of social care assessment is evident from attempts to identify types of need which may be assessed (identified above in the section on need). It is also evident in suggested formats for comprehensive assessments, which are highly prescriptive.

However, the care management *process* is itself prescriptive, and this is technicalised in two particular ways: in the demand for precision in the identification of need and cost of services, and in the assessment and review of services provided. Hence the

assessment of need (stage three) includes the practitioner in clarifying expectations, determining eligibility of consumers for services, setting priorities, agreeing objectives (considered 'the key to effective care management' (Dept of Health, 1991b, p 55) and recording the assessment. Care planning (stage four) includes discussing options, establishing preferences, costing the care plan and establishing financial means, agreeing service objectives. Stage seven, 'Reviewing', includes reviewing the achievement of care plan objectives, evaluating the quality of care provided, reassessing current needs and revising care plan objectives. This technical approach is underwritten by a range of proformas which must be completed whose design is profoundly influenced by the care management process as outlined in government guidelines. It is a means of 'channelling' the process of assessment and review in a particular way.

Obviously this approach requires practitioners to be proficient in skills of assessment and evaluation. Alongside this, however, they are required to manifest appropriate interpersonal skills. Smale et al (1993) indicate a number of these, all of which will be familiar to social work practitioners. These include authenticity, empathy, and respect as interpersonal skills. They also include, as patterning and arranging skills:

- the skills of marginality (the capacity to join with people but remain impartial);
- challenging (confronting people with behaviours obstructing need resolution);
- conceptualisation (the ability to pattern and make sense of data in whichever form it is presented);
- reframing (the ability to help redefine circumstances in ways which lead to problem resolution);
- social care planning (the ability to contribute towards understanding and systematically planning responses to pattern of behaviour which precipitate and perpetuate social problems).

Quality assurance is expected to be carried on alongside this process of care management and social care provision. It operates in two ways: in focusing on the quality of service provided by the care manager (and is in this respect linked to accountability) and in the social care provision given to consumers. Local authorities are expected to identify and publish in their guide to assessment, the quality by which procedures should be monitored (Dept of

Health, 1991a, p 48). This should help users and carers know what standard of service to expect, to enable them, if necessary, to make representations under the complaints procedure. It should also provide information by which staff will know the standards by which their performance will be measured. In examining the quality of service provided by the authority as a whole a checklist is suggested, including, for example, economy (time in producing care plans); effectiveness (number of users satisfied with the outcome of assessment); degree of choice; collaboration with other agencies; and levels of expertise and number of assessments completed by different 'levels' of staff.

This quality assurance is closely linked to service planning. Care management is considered most useful when a range of resources provide choice for the user. Care management must therefore be backed by a commitment to service planning and development, which is primarily the responsibility of staff other than care managers. The development and contracting of services involves also some quality assurance. This requires all agencies to develop, monitor and maintain specific quality standards. Statements on standards are expected to be incorporated into the specifications for all services. Standards of practice and monitoring mechanisms are expected to be developed by all local authorities to ensure that all staff with care management responsibilities are offering a quality service These should include factors such as response times, sharing information, user and carer involvement, open recording and decision making according to specific criteria (Dept of Health, 1991a, p 69).

CONCLUSION

Clearly care management embraces a particular philosophy of social care. Indeed, it remains to be seen how successful it is by its own terms of reference. How far, for example, is there a conflict between the 'efficiency' and 'quality assurance' dimensions of care management? How effectively will it bring in competition rather than two monopolies (of care managers and care providers)? These are, of course, empirical questions which may only be resolved in the fullness of time. There are, however, questions relating to the 'philosophy' of care management – what kind of social care system that has been devised – which can be examined in more detail. This entails going beyond the bland commitments and practice prescriptions of the official guides to a more analytic understanding of what practitioners are really committing themselves to when they undertake care management.

It is important to realise that, as written in official documents, information about care management has something of the quality of a manifesto. It is possible to get at the main dimensions of care management but much of what is written represents assertions or expectations about care management rather than actual outcomes. This is, of course, necessarily the case, given its early stage of development. However, we may, even at this stage, subject care management to close conceptual scrutiny. *Criticism*

A number of themes have emerged from this chapter which will be explored in the following chapters. Care management involves a strong emphasis on the concepts of need and empowerment and consumer choice. What, however, when we subject this to greater scrutiny, does this actually mean for the provision of social work? A number of measures have been taken for the technicalisation of services and increased accountability. What does this imply about the professional status of social work, their degree of independence of action and their relationship with the bureaucracy in which care managers are situated? Is it about devolution of responsibility, or a subtle form of managerial control and deprofessionalisation of practice. There is a commitment to a market in social care and efficient use of resources. How far does this reflect a tradition more associated with private enterprise, alien and inimical to welfare practice? what are the implications of the more managerial environment on social work practice? Is this the New Right finally marching into social care?

Before we examine these issues, and the implications for the professional status and practice of social work, it is first necessary to examine in more detail the nature of social work itself, focusing in particular on the extent to which it contains elements which make it adaptable to the care management environment.

Chapter Two

Normative concepts of social work

The definition of social work – of what it is centrally about – is not something which has traditionally commanded a great deal of consensus. Indeed, this is an issue which has frequently not generated a clear answer at all. To ask what medicine is about might generally lead to a quick answer: the promotion of health. To do the same about social work might generate an embarrassed silence or comments to the effect that any kind of definition is elusive with such a complex 'animal' (Huntington, 1981; Butrym, 1976).

Nevertheless, there have been clear attempts to address this issue and these represent different, and competing, traditions within social work. This chapter will seek to examine these different approaches with reference, in particular, to the extent to which they present an understanding of social work which fits comfortably with developments in care management.

SOCIAL WORK AND SOCIAL FUNCTIONING

Bartlett's seminal work emphasised the importance of the development of concepts which promotes synthesis of thinking if we are to make sense of social work as a distinct enterprise. We might add also that those concepts should help identify what is distinctive about social work if it is to be clearly distinguished from other enterprises such as psychotherapy and counselling. The key concept in Bartlett's thinking is that of social functioning. It is this concept which, she thinks, most adequately fits with the 'person in environment' (or person in situation) approach of social work. It should be clear at the outset that social functioning relates to the purpose of social work: social work is about promoting social functioning. This is centrally related to our developing understanding of this concept: 'as more adequate knowledge regarding social functioning is built up by the profession, practitioners will be better able to foresee the possible and probable consequences of the various patterns of exchange between people and environment' (Bartlett, 1970, p 111 cf Butrym, 1976).

Social functioning is presented as a concept wide enough to embrace all aspects of practice, yet precise enough to distinguish social work from other activities. At its most abstract level, Bartlett thinks (1970, p 102) it refers to the interaction of people in the environment. There are two central 'sub concepts'. Tasks are activities which people may have to fulfil in life such as child rearing, transition from hospital to home and so on. Task performance may relate to a person's innate abilities, a lack of opportunity to learn appropriate behaviour or to environmental disadvantage (creating stress). The other concept is coping. When the demands of the environment are excessive in relation to a person's coping capacities, they may become helpless or overwhelmed. Poverty, racial discrimination, lack of access to jobs and so on can lead to alienation and anxiety. Social workers are concerned with the balance between people's coping efforts and environmental demands. As such social workers may focus both on the individual and their environment with a view to improving social functioning.

Bartlett is not alone in her concern with social functioning. For Goldstein (1973) improved social functioning is a matter of social learning. Social work becomes the means 'by which a person can work out, find alternatives for...[and] deal with conditions...which interfere with productive social living...[it] provides a context in which the possibilities of improved social learning may be maximised' (Goldstein, 1973, p 5). Pincus and Minahan (1973) build on Bartlett's work, and in particular the concept of 'life tasks'. They stipulate in more detail what they regard to be the social functioning concerns of social work. They are to:

1. enhance the problem solving capacities of people
2. link people with systems that provide them with resources, services and opportunities
3. promote the effective and humane operation of these systems *and*
4. contribute to the development and improvement of social policy.

In both Goldstein and Pincus and Minahan's models there is a shift to a more interactionist model from one which focuses primarily on the individual. The effect of this, they think, is to encourage the practitioner to look for problems and needs arising from this interaction rather than solely within the person requesting intervention. However, there is a failure to explicate how the social context of practice might be better understood (particularly in relation to social theory) and hence a failure to provide an explanation to account for the nature of the interdependence between the individual and his or her social location. While, therefore, a greater emphasis is placed on social environment the central locus of intervention tends to be around the person in this environment with a greater emphasis on an individualist approach than suggested by the authors.

There is, indeed, remarkably little sociological analysis – a necessary element if social workers are seriously to engage in action in the social environment – of any substance in the writings of these theorists. Surprisingly, perhaps, it is Hollis (1972), a writer heavily influenced by psychoanalysis and who is committed to a 'person in situation' rather than environmental-interactionist approach who refers most extensively to sociological ideas. In the second edition of her book *Casework: A Psychosocial Therapy*, in addition to introducing the concepts of social adjustment and systems thinking, she also refers to role and reference group. However, even this is very brief and represents a set of disconnected concepts. The ecological thinkers, it must be said, provide no more than a model, or at best a metatheory, for thinking about practice. Whittaker and Garbarino (1983) developed a four fold distinction. Microsystems represent the immediate social network of individuals – their family, school, immediate workplace and so on. Mesosystems are the relationships between these microsystems (eg between home, school and work related groups). Exosystems are situations that effect a person's development, but in which the person does not play a direct role (for example, political agencies, centres of economic control). Macrosystems are ideological and cultural expectations in a society: they reflect shared beliefs creating behavioural patterns. However, these ideas have practically no explanatory value and hence provide little guidance at the strictly theoretical level.

There are further problems with the concept of social functioning. It is difficult, as Platt (1981) has observed, to conceptualise social functioning or social adjustment without some reference to role performance. This, however, has a tendency towards a consensus and individualised notion of social functioning. If we are to measure role performance, how do we do so without some reference to a generalised notion of the rights duties and expectations of that role? The consensus commitment is largely unstated, but reflected in the paucity of sociological analysis which accompanies the discussion of social functioning. Furthermore adjustment to role fails to recognise the deep ideological disagreements about whether a particular role is in the individual's interest in the first place. This is most obvious in feminist criticisms of traditional role stereotypes and their association with depression. Where, for example social functioning in a mother is measured by their performance of the traditional role, we may question whether this is an approach which is in the client's interests at all.

Finally the concept of social functioning possesses a generality which renders it difficult to be applied specifically to social work. Social workers are largely involved with relatively specific areas of human life, and these generally appear in legislation (such as child abuse, mental illness and offending behaviour). Poor social functioning might be a label applied to someone performing poorly at work and in their relationship with their colleagues, or to a tramp who chooses to be 'on the road'. Neither would be referred for social work help *simply because* they were a tramp or because they did not get on with their colleagues. Social functioning, in other words, lacks the specificity required to provide an adequate definition of the purposes of social work.

MEANING AND SELF REALISATION

The measurement of social functioning, therefore, in the end depends upon a conception of role. This provides a conceptual representation of the place of an individual in society, in terms of sets of rights and duties appropriate to the role This has been criticised by a group of social work theorists who view it as an essentially arid or stunted view of social work clients (Keith Lucas, 1972; Jordan, 1979; England, 1986; Ragg, 1977; Wilkes, 1981). This is a group who variously describe themselves as centrally concerned with persons, meaning, or more piously, helping. At the heart of this is a view of humans as constituting something more than their roles. If roles represent sets of rights and responsibilities, personhood – the idea of individuals as people or persons – emphasises that individuals have the capacity to decide whether or not to take on particular roles, or how, if these roles are taken, these roles are performed. It is a concept of individual responsibility which is most evident in Existential writing, which has exercised considerable influence on this school of social work thought (Ragg, 1977; Picardie, 1980; Wilkes, 1981). Satre's concept of 'bad faith' refers to circumstances where the person surrenders their individuality entirely to their role – they become nothing more than the role they are performing (Satre, 1948). This is a particularly abject surrender for Existentialists who consider humans to be entirely capable of making themselves. They are free to choose the kind of person they will be by the decisions they make. They are unrestrained by some fixed human nature or other external cause: 'Man [and presumably women!] is nothing else but that which he makes himself. That is the first principle of Existentialism' (Kauffman, 1957, p 289).

The emphasis, then, is on humans as autonomous, or potentially autonomous, creatures, able to take responsibility for their own life and the resolution of their problems. If people possess the power to take control of their lives, it is the social worker's responsibility to help them to do so. This notion of helping represents the more idealised conception of social work often presented by those aspiring to become social workers (and frequently heard at University interviews for places on courses!). It focuses centrally on the client as determinant of the aims of the social work process and the social worker as helper or facilitator of this process. She is the 'good guy', whose only concern is the best interests of the client.

This is not only, however, the sentiment of the well intentioned newcomer. It is an approach taken by some of the most experienced of practitioners. Keith Lucas (1973, chapter 1), for example, emphasises a key aspect of helping to be giving: help is something given by one person (the social worker) to another (the client). It may be defined in terms of *what* is given (material or money help, advice or emotional help). The other side of this helping process is the capacity of the client to make use of this help. Yet, as Jordan (1979) points out, this is, at least in part, a function of the person of the helper. It may not always be clear to the client what these qualities are, but 'somehow, without knowing why, I shall feel better after I've talked to him because I shall not have escaped from anything or twisted anything...but I shall have been recognised, treated as real, by a fellow human being' (Jordan, 1979, p 26).

What, then, is the purpose of this help? the two key, related, purposes evident in this school of thought are, first, self realisation and second, a search for meaning. The issue of self fulfilment or self realisation is a complex one which will be more fully considered in a chapter six. Amongst these thinkers it involves notions of individuals becoming what they have the potential to become. Writers such as Rogers have a fairly straightforward (on the surface) approach to this: for him the individual is best placed to understand him or herself rather than some professional expert (Peck and Whitlow, 1975). This means that – provided they are honest with themselves – it is the individual who knows what they should aim for to achieve self fulfilment.

Keith Lucas (1973) makes a great deal of self fulfilment. For him, this is antithetical to some restricted notion of social functioning. It is, he thinks (p 13), quite different from forcing conformity on a person. Conformity (as in role performance) has no claim to be the goal of helping. Rather it allows clients to explore themselves and come to conclusions which they find satisfactory *for themselves*. This approach emphasises that help is something that occurs in the self. It has to do with personal growth and change. This is an individualising approach: if we are talking about helping someone, we are talking about that someone, an individual, and the change that may or may not occur in them.

Underlying the approach involving a search for meaning is that we live in a world of subjects: of conscious sentient beings who seek to make sense of their world and their experiences. A consequence of this is that the social world, involving subject to subject relations, is one of intersubjective meaning. Where one person can be said to understand what another is telling him, this is the case of shared meaning. Language is essential to shared meaning and shared understanding of the world. Imperfect though it may be language allows us to describe, and convey to others, our perceptions of situations which concern us, our feelings about our situations, our reasons for our actions and so on. Talking is clearly a central part of the social work process. England (1986) emphasises in this context the importance of understanding others. This achievement of 'accurate empathy' – no easy task – is crucial since it is only through the experience of being understood that the suffering individual can go on to transcend the distress and despair which engulfs them. This empathy is achieved largely intuitively and spontaneously, yet ties in to our essential humanity. It is because we all suffer happiness, sadness, despair and joy that we are able to recognise such emotions in others. We may not have experienced the same event that has befallen the client, but we can understand the kind of emotions which accompany it and this is critical to our understanding of the meaning of these events for clients.

While all this is laudably altruistic, this set of views is as important for what is left unsaid as what is actually said. Two key problems exist. First, it is a view which is either untrammelled by the limitations placed on social work by its agency responsibilities or it is laced with the same consensus assumptions underlying the social functioning view. Social workers, at a personal level, may want to help the client grow in their own, self defined way. But it is not an individual's personal agenda which social workers are employed to work on. To be clear on purpose is to be clear about role, and social workers have a number of agency responsibilities – child protection, working with young offenders, compulsory admission assessments in mental health – which they must carry out, and which to a considerable degree defines their work.

Of course, if everybody (including the client) agrees this is their aim then the client's personal agenda will coincide with the social worker's agency responsibilities. This again represents a consensus view of society. We would all have a clear idea of what it is to be a self fulfilled human being and this idea would command widespread, if not universal, support. This will not always be so (and this is axiomatic for those who adopt conflict models of society), however, and where they clash it is the agency responsibilities which must take precedence.

Second, this view does not take proper account of the related issue of the authority roles frequently required of social workers: the social control functions which are an essential aspect of child protection or mental health work. Social control may possess less of a 'feelgood' element than helping for social workers themselves, but without being fully aware of this social work, and its purposes, are not being properly understood.

PROMOTING SOCIAL CHANGE: MARXIST SOCIAL WORK

A number of writers have considered the individualism of traditional social work practice to provide an inadequate base for that practice, and have sought to use Marxist theory in a positive way (Bolger et al 1981; Simpkin, 1979; Jones, 1983; Corrigan and

Leonard, 1978). While some Marxist historians recognise the welfare state, at least in part, as a victory for working class agitation, it is also considered by Marxist social work writers as part of the machinery of class control. Traditional social work emphasises client care, empathy, respect for persons and the like, but its real purpose is a systems conserving enterprise in which the inequality and domination of disadvantaged groups is perpetuated in favour of dominant social groups (Galper, 1975).

Indeed, Leonard concludes that the history of social work and social work education is one, at least in part, of 'massive ideological distortion' (Leonard, 1975). For him, the proclamation of humanist values is largely fraudulent because it prescribes goals which are impossible in the capitalist system. It serves, in fact, a mystifying function, encouraging a misplaced allegiance from people who have a deeply felt commitment to these values. On this analysis, goals like self fulfilment or self realisation are quite simply unachievable because the social circumstances for their achievement do not exist. The goal of social functioning, furthermore, represents no more than the encouragement of social conformity.

This perception of social work is based on a broad analysis of society. Marxism, according to Leonard (1975b) represents a more comprehensive analysis of the human condition than alternative explanations, because, through the analysis of society and its structures, it is able to account for more than these alternatives. At the core of this analysis are two key elements: the analysis of class and class conflict and the examination of the role of the state.

According to Corrigan and Leonard (1978) all aspects of social life, and social problems in particular, may be understood in terms of the dominant mode of production and the domination of one class by another. The determining element of the societal superstructure of social and political institutions and ideology is the economic base. Capitalism's economic base throws up classes of owners (bourgeoisie) and workers (proletariat), the former being in an essentially exploitative relation with the latter. Capitalism, with its emphasis on individualism, competition and inequality permeates all aspects of social life. It throws up a vast range of problems which are experienced by a wide range of people, but which social workers confront on an individual basis. In this context, it is the exploited group, the working class, which represents the progressive force in society.

The state is not neutral in this class struggle. It reflects and propounds the long term interests of the ruling class. This includes the creation of a welfare state which, by its ameliorating impact on the worst effects of capitalism, reduces the potential for revolutionary activity (Miller and Neususs, 1978). It also serves an ideological function, perpetuating the interests and hegemony of the ruling class. Hence, in relation to social problems and the central concerns of social work, an increasing emphasis on social pathology as a means of explaining these problems has developed. This, of course, draws attention away from structural causes of these problems.

Unlike the rational emphasis on individual change, the radical programmatic of Marxists defined positive change in terms of winning more resources for underprivileged and oppressed groups and raising client consciousness. Its ultimate goal, however, transcended these more limited aims. The welfare state, it was argued, cannot solve the social problems of today without the abolition of the capitalist system itself. It is this, therefore, which Marxist social workers should aim for.

How is this goal to be achieved? Crucial to Marxist analysis is the position of social work within the state. For both Corrigan and Leonard (1978) and Bolger et al (1981) contradictions within the state means that social workers, despite being state employees, have room to develop a politicised form of radical practice. The state is seen to be in consistent tension, for example between its position as an instrument of class hegemony and its work ameliorating the worst effects of capitalism.

This, it is thought, leaves social work with considerable potential for autonomy. The social work role in the long struggle to overthrow capitalism has three elements. The first is the raising of consciousness, or conscientisation, a concept drawn from Friere (1972). Essentially, this is the development of social and political consciousness in clients by drawing on their experience to develop a critical reflection of their social reality, as well as the encouragement of their subsequent action on that reality. It is about developing a consciousness of oppression, and of their potential, with others, to combat this oppression. Second, social workers should be allied with the major forces in the working class. In particular, they should be members of trade unions which can both provide a defence against powerful reactionary forces and provide a context for the defence of welfare services and the development of a wider political consciousness. Third, collective action is emphasised. Within the social work organisation this involves working with colleagues in a collective manner. With clients, this involves linking with organisations representing oppressed community groups, such as local action groups and claimants' union.

For Marxists, therefore, all personal problems are public issues, and this is reflected in their practice. Halmos (1978), however, suggested that the 'personal' and the 'political' represent exclusive areas in social life where solutions reside in different domains. We cannot, he thinks, affect social change by a personalist involvement with troubled individuals. Equally, we cannot hope to affect change in individuals who are personally troubled or have problematic relations with others by focusing on structural change through the methods of the political agitator. Hence, he argues, personalising the political or politicising the personal must fail. Since social work exists within the domain of the personal it is inappropriate and counterproductive to attempt to pursue the political.

Rojek et al (1988) make two further points. They suggest that Marxists make excessive claims in respect of the freedom of social workers to act in ways which are seriously radical within the state apparatus. This would involve a widespread tendency to 'stake everything including their jobs and the security of their families in order to follow their radical aims' (p 59), something they consider to be highly implausible. They also observe that social workers are too widely considered with suspicion or outright hostility by working class clients, the very people Marxists seek to mobilise in pursuit of their cause. It is unlikely that this hostility can be dismantled to the point where the posited progressive potential of the working class can be mobilised.

EMPOWERMENT

Empowerment has become a great 'buzz' word in recent years and has had considerable impact on perceptions of practice. Indeed, as shown in chapter one, the idea of empowerment provides a crucial dimension to the official definition of care management. Despite – or perhaps because of – its popular use, empowerment can really be considered a 'second order' concept: it has a diverse range of possible meanings and it does not unproblematically, of itself, give us the precise purpose of practice. It really depends upon the assumptions about the circumstances under which an individual may be empowered. Is a person empowered when they are capable of manifesting adequate social functioning? or when they realise their true potential? or when the barriers created by an unjust society have been removed? To be empowered in a sense implied by a Marxist analysis is quite different from being empowered in a sense suggested by a functionalist analysis.

Empowerment, then, reflects the social philosophy of its particular proponents. However, it contains within it the notion that individuals who are in some sense disadvantaged or (relatively) powerless should have that power enhanced. Power itself is a multifaceted phenomenon and its examination in relation to social work practice is complex (Lukes, 1974; Gould, 1995). Nonetheless, the power concerned represents, in whichever way formulated, the power to exercise choice in a way which influences the direction of one's life (or that part which is the concern of social work practice). This consistent element in the approach to empowerment is evident in the intentions underlying notions as diverse as partnership with consumers on an individual or familial basis and areas of community oriented practice. The latter, on a group basis, involves the development of collective involvement and participation in order to influence the direction of the community (Thomas, 1985).

Put in this way – in terms of the exercise of choice – it is perhaps helpful to identify two fundamental formulations:

- Individuals (or groups) are empowered when those factors limiting or preventing them having equal opportunity to exercise (and act upon) choice are overcome.
- Individuals (or groups) are empowered when they gain a greater understanding of their 'true' interests and are able to act upon them.

Although the latter can, in principle, encapsulate the former, it is equally possible for these two approaches to reflect quite different assumptions. Drawing on Berlin (1969) we can distinguish between the 'empirical self' and the 'potential self'. With the former it is assumed that the person knows what they want (and are the best judge of what they want) and can be helped to articulate this. With the latter, matters are different. Here the focus is not in expressing current wishes, but helping the consumer reach a 'higher level' of understanding of their situation and through this are able to exercise choice based on this higher understanding. These two alternatives can be examined through two illustrations.

The empowerment alluded to in official care management documents (see chapter one) provides an example of 'empirical self' empowerment. The maximisation of choice and encouragement of individual independence provide key elements of the empowerment process. It aspires to create a non hierarchical relationship between social worker and client. The power to exercise, equally with others, choice, is a necessary ingredient for asserting one's individuality and worth as a person (Weick, 1981).

At least three key elements contribute to this non hierarchical relationship. Stigmatising disadvantaged and disabled individuals can profoundly undermine their ability to take themselves, and be taken by others, seriously. (Holdsworth, 1991). More generally two further factors contribute to disempowerment: the power of the professional to define the client and their problem and the different subjective world of client and professional which can lead to conflicting definitions (Robinson, 1978). The problem arises where the professionals 'world view' is automatically deemed to take precedence over the client's. Their 'correct' understanding is derived to a considerable degree from professional training, which is deemed to give them a deeper understanding of problems. However, Robinson (p 18) suggests the socialisation processes of training leads to a certain (professional) viewpoint which gradually blocks out other ways of seeing things. Where views of client and worker clash and where the worker has the power, the client's capacity to influence matters is considerably reduced. Hence the empowerment proposals in care management, detailed in the previous chapter, to a considerable degree, are designed to combat the power to define and act being centred on the care manager.

We can draw on an example from Feminist practice – itself a diverse school (Graham, 1991) – as an illustration of an approach enabling individuals to reach, and act upon, a 'higher level' of understanding of their circumstances. Throughout Feminist social work there is an insistence that women need to recover control over their own lives. This centrally involves appreciation of their oppression and how this affects them as individuals, and includes the development of self confidence and esteem, the better to achieve this potential. There is concern that many social work techniques perceive and assess women in ways that have no bearing on their view of the situation and what their life means to them. It is important that women should speak for themselves and that social workers should listen. As Rose (1982) points out there should be a focus on the 'subjective shared experience of oppression' and feminist social work should develop its understanding from the day to day experience of women clients and workers (Hudson, 1985).

For many women their experience of oppression can be miserable in the extreme. The psychological toll, in terms of depression, for many feminists, represents an understandable response to the oppression women experience in everyday life (Corob, 1987; Penfold and Walker, 1984). Feminist practice involves helping women reframe and reconstruct their experiences in a manner which will help give them greater control over their own lives.

This, of course, entails the development of a 'higher level' of understanding. However, what are we to make of women who are not miserable? Sibeon (1990) points out that some writers subscribe to a notion of false consciousness: an idea that an individual is mistaken because they do not have a full understanding of their true situation (and interests). Dominelli and Mcleod (1989, p 80-81), in rejecting evidence that some women may be happy with their lives refer to a mistaken sense of 'contentment'. They argue that 'the revelations from feminist work questions whether the contentment of an unknown number of women is being bought at a morally unacceptable price in terms of reinforcing a set of social relations that are fundamentally detrimental to women's emotional welfare'. This notion of false consciousness more clearly than anything illustrates this notion of 'higher understanding' since the false consciousness of one group of women can only be deemed so by reference to some higher (more accurate) level of understanding against which their perceptions can be considered.

The central problem with the notion of empowerment is its sheer diversity of interpretation. If its meaning depends on one's social and political creed, as has been suggested, it can have as many meanings as social and political creeds available. Beyond this, the distinction between empirical and potential self formulations present a real conflict of definition. An empirical self formulation presents the individual as (generally) the best judge of their wishes and best interests. This is in direct contrast to the potential self formulation, for, with its emphasis on higher understanding, this formulation denies that this can be the case (except for those who have achieved this higher understanding). The task of empowerment is to change the individual from their (current) empirical self – who is actually disempowered – to their empowered potential self. These two positions are clearly not consistent and highlight fundamental contradictions in conceptualisations of empowerment.

Finally, we may question the basis on which claims to 'higher understanding' are made. This is best illustrated by a revealing quote from Betts (1986):

> How is it that the observer, who is also a member of society, buffeted by all the ideological winds and social pressures that beset [everyone]...can arrive at an 'objective' definition of interests, when they themselves cannot do this? How can we tell that this...is not itself an attempt to impose an alternative dogma?

Her answer is that we cannot. Clearly there can exist a fear that the so called empowering approach may itself be experienced as oppressive by others, particularly if we accept that humans are simply beset by competing ideologies without clear criteria for identifying, with some certainty, what exactly constitutes 'higher understanding'.

CONCLUSION

The understanding of social work as presented by its theorists represents a diverse set of views. The lack of consensus, and in particular the more radical views of social work, has provided fertile ground for those who would suggest that social workers do not really know what they are about, or that when they do their concern is more about social revolution than day to day issues of helping individuals (Brewer and Lait, 1980). It must be said, however, that these diverse views have plagued the academic arm of social work rather more than its practice arm, where its more grand pretensions have been tempered by the immediate concerns of practice. One is tempted to suggest that people take less notice of what is said and more notice of what is done.

The different approaches clearly represent quite fundamental disagreements in the way humans and society are constructed. Compare the intensely humanist orientation of those who seek self realisation with the social role adjustment models of those emphasising social functioning with the radical orientation of Marxists. However, a key to this is the assumption underlying all these approaches of the appropriateness of normative rather than positive theorising about practice. Durkheim (1967) distinguishes between normative and non normative (or positive) theory. The aim of normative theory is to modify what exists. Non normative theory seeks only to express what is or has been. In social work normative theories seek to conceptualise practice as it could be; positive theories seek to conceptualise practice as it is. Each approach has different strengths. Normative theory is not constrained by existing approaches and encourages imaginative conceptualisations of what social work *could be*. However, a corollary of this is that it is unconstrained: social work can be portrayed as diversely as the range of political affiliations allow. Positive theory, conversely, is restrained by its examination of what already exists. It cannot take imaginative flight in the way normative theory may. However, its very rootedness in that which exists provides a picture which is recognisable to, and usable for, practice. If practice is expected to follow the social policy directives of the state, then it is positive theory which will most clearly reflect this.

These normative approaches have certain themes in common. They present social work, or social workers, as entirely able to determine their own definitions and purposes, as able to determine themselves the nature of social work. This is highly questionable where social work is overwhelmingly undertaken in a state setting within bureaucracies which have an interest in what social workers do. It also allows particular proponents to present a particular view that they happen to have. The result is an unconstrained and diverse set of views of the 'nature' of social work, which is often more about what the proponents would 'like' it to be as what is really taking place. Self realisation may be a fine idea, but it stretches credulity to maintain that this is the purpose of practice with chronically disabled families which takes place over a number of years. Sometimes metaphorically 'keeping their heads above water' is all that may be hoped for.

These definitions operate, furthermore at a degree of abstraction and generality which, at times, make them difficult to apply to particular pieces of practice. This is very much in line with the previous comment on self realisation. However, a further problem arises from the apparent diversity of meanings which can be placed on particular concepts. This is the case with the concept of empowerment, the meaning of which depends upon the assumptions being used by its particular proponents. Such terms can have as much importance for their emotive meaning as the precision with which they define and describe the activity of social work.

Finally, these notions show little evidence of the constraints on practice of social work's occupational setting, in particular the importance of agency function. If social workers are *at times* concerned with some concept of social functioning, it is in relation to specific groups. Self realisation may have no part to play in much social work practice, while particular approaches to empowerment my not be consistent with the requirements of agency function. This is certainly the case with Marxist approaches. As Davies (1981, 1986) has pointed out, it is difficult to envisage the state paying an occupation group whose widespread aim was the overthrow of the very same state. The passage of time has demonstrated how far these ideas were in fact radical fantasies. Rather than rely on normative approaches to theorising about social work, it is perhaps better to focus on positive theorising. It is with such an approach in mind that we turn to considering the idea of the social worker as state functionary.

Chapter Three

The social worker as state functionary

It is, perhaps, obvious, but it is nonetheless crucially important to understand that social workers have been overwhelmingly employed by state authorities. This association of social work with the state is so marked that we might expect it would excite the immediate curiosity of any interested observer. It is not coincidental. To understand social work is to understand its relationship with, indeed its place within, the state.

State social work is an occupation which has, in a sense, been socially constructed or created. It has been created to deal with certain areas of social life: to work with older people with welfare difficulties, offenders, the mentally ill, to protect children. It is, in this sense, profoundly interventionist: social workers intervene in the lives of people, sometimes with their agreement, sometimes without it. This claim to intervene in areas of social life may be understood in terms of two central elements. First, social work is one of the occupations (and institutions) which is, in some respects concerned with the problem of order in society, one closely associated with the consensus and functionalist tradition (Strasser, 1976). If a society can be maintained, or orderly progress can be maintained, only by the widespread observation of certain basic rules of behaviour, then certain institutions will be concerned with circumstances where these rules have been transgressed. Examples of this are the police and courts, indeed the whole judicial system. Social work is involved with the issue of order in, for example, its work with young offenders, or as probation officers. This concern with the issue of order to a considerable extent, defines the 'control' aspect of social workers' work.

The second element relates to the ethic of state intervention. Weber (1946) refers to the 'ethic of responsibility' which exists in societies where a belief is widely accepted that human problems are responsive to intervention, and the greater the influence of this ethic, the greater will be the attempts to intervene and solve these problems. Social work may be seen as part of a welfare apparatus in which the state has increasingly laid claim to intervene in certain aspects of the lives of individuals and families. This is clearest in relation to child care. Fox Harding (1991) has shown how quite different philosophies have governed the state's approach to its relationship with families in different historical periods. During the nineteenth century, a more laissez faire approach to these relationships was adopted, in which the family was largely seen as sacrosanct and the child's welfare and development the responsibility of parents. During the twentieth century a more interventionist approach emerged in which responsibility for the welfare and development of children was considered to be an issue for the state as well as the family, and in which intervention might occur when the quality of parental care was inadequate. Timms (1983) has referred to the streak of paternalism in social work (maternalism may be more appropriate given the number of women social workers). This is not simply about the right to intervene in the lives of citizens, but an accompanying belief that the state (or social worker) knows best (at times). Hence, for example, it is the state (through statute) and the social worker and courts (in practice) which decide when parental care is inadequate and state intervention is necessary.

On the foundation of this concern with order and the right to intervene, social work may further be seen to occupy a particular occupational 'space'. This space is identifiable in terms of a number of key elements: a concern with certain areas which are officially defined as socially problematic; a focus on individuals defined in this way (socially problematic); an orientation to this socially defined individual as a subject and an emphasis on an interactionist context for understanding these subjects.

SOCIAL WORK'S SOCIALLY DEFINED CONCERNS

State social work is centrally concerned with social problems. The clientele, or consumers, of social work are people who have been defined in some way as socially problematic. When we speak of child abusers, the mentally ill or young offenders (juvenile delinquents) we are speaking not simply of people with whom social workers work, but those who have been defined in this way. The social problem may itself be child abuse (or mental illness or juvenile delinquency). The individuals with whom the social worker works are, in a sense, the 'individual manifestation' of those social problems. Those who are socially problematic may be broadly divided into two: those who are problems and those who *have* problems. Problematic individuals might be considered in terms of those for whom the problem of order arises, those such as young offenders. Those who have problems may be, for example, older people in need of residential accommodation. Theirs is more overtly a welfare problem. Of course those who are problems may also be considered to have problems. Offending behaviour may be associated with familial problems: indeed much social work with offenders is based on this kind of explanation. Hence, the two issues of welfare and order may be closely tied up in individual instances of those who are 'socially problematic'.

When we speak of child abuse or offending behaviour we are not speaking simply of some objective category which unproblematically is obvious to all who gaze at it closely enough. We are speaking of particular kinds of classifications of people or behaviour which in part reflects the values and commitments of those who do the defining. Thus, the concept of a social problem is a 'category of thought, a way of seeing certain conditions as providing a claim to change through public actions' (Gusfield, 1989, p 431). It is part of the way we think about and interpret the world about us that [1] we perceive many conditions as not only deplorable but [2] as capable of being relieved by and as requiring public action, most often by the state. Definitions of social problems are expressed in terms that describe the condition, reflect attitudes towards the condition and give numerous hints about how that condition is considered offensive or problematic.

The definition of a social problem by members of a society is, Spector and Kituse (1977, p 76) think a social process. The emergence of a social problem is contingent upon the organisation of activities asserting the need for eradicating or ameliorating some conditions. Claims making is always a form of interaction: a demand made by one party to another that something is done about some putative condition. That social problems 'emerge' in this way shows the extent to which they are 'socially constructed': what is considered a social problem in one society or historical epoch may not be considered so in another.

While the definition of social problems is a social process, the conditions which they describe are not. These are generally ascribed an objective status (Woolgar and Pawlich 1985a and 1985b). Thus Gusfield (1981, p 8) for example, comments that the 'social construction of social problems implies an historical dimension. The same objective conditions may be defined as a problem in one period, not another'. Likewise Conrad and Schneider (1980, p 1) state that the transformation of deviance has not reflected 'a change of behaviour as such, but in how the behaviour has been defined'. As Woolgar and Pawlich note (1985a, p 257) this understanding of the social construction of social problems reflects a Realist approach. This combination of variable interpretation of objective conditions is according to Scheffer (1967, p 12-13) only to be expected: 'interpretation must...be interpretation of something, and that something must itself be independent of the interpretation if the interpretation is not to collapse into arbitrariness' (cf Hazlerigg, 1986).

This emergence of social problems is well illustrated in the example of child abuse, an issue of central importance to social work practice. Two accounts (Pfohl, 1977; Parton, 1979, 1985) detail the natural history of child abuse. The definition of certain practices as child abuse is a relatively recent phenomenon. Prior to the twentieth century child beating was believed to be necessary for discipline and obedience. While an increased interest in child welfare on the part of the state developed in the twentieth century this did not focus attention on the perpetrators of abuse. Child welfare agencies were either unaware of abusive behaviour or constrained by a model of casework that focused on psychic disturbance rather than family politics. Doctors directly involved with children were generally unwilling to believe that parents could harm their own children or were reluctant to interfere in family affairs. The identification of child abuse came during the 1960s through an alliance of medical specialists whose professional interests would be advanced by acceptance of child abuse as a social problem about which something should be done, radiography, paediatrics and psychiatry. The result was the generation of the term 'battered child syndrome' around which child protective work could develop.

While social work has long been concerned with issues of child welfare, the extent to which child abuse has become central to social work practice post dates the generation of the term 'battered child syndrome'. This example, therefore, is instructive for our understanding of social work. It is, of course at the point of acceptance of the existence of child abuse that social work begins to take a role in relation to that particular social problem. While it is important to recognise that social problems are socially defined through particular social processes their importance for social work lies less in whether or not these definitions are widely contested than the status of these socially defined categories. In this respect, we may distinguish between social problems as a campaigning issue and social problems as a professional concern. What marks out the involvement of social work with particular social problems is the institutional acceptance of the definitions of these problems as legitimate, and that social work is an appropriate means for working with these problems. In this sense, social work is the product of the successful pursuit of claims: one which has been institutionalised and legitimised, accepted by the state and enacted in the form of legislation, official guidelines and procedures. In so doing they accept and 'buy into' the definitions given. Social workers know this in a very practical way. Their practice in, for example, child care and mental health is not just influenced by the Children Act and Mental Health Act, but, to a considerable degree, is governed by these acts. Furthermore, as legislation changes, so do specific areas of concern, and even philosophies of practice (Fox-Harding, 1991).

Social work then becomes concerned with certain categories of persons, child abusers the mentally ill etc whose status has been constructed and yet whose official definition is regarded as the only relevant one. These definitions may remain contested, although institutional acceptance implies a high degree of consensus exists. For example, the Paedophile Information Exchange would (I assume) contest that their activities constitute child abuse, and even that the child should be allowed to make up their own mind over sexual relations with adults. In other areas (for example offending behaviour) there my be a wider variation of views. For the social worker *qua* social worker, however, sexual relation between an adult and young child is an issue for child protection and legally sanctioned intervention as is the case, where appropriate, with adolescents referred for social work intervention where that referral was related to their offending behaviour.

The distinction, therefore, between the social construction or definition in understanding the generation of social problems and the objectification of them once they are accepted by the state (ie that they 'really' exist and are the appropriate definition) is the difference between outsider and insider definitions. The analyst of the generation of social problem definitions may understand the social processes by which these definitions are generated. The practitioner as insider is 'presented' with these definitions as the stuff of their work. They are, for them *qua* social workers the relevant representation of the focus for their work.

SOCIAL DEFINITIONS AND STATE FUNCTIONS

The second key aspect of state social work is the delegation of authority to this professional group by the state. State social work is the very creation of the state - a strategy if you like - specifically to deal with certain social problems or areas of concern in social life. Social workers are not, it should be clear, primarily created for the purpose of political activism, but in the role of individual practitioner or technical expert whose purpose is to deal on a personalised basis with those who are in specific respects, socially problematic. The politicised actions of those who seek to gain acceptance of a particular social problem as legitimate, in this sense, therefore, p*recede* social work involvement with these social problems. Social workers become involved when the case is won, the definition institutionalised and the task of management is delegated to social workers.

Social work is political, but only in the sense that social workers become involved once the political case has been won. This means that the political position of social work is inevitably tied to that of the status quo. It has often been commented (Gusfield, 1989; Wilding 1982; Morgan, 1980) that the involvement of social work in a socially problematic area, is the mark of the depoliticisation of that social problem. It is removed from the arena of the political crusader into the hands of the technical expert or individual practitioner. As Wilding (1982, p 63) comments 'the professions have contributed to a depoliticising of social problems, treating them rather as personal problems susceptible to individual solutions by experts'. He goes on to suggest that this has implicitly propagated the notion that the problems with which they deal could be solved within the existing pattern of economic and social relations; that such problems were marginal, technical and susceptible to solutions through the technical expertise of the practitioners. In the process people with these social problems are relegated to a residual category: those who do not care adequately for their children, who offend and who are mentally ill are relatively small as a proportion of the total membership of society.

This is, furthermore, reflected in social workers' concern, not with the social problems *per se*, so much as those individuals who are socially defined as socially problematic in areas of concern to the occupation. In this sense, theirs is a case based approach. The delegation of responsibility for working in these areas of concern reflects the individualising influence of the definitions of the problems themselves (Best, 1987). Social work is clearly not concerned with all areas of life considered to be social problems. It does, however, represent an institutionally accepted (and devised) solution to the resolution, amelioration or management of particular kinds of social problems. When these problems are delegated to social workers, the institutionalised definition of the problems and the appropriate responses constrain the activities of social workers. While social workers are generally far too sophisticated to buy into a simplistic social pathology approach (or such an approach alone) (Hardiker, 1981) their scope for working on wide range structural factors is limited or non existent.

This can be illustrated again with the example of child abuse. Gil (1975) has commented that the way in which child abuse is defined as a predominantly familial issue in which the perpetrator is frequently, or generally, an adult member of the family, operates as a 'smokescreen' which covers the abusive behaviour in the wider society and the result of the impact of powerful social institutions. We may, he thinks, be shocked when we find a young child has been injured or killed at the hands of its parents, but abuse may occur in institutions failing to provide children with material and emotional means for their development and in a society where policies do not actively intervene to limit poverty with its accompanying inadequately nourished, clothed and educated children and where infant mortality is far higher among the poor. It is this dominant, individualised and family focused definition of abuse which characterises social work practice, even though social workers are often well aware of the influence of poverty and disadvantage in the capacity of many of their individual consumers to care for their children.

As state functionaries the practice of social work is carried out within the framework of agency function. The setting for state social work practice is the state agencies - generally local authority social services or probation departments - which employ them. While in some aspects of practice - most notably compulsory admission assessments under the Mental Health Act - responsibility is directly delegated to the social worker by legislation (Sheppard, 1990), the authority of social workers to act is largely derived from their position within welfare agencies. This places them within a bureaucracy, with a hierarchy of authority and responsibility (Hugman, 1991). These agencies are subject to laws and government department circulars which are implemented through these agencies which themselves develop procedures for the enactment of their responsibilities. All these have a profound impact not only on practice, but on the definition of what that practice should be. It is in this context that the accountability of individual social workers may be understood, and decisions involving key areas of practice or the use of resources are rarely, if ever made without senior consultation (Howe, 1986).

It is through the agencies within which they are situated, then, that the very definition of social worker's tasks and functions arise. This is evident from a cursory reading of any general textbook (eg Davies, 1986) and has been recognised for some time. Howe (1979) has argued that agency function is one of the defining characteristics of social work. Others have made similar associations Timms (1963, p 8-9) argued that 'the most important aspect of agency function is that it constitutes the meeting point of social worker and client; it is what brings them together and gives meaning and sustenance to their continued contact'. Warham (1977, p 52) argues that social work 'has to be defined in relation to the circumstances in which social workers find themselves: it is not of a kind which it is at the discretion of the profession itself to determine without reference to the essentially public nature of the situations in which social work is employed'.

Social work, therefore, through employing agencies, involves carrying out certain state functions, and, as we shall see (chapter 4) various bureaucratic mechanisms are in place to make sure this happens. The core framework for these functions lies in the law, in the forms of rights and duties which constitute roles which the social worker is expected to carry out (Downie and Telfer, 1978; Howe, 1980). This emphasises both the source of the social worker's authority (indeed *raison d'etre*) and the extent to which this authority is delegated to them. Social workers, by the very nature of their job, intervene in the lives of others. If such intervention is not to be arbitrary, then they must have a *right* to intervene. These rights come from the law, as do associated duties. There are, of course, innumerable examples. In mental health, section 13 (4) of the Mental Health Act, 1983 illustrates exactly this relationship between law, agency function and social work role. Here, if requested by the nearest relative, the local social services authority is required to direct an approved social worker to make an assessment of an individual with a view to possible compulsory admission to hospital. If they do not then make such an application, they are required to inform the nearest relative, in writing, of their reasons. Here the nature and origins of the duties are clear: the origin lies in the law. However, it is, first, the agency authority which is required to direct the ASW to take action. It is then that the ASW's duties of assessment and communicating with the nearest relative arises. Likewise, under section 115, an approved social worker has the power (hence the right) to enter and inspect premises occupied by a mentally disordered person, provided it is within her social services authority.

Social work, then is about particular roles carried out in pursuit of agency function and designated by law. This is fundamental. The law provides the very framework for the conduct of social work practice. More than this, to a considerable degree, it defines the nature of social work. It is through the law that the rights, responsibilities and duties of social workers in relation to socially problematic areas are defined. There is, then, a close relationship between the socially defined areas of social work concern and the law, which creates and provides the framework for the social work role and hence social work actions.

The individualised nature of social work practice is evident in one further aspect. The work of social workers represents the delegation of certain powers to deal with individual situations to a particular occupational group. There is, in this sense, a difference between the broad category of the social problem, which is the state's (law enactor's) concern, and the individual instances, which are the concerns of social worker. While law may indicate areas of social life in which the state has particular interests, such as offending behaviour or, in some conditions, mental health, it is the job of social workers (amongst other things) to recognise individual instances of these concerns and, where appropriate, act on them. In this sense, they act as the 'definers of the individual instance' of a social problem. This is most obviously the case for social work (often in concert with other agencies) in relation to its child protection functions. In other cases, other agencies may define the individuals' status (the courts define offenders and doctors may define the mentally ill) who are then referred to social workers.

This relation between 'the general' and 'the particular' is clear with compulsory admission assessments. Here approved social workers are involved in a process where the general rules in the Mental Health Act are sufficiently imprecise when applied to the particular situations (what Hart (1961) calls the open texture of law) that the professionals concerned have considerable discretion in the decision about whether an individual may be defined mentally ill and admitted compulsorily to hospital (Sheppard, 1990).

As with the delegation of responsibilities to other professionals (such as teachers and doctors), there is an assumption that some kind of expertise exists at the individual level in managing this problem. This may be tenuous, and, as we shall see in the next chapter, scepticism about expertise can threaten the position of that profession. This is sometimes an explicit requirement, as with section 114 of the Mental Health Act which requires approved social workers should have 'appropriate competence'. This may be termed the expertise of the recognition and management of the individual instance. This kind of emphasis on expertise arises, as Parsons (1949) has noted, in the context of the widely held belief in modern industrial societies in 'the primacy of cognitive rationality'. This belief, together with the individualising approach to social problem management gives professions like social work a crucial role. As Wilding (1982) notes, a system which deals with deviance simply by punishment has no need for experts except in the rather narrowly specialised fields of the technology and techniques of punishment. The belief that what is required is 'treatment' and that there are people with skills and techniques to administer such treatment does much for the power and status of such groups (Packman, 1981).

INTERACTIONAL FOCUS

This concern with socially defined individuals is associated with an interactionist focus. Social work has long possessed what has been termed a 'dual focus' on the individual and society. In this formulation the social worker works on the interface between the individual and society. Haines (1981, p 5) remarked that social work concerns itself 'both with the individual and society and is particularly interested in the relationship between the two' (cf Younghusband, 1971; Sainsbury, 1970). This formulation draws attention to the abiding focus in social work not simply on the individual themselves, but on the individual in their social relationships, with other individuals, groups and social institutions. This focus has, furthermore, been consistently present in all approaches to social work practice. It is evident in three ways: in the social definition of the consumer; in the context for analysis and intervention and in the focus on the 'subject' status of the consumer and the key values underlying this.

Role Relations

An interactional dimension, encapsulating the consumer and those with whom they are in some form of social relationship is evident from the analysis of the 'socially problematic' nature of the social work clientele. The socially defined nature of the social work clients' status is evidence that, in order to qualify as the focus for social work concerns they need to be defined, either by the social worker themselves, or some other professional or social institution as socially problematic. The relationship between social worker q*ua* social worker and their client *qua* client is necessarily a role relationship. The interaction between worker and client can only be understood in terms of the socially defined nature of this role relationship. In this respect, the 'environment' to which theorists refer cannot simply be that of individuals, or subjects, groups and their physical setting. It is, in a crucial respect, symbolic. In this sense a prerequisite to state social work - the existence of socially defined clientele who are the concern of social work - is the interactional dimension which places the consumer in their social context.

This role relationship has become central to recent formulations of social work practice, although it does no more, in this respect, than systemise conceptually a relationship that is inherent in state social work. Anderson (1984), Schwartz (1977) and Shulman (1992), three leading exponents of this interactional approach, emphasise that this model focuses on the connections among three sets of relational processes in any practice situation. These are the consumer, the environmental resource systems that impinge on the consumer and the social worker. This formulation invites consideration of the role relationship between the (socially defined) consumer and social worker, and by extension, both of these and other social relationships.

It is clear that social work action both with and on behalf of the consumer is predicated on this socially defined role relationship.

If, for example, the social worker approaches a parent of a child who persistently fails to attend school (a 'truant' or 'non school attender') in order to secure their help with school attendance, they do so in a capacity in which the rights and duties of their post are inherent in their relationship. This is particularly clear in some social work texts. Shulman (1992) for example, emphasises the importance, right from the outset, of the practitioner being clear about purpose - that is why they are there. This not only reflects the role relationship, but is also presented in terms of honesty and authenticity. If the social worker does not state clearly their purpose (and make sure the parent has understood it) they may consider them merely as some kind of 'friend', simply trying to be helpful over their son or daughters difficult school behaviour. Under these circumstances it might come as some surprise if they (the parents) were then confronted with powers to accommodate that young person if they failed to improve their school attendance.

The relationship between social worker and the consumer's 'environmental resource system' is, therefore, as much predicated on the socially defined role and function of the social worker as the relationship with the consumer himself. In this case the parent is involved qua parent, where the notion of parental responsibility, as outlined in the Children Act, is significant. While anyone (a friend, for example) might be enlisted to encourage the young person in their school attendance, their involvement does not carry with it any special responsibilities. An approach by the social worker to the parent therefore has, by the very nature of legal expectations, carries with it particular expectations. The interactional context, therefore, begins not with John Smith (who happens to be a social worker) contacting George Brown (who happens to be a parent) about his son Gordon. It is, first of all, an interaction between social worker, and parent about the consumer.

Interactional Context

The interactional dimension goes beyond the symbolic dimensions of the socially defined role relationship between the various participants in the social work process. The straddling by the social worker of both consumer and environment reflects an emphasis on the environment as a context for understanding, as well as working with the consumer. This is a consistent theme of all social work formulations. It is as much a feature of approaches which place greatest emphasis on the environment as those which emphasise most the individual. As Webb (1981, p 147) comments:

> Whether it is radical or traditional, social work can overlook neither the person nor society and to talk of the configuration between the individual and social structure is to speak within the rules of formation that lend the distinguishing characteristics and constraints to the social work discourse...Both traditional and radical theorists are therefore engaged in the task of articulating the links and interdependencies between the individual and society.

This theme is consistently evident in social work formulations. In the United States, as early as 1928, the Milford Conference agreed that social work concerned the 'individual's capacity for self maintenance which is always relative to a given setting' (Milford Conference in Anderson, 1988, p 5). Likewise, Hamilton considered humans capacity to adapt and integrate should be seen 'within a changing environmental matrix' (Hamilton, 1941) and Towle (1969) emphasised the importance of psychological, familial and social forces - the social environment - in understanding the human situation. In Britain Younghusband (1951, p 3), in a semi official report commented that social work is concerned with 'mitigating in the lives of individuals, ills whose roots lie in social and economic conditions'.

More recent formulations have continued with this broad approach while changing in detail as a result of changing theoretical or model formulations. Hence BASW (1973) stated that social work 'is concerned with bridging the gap between the individual and society'. Pincus and Minahan (1973, p 9) state that 'social work is concerned with the interaction between people and their social environment which affects the ability of people to accomplish their life tasks, alleviate distress and realise their aspirations and values'. Hollis (1972, p 9) suggested that social work has 'always been a psychosocial treatment method. It recognises the interplay of both internal psychological and external social causes of dysfunctioning'. A rather grander perspective was presented by Schwartz (1977), who suggested that the social work function was 'to mediate the process through which the individual and his society reach out for each other '. Likewise, Schulman (1992, p 6) very recently emphasised that social workers concentrate 'on the way in which the client and the client's important systems are interacting', while Anderson (1988, p 5) argued that 'almost all recent attempts to define social work have taken as their starting point the interaction between individual and the environment'.

This contextualisation of the consumer may be considered in two dimensions. This involves, first, the extent to which the focus of practice is on both consumer and environment and second, an understanding of the client/consumer is act*ed* upon (by the environment) and act*ing* upon (the environment). Inevitably, perhaps, those approaches which emphasise the importance of environment to the understanding of the consumer's situation focus most strongly on the environment. Of course, the degree of emphasis on the environment is variable, and may, perhaps be presented conceptually as a continuum with the individual at one end and the environment at the other. In its most extreme form it occurs in radical approaches, which, it must be said, represent a pretty diverse group. In a quote from 1975, which applies equally well today, Bailey and Brake (1975, p 3) emphasised that 'radical social work ...is essentially understanding the position of the oppressed in the context of the social and economic structure they live in'. Hence the focus is on the social processes by which people are labelled, stigmatised, degraded and the social structural characteristics through which various groups with whom social workers are involved - the poor, women, black people, the old, disabled people - are oppressed (Langan and Lee, 1989).

More individual formulations, such as casework, undoubtedly focus with considerably less interest on the social context or environment. Yet it is not excluded, and is indeed placed in crucial relationship with the consumer. Hence Bowers, in the 1930s (quoted in Plant, 1970) considered casework involved mobilising 'capacities in the individual and resources in the community appropriate for better adjustment'. Hamilton (1953) also formulates a 'person in situation' conception and Hollis (1972, p 35) recognised that the person 'must be seen in the context of his interactions with the external world [particularly]...the external world with which he is in *close interaction* [my italics]'. The diminished emphasis on the environment is evident here from the concentration on its micro social dimensions as well as the limited sociological analysis evident in the traditional approach. Where it does occur, as with Hollis (1972), it is tentative and schematic, and in its concentration on concepts like social adjustment, role and reference group, tends to emphasise a consensus model of society.

The other key interactional dimension involves the notions that the consumer is both acted upon and acting upon (the environment). That they are acted upon is, implicitly or explicitly, evident from the emphasis on social environment. Explaining the consumer's predicament in terms of social processes and social structure is a central theme of formulations emphasising the environment. However, it is also clear from the notion of *inter*action, which is evident in casework formulations. This term entails the notion of being acted upon as well as acting. The consumer as actor is clearly embedded in traditional formulations. Hollis (1972, p 38), for example, states that 'it is assumed that [hu]man[s are]..not only acted upon, but [are]...capable of spontaneous activity, that [they]...have some measure of control over their own fate'. Indeed, some emphasis is placed on the human capacity to develop understanding of their situation. This perception of the human as actor is evident in formulations which place greatest emphasis on social processes. Thus Pearson (1975) recognised that what may appear as maladaptive behaviour is in fact intelligible once we acknowledge that people actively engage in the world by interpreting their circumstances and acting accordingly.

There is, then, a persistent interactional dimension to social work. The discussion so far has emphasised a dualist notion of this interaction: one which distinguishes person and situation or environment. More recent formulations might be termed Reciprocal-dynamic, those which take a systems or ecological approach (Goldstein, 1973; Pincus and Minahan, 1973; Whitaker and Garbarino, 1983). This emphasises the place of the client consumer as part of a system, the components of which constantly act, interact and act back on each other. There is, it is intended through this approach, no longer the implicit tension derived from the dualism of person in situation or individual-environment distinctions. It represents an attempt to view the individual in their environment. However the intentions of its proponents are more firmly interactionist than ever, and they seek both to gain the advantages of viewing the consumer in the context of their environment while not separating the two out in the way previously undertaken.

THE ORIENTATION TO THE SUBJECT

So far, we have concentrated on the consumer as socially defined being. However, social workers are concerned with *subjects* who are socially defined. That is, while social workers are involved because of the socially constructed nature of the consumer's status, they are centrally concerned with that consumer as subject. It is this which leads Ragg (1977) to proclaim an emphasis on 'People Not Cases'. Bartlett (1970, p 118) recognises this as the primary social work orientation: that social workers 'characteristically begin by trying to understand a situation from the viewpoint of the people involved in it'. This 'starting where the client is' (Haines, 1981; Compton and Galloway, 1989) is tacit recognition of the subject status of the consumer, who is able to make sense of situations and act on them by their own conscious effort. It is this also which underlies England's (1986) emphasis on the 'search for meaning' in which the social worker consciously attempts to make sense of the client's perceptions of their situation. For the social worker, the consumer is an individual, a conscious sentient being, with their own aims, wishes, hopes and fears.

The significance of this lies in the 'object' qualities that are inherent in the socially defined status of their consumers. To describe someone as mentally ill, a criminal or offender or disabled, is to categorise them in term of particular class rather then an individual person in their own right. Indeed, these categories generally contain some negative evaluation embedded within them. It is in the emphasis on the subject that the social worker may be said to operate between the individual and society. The individual is the particular subject with whom the social worker is involved and the 'society' represents those social institutions which define them (the courts, psychiatrists etc) or those rules or norms by which the individual is defined.

Philp (1979) argues that, while in any particular case the social worker is involved with this individual subject, this is predicated on social workers operating within a world of universal subjectivity - that is that all their consumers (and people in general) are subjects. They therefore straddle, on the one hand, the socially defined nature of their clientele, and on the other their subject status. He suggests that this has arisen within a specific socio-historic context in which the social worker mediates between the deviant or socially defined and the wider social institutions with which they are involved. However, the central position of the subject in social work also reflects the influence of humanist thought in practice. In this process, the social worker produces a picture of the individual who is at once both subjective and social.

This is evident in the various forms of practice. 'Starting where the client is' is an obvious example. However, it is evident also, for example, in the writing of a court report. Here they are involved in what Philp (1979) calls 'the creation of subjects'. In a court report the social worker is not simply presenting the 'facts of a case' - age, sex, crime, income etc - but is also attempting to portray the subject: what it is like to be an individual with these characteristics. It is presented in such a way as to give a picture of the subject's essential humanity and potential for sociability, if this can be done. In the foster placement the social worker may try to get the foster parent to understand the 'real' nature of the adolescent's 'acting out', to see beyond the mere behaviour to the subject with their fears and anxieties underneath. When an older person is considering residential care, the social worker will often give the establishment a 'picture' of them as a person, and provide them with opportunities to visit before taking up residence. It is not just individual rights, but the sense of the person as a subject which makes a failure to perform (or arrange for performance of) these functions appear abusive.

In this emphasis on the subject status of consumers, social workers are drawing upon values which are widely considered fundamental to the profession. When the social worker speaks of (and for) the consumer, they speak of their potential, the possibilities, their underlying nature and essential humanity. They speak of a subject marked by their capacity for self determination, responsible citizenship and general sociability. The core value of respect for persons, which as is generally appreciated cannot be requisitioned for social work purposes alone, underlies this particular emphasis on subject status (Plant, 1970; BASW, 1975; CCETSW, 1985; Horne, 1987; Butrym, 1976; Watson, 1978). Universally espoused as the core value for social work, this principle is, in fact, morally basic: that is, it is a presupposition of having the concept of a moral principle at all (Plant, 1970; Downie and Telfer, 1969).

This attitude of respect involves recognising their inherent worth as humans, independent of their empirical (or socially defined) qualities, and of treating them never simply as means (to some other end) but always at the same time as an end (Paton, 1949). Respect for persons is pretty well universally recognised as core to social work: it cannot, indeed, be otherwise if social work is to be carried out in accordance with a system of values. Yet in a social work context, it is profoundly problematic. Personhood implies either the possession of, or potential for, rational action.

Such a view would, some think (Timms, 1983) have the effect of actively promoting discrimination against those who do not count as persons. In order to retain the notion of personhood some convoluted, and rather dubious, definitions are required. Budgen (1982) has suggested that children may be seen as potential persons, the senile are lapsed persons, the mentally ill are temporarily lapsed persons, and those with learning difficulties, permanently potential persons (!). Watson's solution (1980, p 61) is to develop a principle 'respect for human beings', on the grounds that it is more all encompassing than respect for persons and as a result would cover all consumers. Respect for human beings would involve valuing the capacity to be emotionally secure, the desire to give and the capacity to receive love and affection , as well as the distinctive endowments of human beings.

What appears to be involved here is a combination of the state paternalism (or maternalism) outlined earlier and a particular reading of the notion of respect for persons. Paternalism may generally be considered to be about abrogating to oneself (or a state institution) the right to make a decision about them, which will override their views, on the basis that it is in their interests or actually furthered their welfare (Timms, 1983). It is possible, for example, to listen and try to understand the position of a child without considering they are capable of making fully rational decisions about themselves currently or in the near future. It is surely this which is involved when the social worker is required, in the Children Act to take account of the 'wishes and feelings of the child'. The same may be said when a social worker tries to ascertain the views of those with learning difficulties (although many will be quite capable of making their own decisions). Acting in their interests requires consideration of their views, and this in turn involves treating them as a subject, even if they are not fully capable of rational behaviour.

The other relates to the peculiarly consensus assumptions which underlie the practice of state social work. This is evident in the 'symbiotic assumption' of social work, with its emphasis on the mutuality of the individual and the wider society in which they are situated (Shulman, 1992; Anderson, 1988). Schwartz (1977) has considered this 'a relationship between the individual and his nurturing group which we would describe as' symbiotic' - each needing the other for its own life and growth and each reaching out to the other with all the strength it can command'. There is here, an assumed symmetry between the interests of the individual and the society in which they are situated. The needs of the individual, it is assumed here, are best served within the existing framework of institutional relationships within society. This symbiosis is predicated on a notion of action which is rational if it operates at the level of social morality, which in turn reflects the norms inherent in the socially categories defining the social work clientele (Milne, 1968). If it is rational to observe social morality, then it cannot be rational, for example, to be an offender. If the social work task is to return the consumer to 'civil society' (Philp, 1979), they do so by a more rational understanding of their actions. The issue is complex, and will be examined in more detail in chapter six: we may note for now, however, that there is a relationship between the notion of the subject and that which might be considered reasonable behaviour.

CONCLUSION

State social work may, then, be considered a socially constructed profession, in the sense that it has been created as a means for working with certain individuals who have been defined as socially problematic. Its focus is one on individual-environment interaction and its orientation is towards these individuals as subjects. Its is in the combinations of these elements of concern, focus and orientation that social work may be most clearly 'marked out'. This formulation helps both to define social work and to distinguish it from other activities.

It is only when an individual is socially defined (by the social worker or other defining agents) that they become relevant to the social worker and then in terms of this social definition, such as the official status of offender. This is quite different from the more personalised concerns of, for example, the counsellor, who may be legitimately involved with a client because of a personal problem, such as unrequited love, disappointed friendship, frustrated ambitions and so on. However, their concern for the subject is one which distinguishes social from, say, police work, despite the pejorative term 'soft police' being, at times, applied to social workers by young offenders. Likewise, the political concerns of the social worker are limited to that consistent with the status quo. Social workers *qua* social workers are not in the business of political campaigning or agitating. They may campaign outside their work, informed by what happens in it. They may advise political or official committees as expert witnesses. But as social workers they are individualisers of social problems.

This understanding of social work, rooted in the reality of practice - one characterised by positive rather than normative theorising - is one which presents a practice role apparently most relevant in the new climate of social care. This is because the development of care management clearly reflects the notion of practice in social care as the result of social policy directives. The notion that social work is a created or constructed occupation is one that allows for a degree of change in the focus and even the manner of practice, within the constraints of its interactional focus and subject orientation.

Social work is both created within and constrained by its role or roles. These are carried out under the auspices of agency function and it is in this context that social workers should be understood as state functionaries. While the role defines what it is that social work is about in any specific area, its official aims, those of the social worker qua social worker, are contained within these roles. It is also about the recognition that as subjects consumers may act and change. Where social workers are involved in an Emergency Protection Order, their business is the protection of the child; where compulsorily admitting an individual under the Mental Health Act, their aim is to safeguard the health or safety of the patient or protect others. Of course there will clearly be some room for manoeuvre and flexibility, and for roles and aims which are not specifically set by legislation and agency function. However, these could not occur without the officially ascribed roles within which social work works.

The greater specificity entailed in the identification of rights, duties, roles and aims has the virtue of providing greater clarity in determining what social work is about. Terms like empowerment, social functioning and self realisation are as notable for their emotive appeal as their capacity to describe what is exactly going on. This is not entirely to discount these terms. There may be times when, for example, social workers are indeed, and in one sense or another, in the business of empowering consumers. However, the meanings are variable and while, for example, enhancement of self fulfilment or self realisation may take place in one context it may not in another. Whatever the case, for the activity to be social work, the empowerment, self realisation or social functioning concerned would need to be consistent with the individualising consensus assumptions inherent in social work.

Their work, then, is defined in terms of the roles they are required to carry out in accord with agency function. This has two implications of major importance in social work's attempt to adjust to the care managerial world. Social work is not defined, or defined in part, by the particular form of knowledge which it possesses, as are, say, medicine and psychology. A doctor would normally be considered someone who knows about the subject medicine and (presumably) is accredited with the capacity to put some of its insights into practice. It is not even clear that a separate academic discipline, called social work, exists, as much of the information upon which social work is based comes from allied disciplines. Social workers may need knowledge to carry out their tasks, but it is not intrinsic to the tasks, and, to be justified, would need to demonstrate that knowledge led to the improvement in the performance of social work roles or function. A second key implication is that because social work is 'externally defined' it is vulnerable to alteration from exactly those sources which have defined its role(s) in the first place. The roles might alter; the context change; the expectations of those carrying out the job (for knowledge or the production of paperwork) may differ from previously. The issue then becomes one of the extent to which social work is adaptable to meet the requirements of the new environment. While the state functionary formulation represents an approach likely to fit most comfortably with the new imperatives of social work, Davies (1986) warns that certain conditions are necessary for the survival of social work. First, practitioners must implicitly or explicitly accept a consensus model in the conduct of practice. Second, the state must retain a broad commitment to a fair, just and humanitarian society. What, however, happens when the assumptions underpinning the delivery of social care are fundamentally altered? where does this leave social work. We may examine the extent to which this may have happened in terms of the 'New Managerialism' in social care.

PART TWO

SOCIAL WORK
AS CARE MANAGEMENT

TION: SOCIAL WORK AS CARE MANAGEMENT

n the social work literature, but it is nonetheless
w environment of care management has been
enced by the ideological inclinations of the
overnment. In the light of this, it is hardly
ny social workers instinctively feel uncomfortable
agement. The ideological thrust underlying care management and the intended 'marketisation' of social care involves three elements: a strong belief amongst the New Right in the virtues of competition; an assumption, arising from the same quarters, that public management is less resource efficient than private management; and the development of a quasi market in social care.

The views of Hayek and other neo classical economists have provided the intellectual foundations for the emphasis on competition. Competition is useful, Hayek (1949; 1978) thinks, in just the way that sporting competition is useful. It enables the most proficient performer to emerge. It is the presence of competition which stimulates the entrepreneur to move more quickly and exploit new and untapped markets. If he or she failed, the market mechanism would induce someone to step in and fill the gap (Butler, 1983). Competition achieves three ends (Hayek, 1979, p 74):

- It encourages the emergence of new products. Everything will be produced which somebody knows how to produce and which they can sell profitably at a price which buyers will prefer to available alternatives.
- It encourages the emergence of more effective producers. Everything that can be produced is more likely to be produced as cheaply as possible. If a product can be produced more cheaply, someone will enter the market to undercut existing producers.
- It therefore encourages lower prices.

The market itself is considered preferable to alternatives. Provided it is not impeded by special interests, particularly those abusing government power, the market provides a mechanism that encourages the discovery of the most economic ways of meeting our wants. This is because of the market's special capacity to cope with the unforeseeable. What competition and the market allows us to do is harness the diverse capacities of individuals throughout an economy. This knowledge and skill is very particular (Hayek, 1979). It is the essential quality of the entrepreneur - a kind of 'alertness' to opportunities for production. It is, however, a particular kind of alertness: related to that particular set of products in that particular part of the economy with which they are sufficiently well acquainted to make informed decisions. No centralising authority can possess such a range of specific knowledge(s) and no central planning can adequately substitute for this 'alertness'. Competition and the market, therefore, set human ingenuity free to explore and develop ways of meeting the diverse wants of individuals in a complex society (Hayek, 1978, p 182).

This preference for the market has been allied to a deep scepticism about the quality of management in the public sector. The New Right, in particular the Public Choice theorists, have dismissed the notion that individuals may be inspired by a sense of public duty, and hence that the motivations of public sector managers would differ profoundly from the more self seeking motivation of private sector managers. This view of public duty was succinctly expressed long ago by G.D.H. Cole (1947, p 23); managers and wage earners, he thought, would 'be inspired by different feelings when they are working for a public which regards them as holding a public trust, and they will work the better as a result'. He even considered that public utilities would require fewer bureaucrats than their private sector equivalents.

The attack on this view has been presented by the Public Choice School on two fundamental grounds. Public choice theory assumes that all individuals in government (including public servants) 'serve their own interests within certain institutional limits' (Tullock, 1976, p 2). Niskanen is directly critical of the disinterested public servant tradition, comparing it unfavourably with markets. He considers it implausible that businessmen and bureaucrats are such different people that 'profits are a necessary incentive in private firms, but that the 'public good' is a sufficient incentive in government bureaus, that competition is a necessary discipline in private firms, but that monopoly is a desirable characteristic of bureaus' (Niskanen, 1978, p 164).

While entrepreneurs in the market will be driven by the profit motive, bureaucracies, Niskanen argues, will seek to maximise their budgets, subject to the constraint that its budget covers the cost of production (goods and services). He identified several utilities which the bureaucrat will seek to maximise, including salary, perks, public reputation, power and patronage, all of which he considered would increase the size of the budget (Niskanen, 1971, p 38). The opportunity to budget maximise arises because of a bilateral monopoly, whereby the politician is the sole supplier of funds to the bureau and the bureau the sole provider.

The second ground for criticising public management is on the basis of efficiency. Neither businessmen nor bureaucrats have any inherent motivation to be efficient. Whether they are or not depends on the constraints and incentives under which they operate. Peacock (1980) considers the barriers to efficiency in the public sector to be institutional, while Niskanen attributes it to the lack of profit motive. Wolf (1979) has identified a number of sources of inefficiency: the primacy of goals other than maximising cost effectiveness, the problem of monitoring costs where output is difficult to define and unpredictable, and costly side effects arising from the unforeseen consequences of programmes.

These supposed flaws in public provision have considerable significance for the development of care management. The perceived inefficiency arising from the monopoly of public provision by particular agencies provides the background to the division between purchaser and provider functions. This perception also contributes to an environment of short term contracts and performance related pay for managers in an attempt to provide incentives for efficiency. Finally the purchaser provider split allows for the development of a market in social care, with the perceived benefits, in terms of competition and innovation for the recipients of social care.

The development of a 'Quasi Market' in social care reflects an approach which attempts to bring together the benefits of public and private provision. Although quasi markets are markets because they replace monopolistic state providers with competitive independent ones, Le Grand (1990) has distinguished quasi markets from markets by the following characteristics. On the supply side:

- Like conventional markets, there is competition between productive enterprises or service suppliers: independent institutions competing for customers.
- Unlike conventional markets these enterprises are not necessarily privately owned and they are not necessarily out to maximise their profits (although this does not prevent them from minimising costs). Examples may include voluntary organisations.

On the demand side:

- Consumers' purchasing power is not expressed in monetary terms. Instead it takes the form of an earmarked budget or 'voucher' confined to the purchase of a particular service.
- The immediate consumer is not the one exercising choice (generally) regarding purchasing decisions. Instead the choice is delegated through a third party (eg a care manager).

A quasi market is an attempt to simulate market conditions without complete marketisation taking place. The simulation of the market is evident in a number of facets of social care: the division of demand and supply; the development of a range of provider units leading (in theory) to the opportunity for competition; planning is used to encourage development of resources (innovation) designed more adequately to meet need; and quality assurance and information systems combine to create the same effect (in theory) as that of the pricing and information systems of the market. This simulation is mediated by two factors: social care is predominantly publicly rather than privately funded and its central concern is with need rather than want.

All this is all very well in theory, but much of the New Right's case, it should be emphasised, represent articles of faith, or assumptions about the world rather than demonstrable facets (Heald, 1987). Most importantly we may question whether the motives of the public servant are the same (or even comparable with) those of the private entrepreneur. Those, for example, who enter social work do so, it is arguable, for reasons quite different from those who enter Financial institutions. It is difficult to see how those entering social work are doing so in order to maximise their income or wealth. Furthermore, where vulnerable people are concerned, choosing the most cost effective of limited resources is quite consistent with the motivations for entering social work. Social workers are well used to struggling with small and grossly inadequate resources. It does not follow, therefore, that the 'discipline' of competition will necessarily lead to an improvement in services. Indeed, where costs become of *overriding* importance, there is a danger that quality will be sacrificed to cost. Finally, it is not clear that the previous monopoly of service provision will be replaced by competition. Rather it is possible that duopolies will develop involving service purchasers and individual service providers working in their own discrete area of social care without competition from alternatives (Le Grand, 1993). Whether this will prove the case is a matter for empirical research.

It is important, then, to appreciate the influence of New Right thinking on the development of social care. In the chapters in Part Two, particularly chapter four and five, this influence will become apparent.

Chapter Four

Care management and the new managerialism

Care management represents a particularly profound switch in practice, not simply because of what it means for the individual social worker in their relationship with clients, but because of its impact on the autonomy and control of practitioners. In some respects it involves the old 'profession in bureaucracy' problem, but on its own this underestimates considerably the scale of change. This chapter will first examine the New Managerialism influencing the organisation of social care; it will then examine the failure of social work to establish sufficiently credible professional credentials to resist this managerial ideology; and finally it will examine the impact of managerialism on the conduct of care management.

THE NEW MANAGERIALISM

The organisation of care management involves extolling the manager as hero(ine). There is little that cannot be achieved provided we let managers do their job. This 'new managerialism' has been defined by Pollitt (1990, p 1) as 'a set of beliefs and practices at the core of which is the seldom tested assumption that better management will provide an effective solvent to a wide range of economic and social ills'.

However, the New Managerialism is not simply about extolling the virtues of good management, about which few people would argue. It represents an ideology in which the measure of all practice is the extent to which it fits with management structures and practice (as compared with, say, professional structures and practice). Linked with the New Right ideology, therefore, there is a change in the very language which is used. In Higher Education, for example, notions of collegiality and academic community are replaced by management; in social services, clients (a professional term) is replaced by consumers (or worse, users); in practice, assessment and review are replaced by care management. Management, in other words, becomes the superordinate term defining the whole range of activities which might previously have been constructed in different ways.

The New Managerialism, furthermore, is not limited to social services, but involves shifts in practice throughout the public, and in many respects, private, sector. Michael Hesletine, for long a cabinet minister in the eighties and nineties stated that 'efficient management is a key to the [national] revival...and the management ethos must run throughout our national life - private and public companies, civil service, nationalised industries, local government, the National Health Service (Hesletine, 1980). It is, therefore, an ethos widely influential, not simply confined to the provision of social care.

TWO FACES OF MANAGERIAL CONTROL

An environment as hostile as this was unlikely to leave social work untouched. Historically, welfare state administrators have played little part in the development of managerial ideology. Managerialism, therefore, represents the transfer of a 'foreign ideology' from the private sector to one characterised previously by quite different traditions of thought. It was allied to a political ideology hostile to the public sector. Two key elements are relevant to social care. From the standpoint of liberal economics many public bureaucracies were presented as over large inefficient and wasteful because of lack of competition and alliance with special interest groups (Niskanen, 1973). Second, professions were presented as occupations characterised by a restriction on trade, operating to a considerable degree in their own interests rather than that of their clients. Fear of bureaucracy by the 80s had become a 'raging pandemic' (Kauffman, 1981) and influential groups considered private sector provision a cheaper option than public sector provision (Banham, 1988).

Managerialism, at core, involves an issue of control: managers are those whose authority is derived from seniority (and management responsibility) within the organisation. This contrasts, for example, with a professional ethos where authority (about their area of expertise) is derived from knowledge and skills. The ethos of managerialism is historically an attempt to justify the authority of one group (managers) over another group (workers) (Perrow, 1979). This has broadly two dimensions: the normative and the structural.

The Normative Dimension

Managerialism legitimises the authority and seniority of managers. It involves the idea of the manager as a highly technical function requiring appropriate levels of education and expertise in running the organisation. It is, therefore, a skilled job. Managers, in this view, have gained their positions of authority through widely accepted criteria of ability, reflected in their senior position in the organisation. It follows that managerial prerogatives to direct and control industry should be considered legitimate.

Associated with this is a unitary view of the firm or organisation. By definition business organisation involves some degree of cooperation. Managerialism (see particularly Mayo, 1933) fosters the belief that there is sufficient common purpose and normative consensus amongst all groups for conflict, should this occur, to be contained without disrupting the basic framework of consensus. This is evident in the emphasis of the human relations school which simultaneously provides a model of the firm where 'the managers could see themselves as representatives of shared aspirations, and a reason for employees to accept managerial authority provided they were technically competent' (Child, 1969, p 222-3). This consensus is stressed at the expense of trends towards conflict: the pluralist model of the firm is normally defined in a way that performs the same kind of integrative function as a unitary model and involves amongst subordinates a moral commitment to honour agreements with management.

This normative dimension of managerialism does not simply offer a justification for managerial authority and control, but represents an ideology which of itself exerts control over the actions of subordinates. Where successfully applied, Clegg (1979) calls this 'Hegemonic Control'. This hegemonic control includes elements of the organisation's value system which regulates the conduct and performance of members. Sometimes, as Hill (1981) notes, the dominant values of the organisation transcend the interests of any particular group, but more often they reflect the interests of those with power in the organisation. Where there is widespread acceptance of managerial authority, subordinates s an 'inner commitment' through which they regulate their own actions. 'It is only where hegemonic control slips, assumptions fail, routines lapse, and 'problems' appear that the overt exercise of power is necessary' (Clegg, 1979, p 147). An acceptance, by social services practitioners, of a managerial ideology, is likely to entail acceptance, too, of managerial control, rather than reference to external (to the organisation) professional mores.

The Structural Domain

Structural control may be divided into control by command and control by rule or procedure. Control by command involves a clear statement by a superordinate (manager) made directly to a subordinate indicating what should be done (and often how it should be accomplished). An instruction of this sort might be from a district manager to a social worker that they should transport an older person to a residential establishment for respite care. While such direct commands are clearly made from time to time, used widely this is time consuming and cumbersome, constantly involving the superordinate directly. Simon (1952) suggests that for this system to be widely used, hierarchical differentiation must be relatively underdeveloped and the events of concern must occur within the 'field of vision' of the superordinate. Functional differentiation must also be rudimentary: most individuals should have the same 'rank' in the hierarchy and they must fulfil identical functions. As organisations have grown in size and become qualitatively differentiated, the scope for such direct control becomes increasingly limited (Clegg, 1979).

Control by rule or procedure is much more widely prevalent. According to Dunsire (1979, p 109) they are a 'surrogate for direct supervision'. For managers to gain maximum control over subordinates' work, it is necessary to concentrate important decision making in their hands. Weeks (1980) and March and Simon (1970) distinguish between programmed (routinised) and non programmed (unroutinised) responses. A set of activities is routinised to the degree that choice has been simplified by the development of fixed responses to situations. Where activities are unroutinised, the individual has to think up their own response (having analysed the situation) decide what should happen and carry it out; solutions to problems are novel and unstructured.

Friedman (1977) has distinguished, furthermore, two different management strategies for dealing with subordinates. *Responsible autonomy*, the first strategy, refers to the continuity of the traditional practice of delegation on the basis of occupational principles. This strategy entails conceding elements of control to the workers so that they may use their discretion in the process of production. This strategy seeks to harness workers' own knowledge and abilities to managerial objectives. *Direct control* involves managers directly specifying work methods and compelling compliance. Direct control is held to be more effective in less developed areas and among peripheral workers and peripheral industries. One main reason, according to Hill (1981, p 34) for 'responsible autonomy' is growing worker resistance to rationalisation which compels management to find some other methods of managing.

These different elements of managerial control are brought together by Dunsire (1979), who distinguishes two dimensions influencing the capacity of the superordinate to direct the subordinate through rules and procedures:

1. The degree of uncertainty or predictability of the results of particular actions on the task environment (for example work on child abuse or with young offenders). Where a situation and its consequences are easily anticipated, it is more easily subject to rules or procedures.
2. The degree of discretion granted to subordinates in relation to working on that environment. This is a matter of preference, ideology or attitude, and indicates the extent to which they can decide what to do and act on that decision.

Narrow Discretion: The most controlled situation involves subordinates working in an environment low in uncertainty and given narrow discretion. Dunsire calls these 'Rule Followers'. Monitoring of these rule followers is easiest for management, for example with routine clerical work. Operations can be considered correctly or incorrectly carried out and mistakes traced to the individual concerned. The error becomes visible, measurable and recognisably blameworthy. The other group with narrow discretion, who occupy an environment of uncertainty, Dunsire calls 'Policy advisers'. These people carry very little executive authority of their own, yet deal with high level problems. In the British government such people tend to be professional, scientific and technical advisers.

Wide Discretion: Those with wide discretion, but who are involved in environments low in uncertainty are called 'Judgement Makers'. Their discretion arises because it is felt desirable that the objectives to be pursued are not those of superiors, or only them, but drawn from some extra bureaucratic context - the law or professional standards, for example. It is sometimes suggested that such individuals decide on their own authority and their office is seen as located in two distinct hierarchies: that of the bureaucracy and that of the profession or the law. Those with broad discretion in an environment high in uncertainty he calls 'Problem Solvers'. Subordinates are dealing with uncertainty because superiors are not only unable to specify goal priorities, they are also unable to categorise incoming work or the problems presented to the organisation by the environment. In this case the solution to the problem has to be devised rather than sought. It is a creative (problem solving) activity.

Dunsire's classification, though helpful, is too dichotomous and both discretion and uncertainty may be better viewed as continuums. However, it helps illuminate the effects of a growth in managerialism and direct managerial control for social work. Very broadly, an accretion of power to management would involve a narrowing of discretion allowed to practitioners and hence a reduction in the autonomy of their decision making. Their work would be characterised by an increase in procedures as a determinant of the work they do. We might schematically present this as a tendency to move away from judgement making or problem solving towards rule following.

However, in order to achieve this it is necessary for the task environment, or those aspects defined as important, to have a good degree of predictability. It would need to be possible, in advance, to construct rules or procedures which would be highly likely to be efficacious. The granting of discretion on professional grounds is likely to be based on two key elements. This is, first, an inability on the part of managers to construct rules or procedures which are likely to be generally applicable to the range of client situations, for if they could do this they would have little need for professional discretion. The second is the possession of knowledge and skills on the part of the professionals on a case by case basis which was both applicable and able better to control situations than managerial procedures. Of course, social work involves elements of both, but the balance may be changed in one direction or the other. At the level of ideology, this would involve the presentation of a convincing case that both the defined problem and its resolution was more likely to be achieved through the granting of professional discretion than by more direct managerial control.

THE (PARTIAL) FAILURE OF PROFESSIONALISM IN SOCIAL WORK

How effectively has the case been made? The position of social work as a semi profession, or profession in bureaucracy (Etzioni, 1969) places its practitioners, at times, in an uncomfortable relationship with managers in the organisation. This tension can be exaggerated: for managers of social workers have themselves generally qualified in social work (although this may change). However, these two groups derive their authority from different sources: managers from their seniority in the hierarchy of the organisation and social workers, junior to managers, largely from the knowledge and skills attached to membership of their profession.

The advent of the new managerialism presents social work with a challenge to its traditional functioning, the key to which is the issue of control. The extent to which social work is able to resist this accretion of power to managers in the face of this alternative ideology (managerialism), for the delivery of social care is derived from the success with which they have been able to appeal to a professional status with which they are able to gain, in Friedman's (1977) terminology, responsible autonomy. Social workers, unfortunately, have had limited success in this respect, leaving them vulnerable to greater control in the face of this managerial ideology.

For Freidson (1970, p xvii) control is the central characteristic of a profession, which, he considers, to be 'an occupation which has assumed a dominant position in a division of labour, so that it gains control over the determination of the substance of its own work'. Likewise, Johnson (1972, p 45) considers it a peculiar type of occupational control, rather than a form of work containing certain traits or inherent characteristics. Those in an occupation seeking to gain or maintain professional status, therefore, may be active advocates of this status in their conduct of social or occupational life. Professional status, therefore, entails an appreciation of the way professions are 'made' or 'accomplished'. Thus Dingwall (1976) suggests that professional status is best understood through an explication of the ways ordinary members of particular occupations invoke and employ the term during the course of their everyday activities. Of course, however, occupational members are not the only players in this game, since others, including those espousing a managerialist ideology for the delivery of social care, have a key interest in the status and control exercised by that occupation. (Freidson, 1983, p 27).

Expertise and Control

In a frequently quoted passage, Hughes (1971, p 375) states that the essence of the professional idea and professional claim is 'to know better than their clients what ails them and their affairs'. It is this expertise, successfully claimed, which provides the main justification for professional power. It derives from a scientific rationalism which has gained widespread currency. Parsons (1949, ch 2) calls this the 'primacy of cognitive rationality'. It represents a belief in the value of expertise and those who claim and display it gain status and power. Berger's (1977) concept of 'cognitive imperialism', furthermore, captures the vigour with which this claim is pursued. An inhabitant of a particular world may normally be considered to have an understanding of, and access to, it, denied to the non-inhabitant. Where, however, professional definitions carry the day, unless they happen to coincide with those of the 'inhabitant' then the latter's views will be marginalised or ignored completely. Such is the case with diagnoses of mental illness or definitions of an individual as a child abuser. Professional status gives the individual practitioner greater expertise than the subject of their concern.

A key dimension of this professional expertise, then, lies in the power to define both the subjects of their concern and the nature of the work undertaken with them. Marshall presents this in a highly illuminating way for care management: the professional has the responsibility for giving the client what s/he needs rather than what s/he wants. The professional rather than the client defines the 'real' problem. Where this 'right' to define needs is absent, this represents a significant 'slippage' of control away from the professional, and towards others. The right to define need, it is true, remains with the care manager (Department of Health, 1991b). It is, however, a bounded right. There is a clear official commitment to giving 'users and carers a more powerful voice in expressing needs and influencing the services they receive' (Department of Health, 1991a, p 55). Information systems are required to facilitate this, and monitoring arrangements make sure all care managers are offering a quality service. Indeed, need should be explicitly defined and prioritised in policy statements (Department of Health, 1991a, p 14). The 'terms of discourse' therefore, are, to a considerable degree predefined at a managerial and organisational level.

Of course it is true that social workers, except in their more unguarded and grandiose moments during their psychoanalytic phase (Roberts, 1990) placed limits on their claims to 'know better' than their clients. It is equally true that statutory powers, most notably those of child protection and mental health compulsory admissions continue to give social workers, or their departments anyway, considerable powers of definition. Nonetheless, care management represents an explicit shift, in this respect, from professional to consumer.

Esoteric Knowledge

The extent to which a profession may claim cognitive superiority relates to the extent to which there is 'a systematic body of theory and esoteric abstract knowledge on which the work is based' (Pavalko, 1971, p 18). Medicine provides the paradigm for this, where knowledge fits with the scientific-technical approach which Parsons considered crucial to professional acceptance. This is not always the case, of course; legal practice is based on a highly elaborate system of changing rules and customs. Nevertheless, the claim to expertise rests on the professions presumed mastery of a body of knowledge. The more abstract and ideational the knowledge required, as well as the longer the training (in general) the greater the expertise ascribed to the profession.

However, in social work's case there remains doubts about the extent to which the knowledge claimed can be put into practice in the real world. A number of studies exist questioning the effectiveness of social work (Fischer, 1976; Thomas, 1978), although more recent findings, if at times tentatively, give a rather more hopeful impression of effectiveness (McDonald et al, 1992; Sinclair, 1992). Stevenson (1971) long ago warned against building social work's knowledge foundations on the 'shifting sands of social science', which, however, remains a core element of the social work curriculum. Many social workers, furthermore, have *themselves* doubted the impact of training on practice. Stevenson and Parsloe (1978) found that although there was evidence that social workers used social science concepts to understand clients and their difficulties, there was little evidence that they had been assimilated into an integrated system to guide practice. These findings resemble those of Carew (1979) while Holme and Maizels (1978) found only ten per cent of practitioners they interviewed considered their professional skills and expertise were the most important factor contributing to effectiveness, far less than personal factors.

Not all evidence points in this direction. Hardiker (1981) has argued that the nature of their (social science) knowledge base, and the degree of theory practice integration achieved by social workers leaves many of them unaware of the extent to which they use theory in practice. Furthermore, she suggested that it is crucial to good practice: the lack of adequate theory can lead social workers in completely the wrong direction . Likewise, Sheppard (1991) has shown that crucial differences in the conduct of practice between social workers and community psychiatric nurses may be related back to their theory base.

However, where social workers are themselves such poor self publicists, with such a limited belief in the importance of theory to their own effectiveness, it is difficult to see how claims to professional status can carry conviction.

Technical-Rationalism

This problem has been compounded, it might be argued, by social work's attitude to its own knowledge base. In a society devoted to technical expertise and characterised by cognitive rationalism, social work has shown at times, in view of its search for professional status, an almost perverse desire for alternative forms of knowledge. The energy with which social work has accumulated one theory after another, with little concern for its usefulness or effectiveness, and without discarding previous theory, has been widely commented upon (Payne, 1991; Sheldon, 1979). Hoghughi (1980a, 1980b, 1980c), however, identified the core of this problem.

Of particular significance has been the emphasis on the relationship in practice, without identifying it as an end to social work or a means to some other end. There is, in any case, no reason, he thinks, to believe that social workers are any more capable of establishing and maintaining relationships with their clients than anyone else (a claim, incidentally, disputed by Sinclair (1992)). However, the key to the problem is its identification with a thoroughgoing, and exclusive, humanism, where such exclusivity leads away from a more scientific-rational approach. Social workers, Hoghughi argued, could not hope to be widely considered as a profession with special expertise when they celebrate the 'relationship' at the expense of a more empirical, evaluative approach designed to identify and demonstrate a particular expertise possessed by the profession.

His solution was an approach consistent with the scientific-technical tradition involving a central concern with assessment. He deliberately compared this with the 'diagnostic' approach of the more established profession of medicine and argued that this approach would impose some coherence on social work's understanding of the phenomena with which it is concerned. In brief, this involves a cyclical approach of determining the problem, acting to alleviate it, evaluating the outcome, using this evaluation to improve future work with the problem and so on.

Public Acceptance

Faith in the expert knowledge of a profession is crucial to its public acceptance. Such acceptance is dependent upon a focus on areas of life believed to be of considerable importance, the possession of skills and knowledge which are difficult to understand and a capacity to bring under control areas of life which would otherwise be plagued by uncertainty. Medicine achieves all these qualities. Its 'mystique' lies precisely in the fact that life and death situations, as well as potentially serious ill health, lie within its ambit, and that it possesses the capacity to control situations with potentially serious adverse consequences for those involved. They are capable of creating a 'social distance' from their clientele by their esoteric knowledge and capacity to control the uncertain.

A central problem for social work has been its limited success in gaining public acceptance that they possess specialised knowledge and skills. Social workers appear to deal too much with the stuff of everyday life. If a family has problems with an adolescent this may not appear substantially different from the problems of all families raising children. If residential care is being considered for an older person, it is something a relative could easily arrange. It is the very apparent 'ordinariness' of social work matters which undermine claims to professional status. This ordinariness can go so far as to undermine a belief in the need for training: sound judgement allied to life experience is frequently touted as the 'real' requirement of those entering social work. In such circumstances it is of little use for social workers to point to their wide ranging responsibilities, or that their work involves the conscious use of self or some form of 'uncommon sense' (England, 1986).

Indeed, their areas of greatest responsibility have not been altogether helpful for social workers. They may claim to deal with life and death situations in their child protection functions, and even to argue on this basis for more extensive and lengthy training (Blom-Cooper, 1985) However, the spate of child deaths, when social workers have been involved, have rather overshadowed the frequently excellent job undertaken protecting large numbers of children on a day to day basis. As Wilding (1982) points out, with doctors we only hear of their successes, with social work the opposite is true.

A Stigmatised Profession

Whatever the responsibilities carried by social workers, public perceptions of social work can be affected by their clientele. Social workers have dealt to a large degree with groups who are themselves stigmatised. Pinker (1971) has commented that different values are placed on individuals according to the extent to which they are economically dependent on the efforts of others, a quality characteristic of most social work clients. Groups such as the physically disabled, those with learning difficulties and the mentally ill have historically been stigmatised, and their stigma is liable to 'rub off' on the profession concerned with them.

Hughes (1958) has coined the term 'dirty work' to describe work which is not valued in society. Examples of such work might be that of the dustman or sewage worker. However, it is applicable also to the more 'professional' jobs, particularly where that work involves people. If the people with whom a profession works are stigmatised, that profession is itself likely to be affected by the stigma. While the public may want some professional group to deal with 'undesirables' such as delinquents and child abusers, it is not likely to reward that profession by high esteem. This lack of esteem leaves social work vulnerable to questions about the legitimacy of their professional status and their control over their work.

NEO TAYLORISM IN SOCIAL CARE

The weakness of social work's case for professional status left it vulnerable to a more managerial approach to social care. While recognising the schematic and 'ideal type' nature of Dunsire's classification, the position of judgement makers or problem solvers is one characteristic of professions within bureaucracies (such as accountants) who have successfully pursued their claim to professional status. Social workers have always been subject to greater managerial control. Howe (1986) found that where social workers' occupational skills failed to bring situations under control, in line with organisational goals, the more restricted strategies of managers could be applied through authority based directives or by managerial design and structure. Nonetheless, social workers have been able to exercise considerable discretion, based, in no small part, on the uncertainty of their area of work and the knowledge and skills - not uncontested - to which they have laid claim (Lipsky, 1980; Mechanic, 1962).

Managerial strategies have placed this under increasing threat, with significant portions of social care involved in care management being routinised, with tendencies towards rule following and an employment of less qualified individuals representing a deprofessionalisation of areas of social care. This process of, on the one hand, accretion of power or control to managers and routinisation of tasks of other staff has been identified more widely within the public services as 'Neo Taylorism' (Pollitt, 1990), elements of which represent distinct tendencies in the development of social services delivery. Taylor developed the idea of 'scientific management', which, according to Braverman (1974) is the basic principle of structuring work from early this century to the present day. It involves two key elements: task fragmentation and deskilling of the workforce together with centralisation of work planning (Littler, 1978). Taylor's scheme involved the systematic analysis of the process of production followed by its fragmentation by a greatly increased division of labour. In this way tasks could be simplified, standardised and deskilled. Labour productivity (in theory) would increase, as would profits, once workers specialised in repeated tasks. In the extreme form of time work management, managers would have greater control of production costs through the fixing of standard times and the establishment of payment by results schemes. Evidence of this task fragmentation is apparent in studies commissioned by some social services departments (Abbott, 1992)

Task control is achieved by a 'planning department' which plans and coordinates the manufacturing process. The principle of task control was that managers should plan and direct the organisation of production. This involved two crucial elements. First the standardisation of tasks arose through the prescribing of uniform practices and operating procedures . Second, tasks undertaken, and worker performance generally, became more amenable to supervision as a result of this standardisation, either by more directly determining what should be undertaken or by reducing the problems arising from the incongruence of superior-subordinate skills.

Two consequences are of interest. First, scientific management represented an attack on craft autonomy. Braverman (1974, p 11) commented 'all possible brain work should be removed from the shop and centred in the planning...department'. Second, though Taylor never developed any systematic ideas on training, the move towards job roles incorporating minimal training time was a crucial step towards shifting control of training to the employer.

While it would be foolish to suggest that social care developments meant the introduction of 'full blown' Taylorism, these ideas are illuminating in indicating tendencies and directions. The routinisation of some tasks is most evident in the development of core assessment schedules, through which initial assessments of consumer's circumstances are undertaken. These are structured forms, involving ticking boxes, which direct the practitioner to areas of assessment and supplies them with the alternative responses they may make. These forms are developed on the assumption that the range of consumer circumstances are sufficiently predictable in advance to enable such forms to be developed and used. Its most extreme form is evident where such information is computerised, and programmed to provide care packages unencumbered by the ideas of the practitioner. This degree of computerised routinisation has in the past been more closely associated with jobs such as clerical work in banking where the computer assumes most of the functions of checking the transactions and controlling the work. Because all information about work activities within the firm is centralised, senior managers have the knowledge to direct and coordinate those activities far more thoroughly than before (Weir, 1977). This approach of computerised assessment and management of social care contrasts with the flexible more qualitative approach formerly more (though not exclusively) characteristic of social work assessments. Yet these are, in many respects, the very stuff of professional skill.

A limitation to routinisation arises in relation to 'sentimental work' (Strauss et al, 1982). This refers to work which has to take account the essential subjectivity and value of humans . Morgan (1990) has noted that the scientific management type routinisation to which NHS nursing has been subject has nevertheless been limited by a core of tasks centred around sentimental work, that both resists further deskilling and provides the basis for a claim to wider job control for nurses. However, this depends on the dominant definition of the work content of the practitioner. If managers wish , and are successful in this respect, to define the work content of care management in terms of simplistic and routine tasks, then the elements of sentimental work, such as interpersonal skills and reflexive responses to situations will be marginalised or removed altogether.

A further development partly consequent upon this, is the employment of community care workers, without professional social work qualifications. This is analogous, in many respects to the attack by Scientific management on the craft unions. If forms can be provided, procedures followed, individuals programmed in advance, then there is little need for a higher level professional qualification. These processes, furthermore, are evident in the development of NVQ awards and HNDs in care management, both lower level awards, and in the case of the latter comprising certain aspects of the former social work knowledge basis. Social care, then, is characterised by deskilling of tasks previously widely performed by more qualified staff.

Managerial control is extended in a number of ways. National Vocational Council qualifications (NVQ) awards may be undertaken 'in service' while an individual is employed by a department. An HND may be taken in the same way, and perhaps in a Further rather than Higher Education establishment. A key element, however, is the extension of managerial power to determine, or at least significantly influence, the content of training, with the intention of producing individuals able to carry out agency and managerial policy, rather than troublesome social workers with a capacity to question approaches and procedures. The standardisation of tasks through forms like the core assessment schedule, second, enable managers to exercise far more direct control over practice, by largely determining *in advance* what shall take place, as well as audit what has actually taken place. Third, as the Department of Health Manager's Guide (1991) clearly indicates, care management has the equivalent of a centralised 'planning department' whose role is to develop services and coordinate the delivery of social care.

Large areas of social care, therefore, are characterised by task routinisation and deskilling. It would be wrong to suggest that this is the case for all areas of practice formerly undertaken by social workers. In the child care field, for example, the need for a professional social work qualification is still recognised, and indeed, may soon involve the development of post qualifying accreditation in child care, actually increasing the training required for practice. This is despite the well publicised child deaths involving social work supervision. This may be attributed to a continuing recognition of the uncertainty of the area of work (Dingwall, 1989) together with the disastrous consequences where mistakes are made. The level of responsibility involved, together with the uncertainty, would appear to require levels of judgement, the existence of professional virtualities and a capacity to follow procedures which requires a high level of training.

An associated trend is the development of accountability. This is interesting, because it provides an impression of greater responsibility - and hence professional status - being granted the practitioner. This is closely related to an apparent opportunity to devolve budget holding - and hence power - to practitioners (rather than managers). Perceptions of professionalisation are, however, largely chimerical, and may be better tied with managerialism, for it is the terms under which these developments are occurring that are critical. Devolution of budget holding (where it occurs) takes place in a context where the procedures for coming to decisions have become more circumscribed. Where practitioners tasks are largely defined in terms of rule following, particularly where computers are used, then managers retain real control by setting the rules to be followed. Accountability, furthermore, is set in terms of the capacity to follow rules and procedures rather than on professionally defined competencies and virtualities. Hence, the Department of Health Managers' Guide (1991, p 50), while supporting a balance between regulation and discretion, and even a trend towards the latter, nonetheless states that, in the last analysis 'there has to be enough regulation to support the achievement of policy objectives'. These rules, then, by making practice more 'visible' enable managers to exercise greater 'arm's length' control.

CONCLUSION

Social work, it seems, is in many respects in a position analogous to that of the craft unions which 'scientific management' sought to usurp. There is a reduction in its control over a number areas of work accompanied by an extension of managerial control. This has occurred within a powerful ideology of managerialism, to a considerable degree imported from outside the traditions of welfare administration. While social work has always been characterised by a combination of procedure based rule following

and professionally based discretion, t
the balance of the two towards the
latter.

There will always be some discretic
tasks, primarily because it is impossib
matter how routine the situation, all i
therefore, no matter how far social ca
following, some degree of autonomy an
Indeed, practitioners may have goals
ways they work with them) in confl
(about managing practitioners) and may at times be able to act as
de facto policy makers (Lipsky, 1980; Mechanic, 1962).

However, social work has also been undermined by a second
element, associated with its weak professional status: an
assumption, widely canvassed in official documents (Department
of Health, 1991a) that consumers should be given considerably
greater say in defining their own needs. This is a limit to the
'cognitive superiority' of such importance to professional
recognition. This firmly places their area of work, at least in part,
in the arena of matters of everyday concern and competence.
There need for any particular expertise is concomitantly reduced.
This is a clear reflection of a consumerist ideology (of which more
later).

Social work is therefore undermined by a 'pincer' movement,
involving on the one hand a growth in the influence of
managerialist ideology and on the other a developing belief in
consumerism. However, *within* this broad trend there are, on the
one hand, certain areas of work characterised by an increase in
professional training, on the other areas of work characterised by
deskilling and reduced professional input. An example of the
former is child care work and of the latter work with older people
. Which aspects of work falls into which camp appears to arise
broadly from two factors: the degree of uncertainty both in the
assessment, management and outcome of practice interventions,
and the seriousness with which the consequences of failure is
viewed. Where child protection is involved, failure can mean the
death of a child, a consequence appalling in itself, but also usually
associated with extensive blame and condemnation, not simply of
the practitioner involved, but of the occupation as a whole. Placing
an older person in a less than adequate residential establishment,
is likely to have less dire consequences, and even if it did, the
outcry would be likely to be considerably less than where children

We may, therefore, predict a better qualified, though number, social work force within social services. At the me, both in planning and direct control of work undertaken, developments represent an extension of managerial control practice, and a greater capacity to determine what level of qualification and skill is required for which area of work. All this, of course, relates closely to the nature of the social work role, outlined in chapter 3. We may explore this further in relation to the concern for efficiently linking needs to resources in the care management process. This will be the subject of the next chapter.

Chapter Five

Care management and the consumer

The term consumer has been widely, and generally positively, used in social work circles in recent years (Shaw, 1976, 1984; Rees and Wallace, 1982; Sheppard, 1992). For some people it is considered preferable to the term 'client'. However, the term consumer is also used in economics, and with the advent of care management, linking packages of care to their cost, this definition may be particularly illuminating. What do we find social workers advocating the term consumer have been committing themselves to? Care management, as presented here may be understood as a form of economic activity whose central concern is social care. This chapter is concerned with what this actually means in theory and practice, and explores the extent to which this is illuminated by neoclassical ideas as well as identifying the limits to their application. This is undertaken in relation to the main concepts in Expected Utility theory (Ford, 1983, 1989; Hey, 1979). Many of the concepts involved in Expected Utility are more easily understandable in introductory texts on cost benefit analysis, also about choice and decision making under conditions of uncertainty, (eg Pearce, 1983 and Mishan, 1971). Although it has become evident in recent years that people do not behave exactly (or only) as the expected utility hypothesis predicts (Ford, 1989; Fishburn, 1983; Schoemaker, 1982; Sugden, 1986), it nonetheless provides concepts whose exploration benefits our understanding of care management. In proceeding with this issue, we shall need to explore the whole question of utility and value in relation to costs.

This will involve, first, examining what it means to call a client a consumer, in terms of the value or utility attached by an individual to social care, concentrating in particular on the monetary expression of value. This essentially links cost of social care to its benefit to the consumer. Second, we will examine rational choice of care package: choosing the care package providing the greatest benefit at any given cost. Third, we will examine the difficulty identifying the care package with the greatest utility (benefit) because of the uncertainty over outcome of provision of any care package. *As a response to need, therefore, care management is presented as an activity which seeks, by rational assessment, to maximise the utility of the consumer, by choice of the care package providing them with the greatest benefit compared with alternatives, as far as this is possible to determine where the outcome of social care is uncertain.*

THE CLIENT AS CONSUMER

Care management is concerned, with maximising the benefit to a consumer, of social care, at a given cost. In economic terms 'utility' refers to the benefit or satisfaction an individual gets from the consumption of a commodity (good or service). It represents the value they place on that commodity. Conventional neoclassical economics assumes each individual will seek to maximise their utility and will do so in relation to the range of goods or services available to them (Parkin, 1990; Phelps, 1985; Samuelson and Nordhaus, 1989). This is not a uniform matter: each individual will place different values upon the same good or service and any single individual will place different value on different goods.

The individual's consumption, through which they attempt to maximise their utility will be related to disposable income and the prices of goods and services. A higher disposable income (DI) or reduction in prices provides the opportunity for increasing a consumer's total utility through the purchase of more goods and services, and vice versa. However, they are also likely to change the consumption pattern. With a lower DI the consumer may concentrate their entire DI on essential goods - food, rent, energy costs and so on - while with a higher DI that consumer may devote considerably more of their DI to luxury goods such as cars, dishwashers and microwave cookers (to bring out key characteristics, the issue of elasticity of demand is not dealt with here, and may be examined in any basic Economics textbook (Samuelson and Nordhaus, 1989)). In maximising their utility, therefore, an individual will seek, within the constraints of their DI and prices to obtain that combination of goods which maximises their utility. In the neoclassical world of perfect competition, the achievement of this is called consumer equilibrium.

This process involves choice, since an individual will have a limited DI reflecting, at an individual level, the scarcity of resources available in the economy. An individual, therefore, has to order those goods in terms of their preference and amount in order to maximise their use of resources. This is exactly the problem confronted in care management, where individual need, and the necessary social care, confronts the limited budget available. Neoclassical theory copes with this with a belief that at the margins (ie the last unit of a commodity bought) the utility per £ (ie value÷cost) spent on all goods is equal (Parkin, 1990). We may doubt that economic agents can perform the complex calculations necessary to maximise their utility in precisely this way: they may rely on rules of thumb to govern their behaviour (Simon, 1955; Schotter, 1990, p 31)

This does not prevent care managers from acting, as far as possible in a rational manner in relation to the benefit provided to a consumer by a package of care. Within the restrictions of a budget the care manager's task is to achieve for the client consumer equilibrium: they seek to achieve that combination of forms of social care which will maximise total utility (per £ spent). However, care management differs from wider application of marginal and total utility since the latter is generally used to account for indifference between all commodities available to consumers, as widely variant (potentially) as health care insurance, purchasing a car, a holiday and so on. Care management involves a budget earmarked for one purpose only: social care. The choice, therefore, is restricted to the market in social care and indifference will be expressed only in relation to and between those social care commodities.

Utility, therefore, introduces the basic element of linking costs and benefits which form the key elements of care management. Care management seeks to relate the benefit from a given service or range of services to its cost, and to seek to maximise the client's utility ie provide them with the maximum possible benefit. We shall now seek to explore what this means in detail

Social Care as a Commodity

Utility or value may, basically, be divided into value in use and value in exchange. Value in use reflects the value that an individual personally places on something rather than its actual price. I may personally value highly a drawing from my child which would have no market value whatsoever. The intrinsic value of something has nothing to do with economic conceptions of value. It does not, furthermore, involve issues of morality - what we should do or the way we should behave. A moralist may value something because of the good it does, such as being kind to someone regardless of whether it costs anything. 'Being kind', however, is not something we can exchange. We cannot 'buy' that good act (or the good intention underlying it) from another so that it becomes a property of ourselves. This, of course has implications for social morality: economic concepts of value have no concern with the distribution of commodities or more generally with social justice. (Macintyre, 1967; Sen, 1970).

An economist's sense of value is always value in exchange. J.S. Mill puts this well (1909, p 436):

> ...the word value, when used without adjunct, means, in political economy, value in exchange...political economy has nothing to do with the comparative estimation of different uses in the judgement of the philosopher or moralist.

Value in exchange concerns that which is tradeable. Exchange value is a value which occurs in a market. With the commitment to a market in social care, exchange value becomes a key dimension to the conduct of care management: the exchange value of various forms of social care.

Value in use and in exchange, even without reference to the moralist or philosopher, can contrast sharply. Adam Smith (in Schotter, p 28) wrote that:

> ...the things which have the greatest value in use have frequently little or no value in exchange. Nothing is more valuable than water, but it will purchase scarce anything; scarce anything can be had in exchange for it.

The low exchange value attached to water contrasts sharply with the high value attached to diamonds, yet water is an absolute essential, without which survival would not be possible. This conundrum, which so perplexed Smith was eventually 'solved' by Marshall, with his law of diminishing marginal utility (Marshall, 1947). At base this is very simple: the more of a commodity consumed by an individual, the less they value it. Water is plentiful, diamonds are rare, hence the exchange value of diamonds is greater than water.

Willingness to Pay

The medium through which an individual's preference is expressed is money. This represents the exchange value of a commodity. The context in which this exchange takes place is the market - in this case the market in social care. With care management the money available is formulated in a voucher or budget with which the care manager is able to purchase a package of services.

The amount an individual is prepared to pay for a good reflects the value, expressed in monetary terms, they place on a good. This is termed their 'willingness to pay' (WTP) (Pearce, 1983). This is the maximum an individual is prepared to pay in order to avoid foregoing the benefit (utility) obtained from consumption of that good. WTP is a monetary expression of value in use to an individual. In a market an individual's preference is expressed by the offer of money in exchange for some benefit received. What is actually paid for a commodity, however, could well be less than the individual's WTP. It cannot be more, because to pay more than their WTP involves paying more, in monetary terms, than the value they place on it. Mill (1909, p 436) again:

> The exchange value of a thing may fall short, by any amount, of its value in use. But that it can ever exceed the value in use implies a contradiction, it supposes that a person will give, to possess a thing, more than the utmost value which they themselves place upon it as a means for gratifying their inclinations

Given that the actual price paid is determined by the interaction of many buyers and a few or many sellers, there will be those whose WTP will exceed the price they actually pay, an excess termed 'consumer surplus'. This may occur with social care, despite the more controlled market of social care, where the need for some form of social care will outweigh (in monetary terms) its cost. In the case of an older person remaining at home, they may feel socially isolated, a problem solvable by day care. The budget available may exceed the cost of day care, although they would have been prepared to use all the budget for this purpose. Their consumer surplus (which might be spent on other social care commodities) would be the difference between the cost of day care and the total budget available to them.

It should be remembered, of course, that while an individual's willingness to pay reflects the monetary value attached to a commodity, it is expressed in the context of their available disposable income. An individual with limited income is likely to have a lower WTP for luxury goods, where most, if not all their income is spent on essential goods, than those with a higher income, where greater resources are available for luxury goods. This is relevant to the context of care management. An individual's choice will, in relation to the range of 'social care commodities' be restricted by the budget available to them. For an older person, the utility, in terms of protecting health and safety, of residential care may be the most significant consideration. They may also be interested in the preservation of independence. However, within the restrictions of the budget, the alternative of residential care may mean a limit on their independence. The consumer's WTP, in other words, is such that the whole budget is used on residential care, despite the limits to their independence which may arise. In this case, the 'essential good' is residential care. Their WTP for alternative resources which may enhance their independence is correspondingly lowered: they are not prepared to pay anything.

This linkage of WTP with money and an emphasis on exchange value as an economic measure of value of commodities has created some disquiet. This is well presented by Shumaker (1973, p 41-2) who has commented, in relation to cost benefit analysis:

> ...what is...destructive of civilization is the pretence that everything has its price or, in other words, that money is the highest of all values.

Cost benefit analysis, in that well known phrase, involves knowing 'the cost of everything and the value of nothing'. Such apparent indifference to social or moral values implies, in terms of the wider market, that it is the market which should determine the distribution of income and wealth. This cannot be said to be the case with care management, for the very existence of care management within a welfare system involves a commitment to welfare which necessarily involves interference in the market's distribution of income and wealth. Welfare costs money, and this is obtained through taxation. The availability of a state funded budget used by care managers involves monetary commitment to certain values of care and support for those defined to be in need (whether this is a sufficient commitment is another matter). However, Shumaker's comment may remain relevant: we may question whether having to consider, from the outset, monetary issues, places an implicit value on money which will somehow interfere with the consideration of need, especially if considered in terms of willingness to pay.

In other respects, care management closely reflects the wider concerns of linking costs and benefits. There is, in fact, at least one hidden value judgement: that it is a good thing that individual's preferences should count. The analysis of utility, therefore, highlights key issues behind two central concerns of care management: linking the social care provided to individuals to its cost and giving consumers the greatest possible say in decisions about the social care they receive. Understanding social work as care management, therefore, clearly involves an economic notion of the consumer and social care. However, the extent to which individuals' preferences do count, or can in fact count, will be considered further later.

Embedded in the notion of care management is a belief that the choice of social care within any particular budget should be a rational one. Rational choice, for the (economic) consumer, is one in which the gains from consuming a particular commodity exceeds its costs, either in the process or outcome of consuming that commodity, or in relation to the alternative commodities foregone. Rationality, in this respect, is closely related to selfishness. Modern free market economics couples a belief in self interest with a belief that economic agents are rational calculators capable of solving the implicit mathematical maximisation problems they face in everyday life. This is a well established position. Jevons (1970) wrote:

> Pleasure and pain are undoubtedly the ultimate objects of the calculus of Economics. To satisfy our wants to the utmost with the least effort - to procure the greatest amount of what is desirable at the expense of the least that is undesirable - in other words, to maximise pleasure, is the problem of Economics.

The problem of rational decision making, even at the level of utility adopted in Economics, involves complex issues in which the benefit of consuming a particular set of commodities must be set against the potential benefits foregone of alternative possible consumption - referred to in cost benefit analysis as opportunity cost (Eckstein, 1958; McKean, 1958) - and the cost of the commodity set against the benefit which may not immediately transpire or be apparent (formalised in CB analysis as time discounting) (Pearce, 1983)). This is obvious, for example in the case of work with a young offender, where that work directly helps prevent them pursuing a life of crime (it should be remembered that we are here writing 'in principle'; it is clearly difficult to demonstrate such an effect in practice) (Thorpe et al, 1980). The costs may in the first instance be great, for example if the young person required secure accommodation. But this may prevent considerably greater cost of policing and imprisonment at a later stage

Expected Utility theory (Ford, 1983, 1989) possesses a number of axioms which formalises this position and links it with assumptions of perfect competition:

1. The axiom of completeness. The consumer is able to order all available combinations of goods according to his/her preferences.
2. The axiom of transivity. If commodity A is preferred to commodity B and commodity B is preferred to commodity C, then A is preferred to C, with ABC normally conceived as bundles of commodities.
3. The axiom of selection The consumer aims for his/ her *most preferred* state (Allais, 1979). Clearly, the demands upon humans as 'rational economic man' are tremendous. To what extent (a) can they be considered realistic and (b) to approximate the position of care manager?

Amongst the assumptions underlying these axioms are three of particular importance. First, that in choosing between different commodity combinations the individual is involved in a number of decisions, the property rights over which are vested in them as an individual. This is about consumer sovereignty, something to which reference is frequently made in official literature on care management (Department of Health, 1991a, 1991b). Second, the consumer knows themselves what is best for them; it is not for anyone else to decide, on value or other grounds what is good for the consumer. Mishan comments in relation to this (1971, p 172):

> ...economists are generally agreed - either as a canon of faith, as a political tenet or an act of expediency - to accept the dictum that each person knows their own interests best.

Third, there is an assumption of 'perfect information' on which to base their decisions. Linked to the other beliefs, about rationality and property rights, this means that, being perfectly informed about all prices, each consumer would be willing to buy only at the lowest price. Indeed, in this world of rational and perfectly informed beings with identical tastes, each consumer would hold out for the best terms, and these would be identical to that of all other consumers (Phelps, 1985, p 236). Such assumptions are, of course, far fetched, and criticised even from the right (Hayek, 1978). However, their exploration may help further our understanding of care management. From the perspective of social care, three issues arise: the extent to which the consumer may be considered sovereign, whether or not self interest is the key to decision making and the appropriateness of utility as the key to rational decision making.

Rationality

The issue of rationality will be dealt with in more detail in the next chapter. However, we may note here that rationality based on utility represents a limited concept of reasoning. Milne (1968) considers utility to be the lowest level of reasoning, above which are, in ascending order of rationality, first, reasons for actions which enhance personal well being, regardless of the wants of the moment (and which may fit with the concept of need in care management); second rational moral agency, involving acting according to the established social morality; and finally - the highest level of reasoning - critical humanism, which is rationality based on that which is intrinsically valuable to us as human beings.

Self Interest

On one hand the social policy context of care management involves a commitment to a redistributive dimension difficult to equate with individualistic self interest; on the other hand care managers are largely expected to act as utility maximising agents of consumers. In social care an issue of equity arises: for if I am wealthy and completely selfish, then I will not be concerned with your access to the same commodities as me, despite your relative poverty. It is clear that, however inadequately, in relation to social care, some weight is attached to distributive goals. Tobin (1970, p 263-77) has commented that economists willingness to accept inequality (in rational humans):

...should be tempered by a persistent and durable strain of...specific egalitarianism...the view that certain specific scarce commodities should be distributed less unequally than their ability to pay for them.

This is clearly the case with care management, where money in the form of care manager's budgets, is available for the purchase of social care, the cost of which may be only partially or not at all carried by the consumer of social care themselves. This indicates a clear tension between the economic theories of the right through which they justify the superiority of the market (Buchanan, 1978; Hayek, 1978) and the context in which this is applied. The social policy context of care management involves a commitment to welfare which takes us beyond self interest and rationality based on personal utility, one which is consistent with Tobin's remarks.

A number of approaches may help explain this limit on individual selfishness. Margolis (1982) has emphasised the importance of participation in limiting selfishness. Here individuals obtain utility through participating in group activities - such as the provision of health or social care - where they are equal members of the group and utility is gained through the process of participating (doing their 'fair share' for society). Sen (1977) has a notion of commitment whereby, perhaps because of some Kantian sense of duty, individuals are committed to the provision of equitable social care. Culyer (1976) has referred to the 'humanitarian spillover', which suggests that individuals care about the health status, or consumption of health care, of others, an idea which may be transferred to social care.

This limit to selfishness may be related to deep psychological needs: pure selfishness may affect an individual's self esteem or give them feelings of guilt. This would be related to an innate feeling for justice or fairness. This is particularly likely to be the case in circumstances where vulnerable and needy individuals are involved, and where these needs are generally accepted within a society. Thus Williamson (1975, p 256) notes:

...that transactions which affect conceptions of self esteem and/or perceptions of collective well being are those for which attitudinal considerations...are especially important.

It is, *in the process of conducting care management,* for social workers to behave, through utility maximisation as if the consumer's interest were paramount, and hence from the consumer's perspective, operate in their interest. Where, for example, a budget is available to a consumer, there is no expectation that they will somehow use some of that budget to contribute to the social care of another consumer. There is no redistributive dimension evident once the budget is allocated to the consumer. The social worker as care manager, is acting as an agent who in principle, is deemed to be working in the self interest of the consumer. Hence the implicit aim of maximising the consumer's (not anyone else or the wider society) utility within given budget constraints. This is the position, it should be emphasised, once the budget is allocated to the individual. Wider resource decisions about how much should be allocated to different groups receiving social care could well involve, from, say, one year to the next, changes in relative amounts set aside for those groups. The issue of the consumer's interest may, however, be examined further in relation to their sovereignty.

Consumer Sovereignty

The care manager, in theory, might be seen purely as the agent of the consumer. The consumer would have sovereign power over decisions within the constraints of a limited budget. In such circumstances the care manager would simply 'take instructions' and carry out the will of the consumer. There are, however, a number of limits to this. First, and this is built into the idea of care management, the consumer is likely to suffer from a limit to information available to them. This information could relate to a number of things, including precisely what their personal needs are, what their legal position is in relation to social work involvement, what are the range and type of resources available to them, their cost, and money available to purchase those resources and the likely outcome, in relation to their personal needs, of the use of that particular resource. The consumer, it might be argued, is as far as possible, to decide what their own needs are. Even where this is the case, however, they may have limited knowledge of the range of alternatives. This can be the case even where circumstances are most auspicious for consumer sovereignty. An elderly woman, for example, who has decided that they wish for residential care, and who is clear about that decision, may nonetheless not know of the range of homes available, which would suit her best, their cost and whether or not her 'budget' would be sufficient to cover the costs. She is likely to have little detailed knowledge of what they have to offer specifically in relation to her needs.

Wherever, furthermore, the care manager possesses some esoteric professional knowledge not immediately available to the consumer, and of relevance to their needs and resources provided, this will place a limit on consumer sovereignty. Where, for example, groupwork is purchased to help an individual with some psychological problem (such as depression) the care manager is likely to be in a far better position to predict its outcome than the consumer (though we should be wary of ascribing too great a capacity for 'prediction' amongst social workers, while being aware that clients may, by their own deliberate acts, influence the course of events (Homans, 1973)).

Second, there may be limits to the capacity of the consumer to exercise sovereign decision making. Some individuals will want to retain maximum autonomy in decision making. Others, however, may be ready to abrogate responsibility for decision making to the care manager. Good practice may dictate that the care manager encourage such individuals to make their own decisions, but this may be limited by an individual who determinedly refuses to do so. They may, in fact, feel some utility (called process utility) (McGuire et al, 1988) from so doing: where a decision is of such moment, it may invoke such anxiety that they feel unable to make it themselves, and try to abrogate decision making to the care manager. Keith-Lucas (1972) describes the task of the helper as frequently one where they must work through client ambivalence to encourage them to make their own choice. In this, they may not always be successful. Furthermore, some consumers may be limited by factors such as learning difficulties. Where, for example, as is frequently the case, there has in the past been insufficient attention given to developing the social skills and decision making capacities of an individual with learning difficulties, severe constraints will be place on even the best attempts of a care manager to maximise their control over their own life. The temptation exists, which is apparent in medicine (Arrow, 1974), for the consumer, both in ascribing professional status to the care manager and consequently attributing greater knowledge to them, to abrogate responsibility to the care manager.

However, there is a more fundamental limit on consumer sovereignty inherent in agency function. These relate also to the difference between wants and needs and the extent to which these limit consumer sovereignty. It is a fiction to consider the care manager will, in many instances, be the agent of the consumer. The care manager exists, at times uncomfortably, between the social expectations manifested in their state responsibilities and the direct relationship they have with the consumer. The care manager is often not primarily answerable to the consumer in the way, for example, a solicitor may be when representing a client. They will be there to make sure certain things happen - for example protecting a child who may be at risk - and that responsibility rests with them, amongst others, whatever the views of the consumer (Howe, 1979). This consumer may be considered to be the child, who is being protected, or the parents, whose parenting capacities it is the aim of the care manager to support and improve. What the parent, as consumer, may want may be to have no social service involvement at all. What they may *need*, according to the agency, is extensive intervention designed to help protect the child. In such circumstances, where there is some risk to the child's safety, either the parents will cooperate with social services involvement, preferably, if possible, in partnership with the parents, or this is likely to take place without their agreement. This is a clear, if last resort, responsibility of social services under the provisions of the Children Act (Department of Health, 1989). An alternative view might make the child, rather than the parent, the consumer. Where the child is young enough, however, it may be difficult to ascribe sovereign decision making capabilities to them, notwithstanding the responsibility in certain circumstances, to take account of the wishes and feelings of the child. The age limited life experience and understanding of young children may not necessarily prevent them from making their wishes and feelings clear, but the care management decision, possibly through a case conference, may, taking all circumstances into account (for example risk to them), not accord with the child's preferences.

Uncertainty
We have so far discussed matters as if the outcome of consumption - the costs and benefits (utility) attached to choices were known. If we make a choice we will know with certainty what will transpire in terms of consumer benefits. This is not normally the case, and expected utility is concerned with decision making in uncertainty. Care management is largely concerned with outcomes, ie choosing that combination of social care commodities which will maximise an individual's utility within the constraints of the available budget. There is, however, a problem: we cannot be sure for the consumer of any particular care package what the outcome will

be. This is the case with even the apparently most straightforward situations. Where, for example, an elderly person displays a clear desire to move from home into residential care, and knows exactly their preferred establishment, we cannot be sure, when provided, that they will be satisfied with it. They may, for example, feel a greater sense of loss for their former home than they anticipated or they may not get on with residents preferring an alternative. Matters become far more complex when, for example, a particular care package is designed to change an adolescent's offending behaviour (Thorpe et al, 1980). The point is, that when putting together a care package we have a particular outcome in mind, and that outcome implicitly involves some prediction of the form: if approach (package) A is applied to problem B then outcome C will occur. Life is, not, however like this, and we cannot make predictions in this way (Howe, 1980). Care management is, therefore in the business of making rational decisions in conditions of uncertainty. Uncertainty, technically, involves two concepts: risk and uncertainty (Mishan, 1988; Sugden and Williams, 1978)). The overall concept of uncertainty, embracing both risk and uncertainty, we shall refer to here as 'overall uncertainty' to avoid confusion with the sub category of uncertainty.

Risk relates outcomes to the probability of them occurring. If rational choice involves weighing up the benefits of any choice against their costs (and comparing this with other choices), then risk involves weighing up the probability of each of these costs and benefits occurring. In this case we would know all the possible alternative costs and benefits associated with a particular course of action and the probability of these alternatives occurring. Uncertainty takes matters one stage further, where although we know all the alternative possible outcomes, we do not know the probabilities of each of these outcomes occurring. For example, for a person entering residential care two alternatives may be that their entry improves social interaction or that it does not (with two alternatives, this is, of course, the most simple possible example). We may, as a rule of thumb, consider the probability of the former is 75% and the latter is 25%. Alternatively, we may have no idea of the alternative probabilities. The former involves risk and the latter involves uncertainty.

The degree of overall uncertainty is liable to vary in particular with the complexity of the situation. Where relatively straightforward practical help is required - eg the supply of aids and home care for an older person with physical disability, there may be greater certainty of outcome. Where a young child has serious emotional and behavioural problems, the care package may include direct work with the child, therapeutic work with the family as well as playgroup and parental skills work. All may be designed to produce an environment more conducive to the child's future well being, but whether or not it will be successful, indeed the extent to which it will be successful, is often not clearly predictable in the everyday world of practice.

The problematic nature of prediction in social work is well illustrated by Dingwall (1989) in relation to child abuse. In general, he comments on the limited nature of models in social work, lacking the well grounded theory that links a set of substantial research findings into a coherent narrative. More specifically, he comments on the failure to construct a generally accepted and used persuasive operational definition of abuse, which inhibits attempts at prediction. The most persuasive definitions indicate an extremely low incidence of abuse. This creates, even with the most sophisticated instruments, the problem of falsely identifying positives (child abusers) in the normal (non abusing) population, where the latter outnumbers the former so greatly. Even a low level of inaccuracy in screening instruments is likely to yield a group predicted as child abusers where the non abusers far outnumber the actual abusers. In one Bradford study this approach yielded a rate of false positives 28 times that of correct positives (Lealman et al, 1983). At an individual level prediction can be equally problematic. In the case of multiple sclerosis sufferers Williams (1990) shows that the course and outcome of the illness, once diagnosed, is so uncertain that it is difficult to evaluate the effectiveness of any treatment let alone predict the likely success of alternatives. This is the situation which frequently confront social workers as care managers. In these circumstances, what is needed is some method for managing uncertainty. Both the principles and methods for managing overall uncertainty become important.

Choices between alternatives can be made on the basis of the relative risk they present. Risk aversive and risk neutral approaches represent two alternative principles for decision making (Pearce, 1983; Sugden and Williams, 1978). Risk aversion entails focusing on the 'worst case scenario': ie making the choice whose worst outcome (*cetirus paribus*) was better than the alternatives. Risk neutral decision making, on the other hand, is not concerned with the feared worst outcome but focuses on the approach with the best possible outcome regardless of its probability and the consequences of choosing that approach and its worst outcome is achieved. In essence this involves gambling on the probability that the best outcome will occur, while disregarding the possible worst outcome (indeed other alternatives). Sheppard (1995) has argued that the nature of social work is such that we should seek to choose, where alternatives are available, that which is least likely to be wrong. This is because, he thinks, we should attempt, as far as possible, to eliminate error, since we are more likely to achieve this if we seek for disconfirming evidence about our hypotheses in relation to any particular case (for example on the cause of an adolescent's offending behaviour, or the best means to prevent further offending), than if we seek to confirm our views. Given the probabilistic nature of decisions in practice, we are unlikely to be able simply to eliminate hypotheses that are in error, but are able to choose that which is, on the available evidence, least likely to be wrong. As a principle this fits with risk aversive responses. Risk aversion is clearly appropriate where the consequences of 'getting it wrong' are very serious although we may be prepared to gamble where the consequences of getting matters wrong are less serious.

The relationship between the range of particular outcomes (costs and benefits) and the probability of them occurring is termed the discrete probability function. This involves identifying each of the outcomes with their probability. In order to make choices care managers need make some estimate (implicit or explicit) of probabilities, and for these to be rational, they need be explicit. There are broadly three alternatives for obtaining the probability function. The first is based on mathematical or physical models through which we are able to predict likely outcomes, which are not really appropriate for social work. The second is to base the probability function on past experience. In cost benefit analysis this might, for example, involve, in building a dam, drawing upon the experience of past dams built. This is more problematic in social work because of the complexity of the subject matter - humans and their environments - and the capacity of humans to decide their own direction and 'act back' on their environment (Homans, 1973; Webb, 1981). Apparently similar situations, such as bereavement may, in fact differ markedly (for example according to the quality of the relationship or the personality of the surviving partner). The use of either approach is called objective probability.

This second approach implies that care management, when managing uncertainty, should encourage the greatest possible systemisation of practice. Where more systematic, it becomes possible to identify key characteristics of cases, and hence both learn from previous experience and identify in which respects current cases differ from previous cases. This is consistent with the tradition of social work as a technical activity, the key characteristics of which have been identified by Sheppard (1990, p 79). In essence this involves classification of case characteristics, informed by theoretical and conceptual elements, which form a knowledge base through which each case may be assessed and examined. The classification is capable of taking in all cases in a specific area of practice. Examples include the Compulsory Admissions Assessment Schedule for compulsory admission assessments under the Mental Health Act (Sheppard, 1990, 1993) and the Assessment Schedule for low support mothers at risk for depression (Sheppard, 1993a). This technical approach is also evident in Task Centred Practice (Reid, 1977; Reid and Epstein, 1972), as well as the work of Hoghughi (1980, 1980a) and Sheldon (1978, 1983). Hoghughi (1980, 1980a) suggests that, in relation to child care at least, the central task is one of classifying problems. These he divides into physical, cognitive, home and family, social skills, anti social behaviour and personal problems. He sees the development of this knowledge as a cyclical and progressive process of determining the problem, acting to alleviate it, evaluating the action, using the evidence of the evaluation to improve dealing with the next problem of the same kind and starting the process again. Every cycle uses evidence from the previous one in an attempt to refine the identification of the problem and ways of dealing with it.

The third alternative is known as subjective probability: this does not rely on objective data, but on judgements derived from assessments by some analyst or expert. This again is more characteristic of social work reflecting a tradition in social work emphasising the irreducible complexity of the human situation with which social workers work, and the uniqueness of each client and their circumstances (eg Wilkes, 1981; Ragg, 1977; England, 1986). Jamous and Peloille (1970) draw attention to virtualities - individual qualities and judgement of practitioners - which are valued by many professionals. This is even evident in occupations with strong bodies of knowledge, such as medicine (Freidson, 1970) which Atkinson (1977) refers to as the 'clinical gaze'. With a considerably less convincing knowledge base, this tradition of an emphasis on individual qualities and judgement is particularly strong in social work. This subjective judgement, however, sits uneasily with the systemisation of practice inherent in the assessment of choices, their benefits and the probability of these benefits occurring. It is arguable, also, that the systemisation of practice based on the technical approach would go far towards developing the knowledge base aiding the more rational management of uncertainty. In all probability the nature of both care management and social work will require a combination of the technical approach and subjective judgement, while, however, entailing a considerable expansion in the realm and influence of the former.

CONCLUSION

Our understanding of the nature of care management is clearly helped by the use of concepts from Expected Utility theory linking choice with costs and benefits of these choices. However, there are limits placed in general by flaws in assumptions, and in particular by the specific circumstances of care management. Care management is clearly, overall, about maximising the benefits to consumers within the constraints of given budgets. It is this which defines its concept of rationality (utility maximising). It seeks to encourage consumer sovereignty, although this is mediated by the care manager as consumer 'agent' and further limits are placed on this by, in particular, wider agency responsibilities. Within these constraints the care manager, by acting as consumer agent, attempts to represent consumer self interest 'by proxy'. Choice is, furthermore, made in conditions of uncertainty, involving judgements about probable outcomes which so characterise social work generally.

The limits to Expected Utility are also clear, however: particularly in relation to rationality, sovereignty and self interest. These may all, however, be related to the context for care management. If care management is already considered to operate in line with established social morality, a position consistent with consensus assumptions about society (Strasser, 1976), then maximising utility within that framework represents rationality at the level of social morality. Similarly, the emphasis on the social care interests of the consumer (as agent of consumer self interest) presupposes a wider concept of social responsibility inherent in the existence of care management in the first place. The limits to consumer sovereignty, furthermore, are consistent with a social morality which gives the state responsibility for care in circumstances of individual failure (Hart. 1963), for example social services responsibilities under the Children Act where care for the child by their parents is inadequate. While at the 'coal face' of the care manager-consumer relationship rationality only involves utility, care management itself involves a higher level of rationality (and morality).

More concern might be expressed, however, about the incursion of the 'cash nexus' into the realm of social care. Some might argue that this introduces financial rigour into practice. Where use value may be expressed by willingness to pay and exchange value is defined in terms of money, however, there is a serious danger that money becomes the expression of value in social care, leaving other values, related perhaps more importantly to the intrinsic worth of human beings, lower in the order of priority. Does care management, in other words, involve an insidious alteration for the worse of the values underlying social care?

However, the concepts analysed here: utility, costs, benefits, rationality and uncertainty do provide the base for the development of the theory of practice in care management. It indicates clearly that the task of the care manager is the most systematic possible management of social care in conditions of uncertainty, linking choice to costs and benefits of alternative care packages. Although this uncertainty itself makes absurd the idea that we may abandon judgement based on virtualities of individual practitioners, this leads us clearly to a greater emphasis on the tradition of social work as a technical activity through which this greater systemisation may be expressed. Care management, therefore, unless it is unnecessarily to lose the advantages of the skills of qualified social workers, involves (a) a form of practice building on social work as it is (b) a necessary further theoretical development, drawing upon existing traditions of social work.

While this kind of cost-benefit analysis tells us something about the nature of care management, there is still the matter of the process and purpose(s) of care management. As chapter 1 demonstrated, need is a key element of care management, and its alleviation is central to its purpose. The analysis of need is the subject of chapter 7. The next chapter will focus on the related issues of empowerment and consumer choice, which may be conceived as aspects of the process or the purpose(s) of care management.

Chapter Six

Empowerment, choice and self determination

A key element of care management is the apparent commitment to consumer choice. It is a key element, as we saw in chapter one, of the notion of empowerment as defined in official documents. The official documents are quite unequivocal in their guidance: the person generally best equipped to decide what they need is the consumer themselves. Consumer choice links two key elements: the capacity of individuals to choose, and the range (and quality) of products from which they can choose. In New Right thinking, this converges with their free market ideology: the individual is seen to be self determining (a morally good thing) and the market is considered to be the best mechanism for generating the range of choices required. It is no coincidence that government policy has consciously attempted to mimic the market: their idea that the individual consumer is in the best position to know his or her needs and hence make choices not only hits at professional claims to 'know best' the needs of their clients, but represents an ideological commitment. The professional task no longer becomes deciding and obtaining what the client needs, but helping the consumer to decide what s/he wants. This chapter focuses on the extent to which the consumer may be considered to be self determining in their choices.

INTERVENTION AND SELF DETERMINATION

McDermott (1976, p 3) states of self determination:

> Interpreted literally...self determination refers to that condition in which the agent's behaviour emanates from his own wishes, choices and decisions.

In this straightforward sense most humans have a capacity for self determination – they are capable of making their own choices and decisions, whether sensible or foolish, advantageous or disadvantageous. It is because it is so obvious – it does nothing to distinguish one person from another – that we rarely add that someone is 'self determining', and that this capacity is taken for granted in care management documents.

Negative Freedom and Persuasion

Self determination is less unproblematic than appears from a common sense definition. The classic modern statement of negative freedom was made by Berlin (1969). This is characterised by the absence of constraints. Freedom exists to the extent that obstacles in the way of exercising one's capacities are removed. Where constraints presented by others exist, I am, to that extent coerced:

> Coercion implies the deliberate interference of other human beings within the area in which I would otherwise act. You lack...freedom only if you are prevented from attaining goals by other human beings (Berlin, 1969, p 122).

It is, then, the absence of constraints which characterises negative freedom, and for this reason the demand for self determination may be equated with the demand for negative freedom.

This is very much the New Right view of self determination. Hayek expresses it in uncompromising terms: 'a policy of freedom must therefore, minimise coercion or its harmful effects, even if it cannot eliminate it completely'. Coercion, he thinks is 'such control of the environment or circumstances of a person by another that, in order to avoid greater evil, he is forced to act not according to a coherent plan of his own, but to serve the needs of another' (Hayek, 1960, p 11-12). Coercion is evil precisely because it eliminates an individual as a thinking and valuing person and 'makes him a bare tool in the achievement of the ends of another' (Hayek, 1960, p 20-21). It is important here that coercion, as Berlin argued also, is a personal attribute, manifested by another, not an impersonal force, such as the market.

A second dimension involves persuasion. To state the obvious, the care management process is an interaction in which the consumer(s) decide, in discussion with the care manager which is their preferred care package (if they qualify for one). In these circumstances, where frequently the care manager has access to far greater information than consumer, and indeed may be expected to act as guide, how can the consumer be said to be self determining? Can the worker legitimately attempt to persuade the consumer to take one course of action? if so how far may they take this persuasion? Benn (1967) usefully takes the argument beyond that of coercion avoidance to one that examines persuasion.

Persuasion, he thinks, is fine provided it conforms to one particular criterion: an individual's freedom is infringed to the extent that his deliberative processes have been inhibited, or some element of action put beyond the possibility of rational criticism. Persuasion is rational, he thinks, provided the persuasiveness lies in the substance of the arguments rather than [1] the manner of presentation [2] the authority of the persuader, or [3] some other special relationship by which one party is particularly susceptible to suggestions from the other. Rational persuasion in short, is impersonal, in the sense that it is the argument, not the person, that persuades. The distinctive feature of rational persuasion is that it invites and responds to criticism. The would be persuader is committed to changing his opinion too if the persuadee gives sufficient reason for rejecting it. Rational persuasion, therefore, is a dialogue between equals. This is not to say that we can always easily distinguish between the case of pure rational persuasion and others. Most cases combine rational and non rational elements: any argument, however good, can be spoilt by bad presentation, and its effect heightened by eloquence.

Non rational persuasion can, of course be resisted by subjects. However, two conditions present a problem: first, deception, involving deliberately withholding (censorship) or falsifying information, and second, any influence likely to lead to future permanent impairment of the capacity to make rational judgements.

An immediate consideration of self determined action in the care management context, then, indicates that consumers are self determining where they are not coerced and discussion both of need and available alternatives is carried out in a rational manner characterised by equality between the discussants. This possesses an immediate appeal. It is quite obvious that care managers will frequently have access to information which the consumer does not and this means that consumers cannot be completely sovereign (ie in total control) as suggested earlier. However, we do not thereby have to abandon the self determined nature of their decision making. The care management process becomes a partnership in which the practitioner and consumer bring different contributions: the practitioner their knowledge of available resources and ideas about their use; the consumer their capacity to decide, from the range of options, what they want. Consumer self determination does not, therefore mean practitioners cannot advise consumers, in strong terms should they consider this appropriate, of their view of the best approach.

The practitioner's task is therefore twofold: helping the client define for themselves their need and helping them choose the best response to it. Their role is facilitating client choice. This is frequently not a straightforward process. The choice may be, for the consumer, fairly clearcut and easily made, and hence unproblematic. They may wish to attend a day centre to make friends, find one they like and go (budget permitting). Other situations may require more deliberation, involving more careful weighing up of options on the basis of their relative utility. Still others may involve choices with, for the consumer, emotional implications, which have to be worked through before reaching a conclusion. An older person considering permanent residential care when currently living at home may have to come to terms with enormous losses, of a sense of independence, of being cut from their personal history, of fond memories associated with their home.

Ragg (1977) and Keith-Lucas (1972) have examined this in terms of facilitating active willing choice. Ragg emphasises the importance of consumer description: their task is to inform, as clearly and accurately as possible, about the way they feel about their options. The key elements for the practitioner are a need for honesty, trust and a capacity, through appropriate questioning, to draw out an accurate picture of the consumer's situation. Description lays bear not only the dilemmas but provides the basis for working on them. It also reveals the emotional work which the practitioner must engage in to fulfil the care management task. A real choice for this consumer is not just some arid calculation of instrumental benefits and costs of different alternatives, but an understanding of the emotional implications attached to them. An active willing choice is one undertaken having worked through these emotional implications at which point the individual may be able genuinely to determine what they want. Although the content of the choice may, in part, be emotional, the process of making the choice can be rational, without coercion and characterised by equality. Additionally, this therapeutic role rather blurs the distinction between care management and provision functions, for although containing a therapeutic element, this is clearly a care management role.

Limiting Consumer Self Determination

Three conditions, thus far, limit consumer self determination: those characterised by coercion, irrational persuasion and specifically censorship (and falsification). We shall consider coercion in more detail later. Situations involving deliberate withholding or falsifying of information likely to affect consumer choice would appear fairly straightforward, and these limit consumer self determination. The injunctions in social work literature to openness and honesty (Perlman, 1979) bear testimony to the long standing acceptance of this in the profession. However, irrational persuasion is another matter, and may be something which is not intended and of which a practitioner is at best only dimly aware. Two examples are presented here which may occur despite the good intentions of the practitioner, and indicate how easily consumers may be deprived of their self determined choice. The meeting of consumer and worker is one potentially stacked with ambiguity and confusion. The potential for disagreement and judgemental behaviour based on competing definitions of the situation are well attested to in client studies literature (Reese, 1978; Sheppard, 1992, 1993). This means that both consumer and worker are not engaged in a common search for some objective and uncontested need but, at best, are in a process of negotiation whereby consumer and worker may reach some common definition of need to which they are both committed. Where differences in definitions exist, however, the opportunity for non rational influence exists.

(i) Situations Not Characterised By Equality

Where a situation becomes 'objectified' ie the worker's view of the world is taken to be the only view, this can limit self determination. We have to draw on a range of background assumptions to make sense of things, many of which are cultural and hence variable. Some of these are so taken for granted that we lose sight of their origin and experience them as 'the way things are'. Where worker-client definitions differ, the insistence, by the worker on one view only can exert pressure on an otherwise reluctant consumer to accept that view.

There is evidence that professionals, furthermore, develop routine ways of defining people, their situations and solutions. This arises partly because of the consistent time and other pressures and the need, in an infinitely complex world, to be selective, to simplify and categorise the world around us. Even professionals committed to responding to consumers as unique whole individuals cannot completely escape this. These 'typifications' are bound up with intervention: the categories developed usually relate to practical concerns and include suggestions about what should be done (in this class of circumstances). Typifications become intrinsic to the way interviews are conducted, involving 'decision rules' about the kinds of evidence that is relevant and 'search procedures' for finding the evidence (Bloor, 1978). Davis and Strong (1976), for example, showed how doctors in routine ante natal clinics typified their major problems as 'worrying mothers', responding to it with routine reassurance, regardless of patient perception of problems.

Typifying, and treating as objective and uncontroversial, definitions of situations which are not unproblematic draw on the manner of the presentation or authority of the persuader to affect the consumer's judgements and hence choice. Indeed, it represents a failure to engage fully in the discussion which is essential if persuasion is not to limit self determination.

(ii) Non Rational Consumer Susceptibility

Represents situations in which an individual is particularly susceptible to the suggestions of another. Non directive approaches, paradoxically, provide a further means for exerting an insidious influence on the client. In certain respects this might appear, on the surface, to represent the approach most consistent with care management values, although evidence exists that consumers prefer some degree of advice or guidance to none at all – to know what the worker thinks (Sheppard, 1991; 1992, 1993). More or less subtle processes of focusing and reinforcement are well established and have been found in even supposedly the most non directive of therapies (Scheff, 1968). Long standing evidence from social work comes from Leonard (1965) who suggested that certain kinds of verbal or non verbal communication (nods, grunts and mms) encourage some disclosures in interviews and not others. This inhibition and reinforcement of behavioural responses he considered to be clearly a subtle form of control. The problem seems to be that however non directive the worker tries to be their perceptions and definitions are likely to appear, if not overtly, then covertly, in their manner of response to the consumer. There is, so to speak, a 'subterranean' dimension to the interview process. An overt stating of the worker's view, attached to a real opportunity to discuss matters openly may be the most honest way to deal with the subterranean influences which can be exerted.

THE AUTHORITY ROLE AND CONSUMER CHOICE

Coercion and in particular persuasion, then, represent areas in which consumer self determination may be, however inadvertently, contravened or restricted. The discussion of consumer choice has so far restricted itself to circumstances where care managers have no authority role in relation to their conduct of the case. However, whatever the aspirations of care management in relation to choice and self determination, social work retains all its considerable controlling functions, most obviously in relation to child care and mental health, and which gives it considerable power over consumers in relevant circumstances. The most well known of these are situations where children may be taken into accommodation by application through the courts or mentally ill people are compulsorily admitted to mental hospital under the Mental Health Act, although social services possess wide ranging powers in relation to these groups.

This raises a number of further issues of self determination. Indeed, some of these issues, in a care management context, may be considered specific to social workers, for they involve tasks which they, and not other professionals will be involved in, in their capacity as care managers. What, however, happens to consumer choice when the care manager possesses some authority role? surely the consumer can no longer be considered self determining, and hence exercising choice, if they are, in some sense, under the authority of the care manager? This involves a number of further considerations relating to self determination.

The Coercion Argument

One approach is to state that the notion of self determination is quite simply incompatible with the authority role vested in social workers and the controlling function they are required to exercise. Indeed this is so widespread that to employ it in relation to social work is to mislead about the nature of the task. Under certain circumstances – and these are clear and well defined in statute – the social work task involves intervention acting on the client and family in ways consistent with their statutory responsibilities regardless of that client's wishes and feelings. The role of social work as one of the methods for securing conformity of individuals and groups to state sanctioned expectations is quite familiar ground. Where, for example, parents do not act in accordance with the minimum expectations, as regards the welfare of the child, of the Children Act, social services may ultimately, through the courts, and even against their wishes, accommodate the child. Child protection work is always, if presented thus, coercive, since there is clearly some constraint imposed through the deliberate interference of another human being. The parents act under duress: if they do not change their child care behaviour, or at least cooperate in the provision of appropriate packages of care, their child may be accommodated. This may be aggravated by perspective differences outlined above: some parents may simply not accept that standards required by social workers are appropriate and consider their interference quite unwarranted.

Three alternatives appear possible with this coercion argument. The first involves distinguishing, as traditionally done, between areas where social workers have controlling statutory responsibilities and those where they do not. There are certainly some non controlling functions: helping an elderly person obtain the best care package might be one, although even here, where dementia occurs, issues such as Guardianship or compulsory admission under the Mental Health Act may arise. We need be more precise and limit this to the non mentally disordered elderly person. However, these are areas where it may prove increasingly difficult to establish social work's sole right to care managerial responsibility, and hence a distinctive contribution.

We may further divide into two those where statutory powers exist, such as child care. Some practice may not involve the likelihood of statutory child protection work, and hence the practitioner is acting solely in support of, and in agreement with, the consumer (parent). This is close to the 'contractual' idea Keith Lucas (1963) presents: the social worker is contracted by the client to carry out certain agreed tasks. We might, then distinguish between cases where controlling functions exist and those where they do not. This would minimise the coercive element of social work. However, statutory responsibilities hang heavy over even these tasks, and clients are quite aware of this. Should the situation deteriorate – and they often do – practitioners may find themselves donning their more controlling hat. If the worker has previously reassured the client that there is no question of their controlling functions arising, no matter how honestly meant at the time, they can look rather like they have acted in bad faith. It would appear that, as agency functionary, in areas where social workers have controlling responsibilities, given the frailty of human foresight, a coercive element is always there. This may be defined as the latent coercion group. The final group is that group of cases where the social worker acts in an overtly authority role: the actual coercion group. This leaves three groups: the genuinely self determining, latently coercive and actual coercive groups.

Hobbes' Paradox

In a further extension of his discussion, Benn (1967) introduces the interesting possibility that those apparently coercive situations of social work control do not in fact infringe self determination. Benn quotes Hobbes to state that 'all actions that men do in commonwealths for fear of the law are actions which the doers had liberty to omit'. To give someone an additional motive for action (ie fear of punishment) to set against any other he has makes him no less free. This contrasts with the previous view which finds self determination and coercion to be quite simply incompatible.

However, Hobbes view does presuppose a kind of freedom. It depends, appropriately in the context of care management, on something like the economic model of a 'rational man [sic]' choosing between alternative courses with different net utilities. The choice may be rigged against him by someone with the power to allot rewards or penalties, but given the conditions he makes his own choice, and by virtue of his own rationality is his own master. The parents who, when faced with the choice of improving – in social services terms – the quality of care for their children or, to put it starkly, face legal proceedings for accommodation, reluctantly agree to change their parenting behaviour in line with social work suggestions, have exercised a free choice in the particular circumstances of the case. They could have chosen not to do so and faced the prospect of accommodation. Such an argument is not implausible, furthermore, because it is certainly true that all choices entail consequences, and these consequences, unless the person acts without reasoning, will be weighed up in making the choice.

We must accept, however, the limits to this Hobbesian sense of self determination. We could, for example, extend this argument to include those in Nazi Germany. On Hobbes' formula, these subjects were no less free to express their opinions or organise and join trade unions than individuals in contemporary Britain. However, the likely consequences in Nazi Germany, that they were killed or at least sent to a concentration camp are such that it is difficult to maintain that they retained an equal degree of freedom to those in contemporary Britain, who at worst might be sacked for trade union activities. If we are to retain this principle in relation to social work, then some distinction between this situation and that in Nazi Germany must be identified which allows us to retain this meaning of self determination.

The Rights Argument

If it is to mean anything consumer choice should be seen as a right, and by implication, therefore, so should self determination. However, if, in order to be a reality, this must be an absolute right, there is clearly a problem, for it leads to the coercion difficulties just considered. Indeed freedom itself is self limiting, in that we cannot all have boundless freedom (Mill, 1972); twentieth century debates have sought to distinguish private areas of inviolable freedom from public areas where behaviour should be enforced (Hart, 1963; Devlin, 1965; Mitchell, 1967). What has been outlined, in fact, is one of three problems outlined by Freden (1991) in relation to absolute rights, ie a clash between two rights, so that the realisation of one can only be achieved at the expense of another. In this case the competing right is the child's right to certain minimum standards of care. If both rights – of parents to self determination and children to minimum standards of care – are absolute this clearly presents a problem. There is no logical solution to the compatibility of two absolute rights which compete over arrangements for desirable human behaviour.

One device for resolving this is to talk of *prima facie* rights. While still allowing for the protective aspects of basic rights, this allows for exceptions to be made. A green traffic light may entitle me to drive down the road, yet siren sounding ambulances, carrying critically injured patients, are entitled to override my freedom of movement by emerging from a side street even where the lights are in my favour. The rights must be considered in the specific circumstances of the case. Here, my right to freedom of movement is overridden by the patient's right to life (or best chance of maintaining life). There are two key issues here. First, we must, as Melden (1959) comments, distinguish between rights and 'right conduct': in any situation we must weigh up supporting considerations for the exercise of such a right. Because we have a pre-existing right, it does not mean that in all circumstances we may behave as if this were the only consideration. Melden's point means that just because we cannot, in this instance, act as we choose, we have not lost the right to self determination. Hence, as a *prima facie* right, consumers still possess the right to self determination, even in cases where social workers have an authority role. Second, as Taylor (1991) suggests, there is an issue of priority (of which more later). Where two competing rights exist, then we should weigh up the merits of each claim. The right to life clearly outweighs that of freedom of movement temporarily restricted.

This is, of course, not an entirely satisfactory solution, for we do not have clear criteria by which to choose between competing rights. *Prima facie* rights remain rights that should always be asserted, but the intensity of that assertion must take account of the possible damage that may be caused to other rights that protect crucial attributes (McClosky, 1985). The clash between mutually damaging *prima facie* rights, thinks Freden (1991) will remain a problem which may only be sorted out by common sense, or indeed fail to be sorted out satisfactorily. Crucial to satisfactory solutions is a capacity amongst humans to exercise practical reasoning.

Positive Freedom

The distinction between negative and positive freedom is commonly made and has quite different meanings and consequences for actions. Taylor (1991) distinguishes between them as, respectively, opportunity concepts and exercise concepts. Negative theories rely simply on an opportunity concept, where being free is a matter of what we can do, of what is open to us, whether or not we choose to exercise those options. Doctrines of positive freedom are concerned with freedom as the exercise of control over one's life. On this view someone is free only to the extent that they have effectively determined themselves and the shape of their lives.

Taylor considers 'internal' as well as external barriers to self determination can exist. This can be understood in terms of an individual's *real* desires. I may, for example, wish to have an affair at the same time as maintain a 'happy' married life (we shall not consider the morality of this for the moment). However, an affair threatens the integrity of that married life. In the long term it is the latter which is undoubtedly of greater import to me, but my immediate desire is for an affair. In choosing the affair, can I be said to be self determining?

Well, at one level, I quite clearly can: no-one forced me to have the affair, and who else is responsible? However, an understanding of internal barriers requires us, first, to understand our real desires and purposes and second, to distinguish between different motivations. How far does one particular motivation (for an affair) assist with our real desire or purpose (a stable married life)? What is important is that we evaluate and distinguish desires in terms of their importance to us. We experience some desires as intrinsically more important than others. Some passing comfort, for example, is less important than the fulfilment of our lifetime vocation. Such judgements of significance, it should be emphasised, furthermore, are quite independent of the strength of the respective desires. The craving for comfort, or the desire for an affair, may be overwhelming for the moment, but the judgement of significance nonetheless stands. What is important is that the stronger desire may lead to action jeopardising the more significant one. Can we really be considered self determining, in the sense of doing what we really want?

An obvious relevant example is that of an agoraphobic who may have significant desires to meet people, go to work, go shopping and collect the children from school. The terror accompanying leaving home prevents them from doing this. The immediate desire, which is overwhelming, is to stay at home, to prevent the rise in anxiety. But this does nothing for the wider and more significant desires for social integration. Similarly, a parent may wish to bring up their young children in the best (and safest) way possible. However, they may also be subject to periodic rages, perhaps related to the stresses of their life situation – poverty, single parenthood, limited opportunity for socialising as well as child care itself – leading to serious physical abuse of their child. Their more significant purpose is jeopardised by the stronger immediate desires. Social work actions can be designed to help them achieve their more significant desires, by for example, helping provide appropriate supports and working on alternative ways of coping with stress and managing the children. In so doing, they are promoting the achievement of self determination by removing internal barriers to the achievement of their more significant purposes.

Positive Freedom and the Exercise of Control

What, however, where the parent is not aware of some higher, more significant, desires, which fit neatly in this way with social work purposes? What if they do not accept their behaviour to be abusive, but an appropriate way of bringing up their children? what, indeed, if they feel such 'punishment' is vital to the development of a well formed character, and a parent who does not punish their child in this way is acting negligently? Where this is examined in terms of positive freedom this brings in interesting new dimensions: that of someone, or official body, deciding what is in fact 'really' self determined behaviour.

Freedom as self mastery is presented as *rational* self direction: the condition in which a person's life is governed by rational desires rather than the desires that they, as a matter of fact, have. Rational self direction, first, involves the possession of a rational will (Downie and Telfer, 1969). A second feature, much emphasised by Kant, involves the ability to govern one's conduct by rules: indeed, more grandly, to adopt rules which one holds to be binding on oneself and all other rational beings. These rules include moral rules and mark the individual out as a moral agent. Yet how are we to decide which purposes are rational and moral ones, and therefore an indication of self determination on the part of an individual? Which rules should I follow and execute?

If we adopt the explicit position of legislation, then the behaviour of parents which social workers are empowered to support and uphold is that of the 'reasonable' parent. This is broadly outlined in the legislation Under section 13 (2) the Children Act states that a care or supervision order may be made if the child is suffering, or likely to suffer, significant harm, and that the care given by the parent is 'not...what it would be reasonable to expect a parent to give him' (Department of Health, 1989, p 25). This is linked to a particular idea of rationality: the rational parent is the parent who observes minimum standards of parenting in line with legislative expectations (as interpreted by social workers, other relevant professionals and the courts). Milne (1968) makes this particular form of rationality explicit: this is rational moral action involving acting both in the spirit and the letter of the society's established morality, in this case enshrined in statute. We are rational, here, to the extent that we act in line with the society's established morality.

If this is the case, it follows that care management activities designed to ensure concordance with this view of rational behaviour, although possibly experienced by the consumer as coercive, are, in fact designed to enable them to become self determining. At the moment their behaviour falls below that of established social morality and is hence not fully rational. The care package developed may include, for example, the use of a family aide, attending personal therapy sessions, attendance at a family centre for parent training and so on. Failure to cooperate may leave concerns for the children sufficiently high for court proceedings to be pursued. On the other hand their decision to cooperate may be seen as an indication of good intent, and ultimately, conforming to expectations as an indication of full self determination. Self determination in this case is something to be achieved by the consumer, not an already granted right, and the purpose of practice is to achieve this self determined state.

The limits to this conception need not be laboured. The first is that such a position assumes a consensus model of society, where particular standards are widely accepted. This may, in the case of child abuse be true, but where it is not then it involves the imposition of the expectations of powerful groups on other weaker groups (Strasser, 1976). Second, this dimension of positive freedom alarms Berlin, and other proponents of negative freedom. The subject cannot be the final authority on the question whether he is free, for he cannot be the final authority on the question of whether his desires are authentic, whether they do or do not frustrate his purposes. Once we admit that the agent himself is not the final authority on his own freedom, do we not open the way to Totalitarian manipulation? This view, he considers, becomes easily transformed into a recipe for controlling and manipulating people so that they come to serve the ends which some authority has decreed to be rational – a view for which there is plainly some historical warrant.

LIMITS TO SELF DETERMINATION

Care management can involve decisions made by carers as well as users: both are considered to have, potentially, a stake in the process (Department of Health, 1990). In this sense the former as well as the latter may be called consumers. At one level this is appropriate: carers have a stake in care packages as well as users. However, this might also be viewed, potentially at least, as a limit to self determination on the part of the user, at the minimum level of not being able to decide for themselves what is to happen, in view of the fact that someone other than the user themselves may influence the nature of the care package. This can occur, furthermore, without reference to any authority role the social workers may have.

This, however, would generally be linked in some way to the capacity of the user to determine what they want. This would be the case, for example, with someone suffering dementia or severe learning difficulties. They would be clear examples of non rational beings, of people who are not capable of determining what is their own interests and forming a coherent plan for achieving them, of, in Kant's formulation, people who are not persons (Downie and Telfer, 1969). This is clearly some positive notion of self determination, but it is linked to other notions by the limited opportunity they are given actually to decide their own care package. This may be decided by the carer, or in part by the carer, and where in the latter case this involves apparently overriding at least some apparent wishes of the user, both cases involve a limit to self determination in the external sense that things are happening to them without their agreement.

In what sense, if at all, can these users be considered self determining? and by what justification does the carer 'inherit' the right to determine what should happen? The key to understanding this is the notion of an individual's interests. Feinberg (1977) suggests that a person has an interest in something when he stands to gain or lose depending on its outcome. He identifies two types. Ulterior interests are based on stable long term objectives, achievement of goals at least partly as ends in themselves, such as raising a family, advancing a cause, owning a home. Welfare interests are interests which are the indispensable means to one's ulterior goals, whatever they may be. They include health, financial sufficiency and the like. Welfare interests are interests that are good for us even if we should not want them.

Welfare interests are the central concern of care management. If a carer is to decide what these are, under what conditions should this occur? This may occur, first, when the carer has 'invested' a desire so strong, durable and stable in the user's well being, that they come to have a personal stake in it themselves. The particular interest of the user becomes, therefore, on of the carer's ulterior interests or focal aims. The carer has an abiding interest of their own in the user's well being which is not merely an episodic 'passing' desire. A complete identification with the interests of the user requires the carer to desire the user's good not simply as a means for the promotion of their ulterior aims that are components of their own good, but quite sincerely as an end in itself. Harm to the user would, then be harm (to the interests of) the carer themselves. No-one would doubt, for example, that someone would harm a loving parent by injuring or maiming their child.

The second condition is when that which promotes the carer's interests promotes also the interests of the user. In the extreme version of this case, where the user is wholly dependent on the carer's help, and so long as the carer's personal interests flourish, the help is likely to continue, the carer's good is, in effect one of the user's welfare interests. Such would be the case where action was taken to improve the morale or reduce the stress on, a carer, by, for example, the use of respite care.

It is, then, first, the identical interest of carer and user, and second, the limited capacity of the user to act to determine what is in their own interests which marks out the circumstances justifying carer's involvement in decision making. Where that identity is complete, we might suggest that the carer is choosing what the user would have chosen for themselves, if faced with their current situation, if they, briefly, possessed the capacity for rational self determination.

Of course the capacity of the user to determine what they want will be variable, and their capacity to be involved in determining their care package will vary also: contrast the situation of the individual with mild learning difficulties and that of those with severe learning difficulties. We may not, furthermore, always assume that the carer will act benignly. This may, first, be deliberate. Where the carer pursues their interests at the expense, or in disregard of, the user provides one alternative. Such acts are likely to result in harm to the user, by for example, using earmarked social security payments not to ensure the minimum needs of the user are met, but for buying luxury clothes and wines. Misguided actions may occur also, for example where a carer of someone with learning difficulties emphasises their disability rather than their potential and thus fails to take advantage of services which may benefit their development on the grounds that 'it would not be fair' on them.

This concern for the individual's welfare, even when not capable of full self determination, represents a form of paternalism (Mitchell, 1967) by the state or even a form of right of citizenship (Spicker, 1990). The circumstances where the carer should abrogate the right to choose and where they should not, are therefore clear. Where the user themselves have limited capacity for self determination and the interest of carer and user are linked, then carer choice may be considered legitimate. Where, deliberately or misguidedly their decisions are against the user's interests the legitimacy is questionable.

CONCLUSION

As soon as we proceed beyond common sense views of self determination, the notion of consumer choice becomes problematic. Self determination may be a capacity which the consumer is assumed to possess, or something which is to be achieved by appropriate intervention. However, the authority role – where self determination is defined as negative freedom – entails coercion in some cases, while still other consumers – those with learning difficulties for example – are assumed not to be fully self determining. There seems, therefore, to be more than a common sense, or even negative freedom, definition of self determination inherent in care management. Some views – Hobbes' paradox and self determination as a prima facie right – provide interesting attempts to retain some conception of self determination, even in the face of social workers' authority role. These, however, possess flaws which prevent their being entirely satisfactory as resolutions for the problem of self determination. It appears that close examination of self determination creates an anarchic situation in which the concept of self determination used varies with different circumstances. There is, in short, no consistency in the conduct of care management.

If we are to avoid such anarchy a central place must be ascribed to positive freedom. Care management – for social workers at any rate – must necessarily encapsulate both authority and non authority roles. If we accept the arguments of proponents of positive freedom, then self determined action requires not only the absence of external constraints but the capacity (internally) for self determination – we must, in short, be able to act rationally. Hence, negative freedom is contained within this conception of positive freedom. A person would not be free if, having made a rational decision, they were constrained from carrying out actions based on that rational decision. However, they would also not be free if they were unable to make rational decisions and act upon them, even if external constraints were absent. They would also be unfree, as a matter of interest, to the extent that the opportunity to develop the capacity for rational decision making was denied them.

Care management as social work, therefore, is consistent with a view of self determination whereby consumers are assumed to be self determining – ie able rationally to decide the right course – except in specific and defined circumstances. These are, for example, where the parent is not acting as a reasonable parent or an individual is suffering from a mental illness or is sufficiently disabled by a learning difficulty to prevent rational decision making. These are areas where the consumer may be considered not to be fully rational. Beating up the kids is not something which is generally considered to be reasonable (or responsible) behaviour on the part of a parent. In these circumstances social workers may take on an authority role, the goal of which is to ensure conformity with accepted standards of 'reasonableness'. In the case of child protection this would involve adequate parenting, in the absence of which social services would be expected to take action to protect the child; in the case of learning disability, this may involve (as with the use of Guardians under sections 7 and 8 of the Mental Health Act), being guided by the carer in decisions about the best interests of the service user.

There are, therefore, explicit circumstances in which the authority role of social workers may be invoked, and they clearly correspond to notions of rational actions. This concern for rational action by social workers *qua* social workers is clearly bounded. They are not concerned – officially at least – with ad hoc definitions of rational and irrational acts. Provided consumers have not acted in a way which requires social workers to act in ways invoking their authority role, social workers have no rights to impose solutions or outcomes on the consumer ie they are not expected to place external constraints on them. Under these circumstances consumers are largely able to make their own decisions which the social worker may not personally consider to be the most sensible, but over which they have no power to enforce compliance.

In these, non authority, circumstances, the focus for self determined consumer decisions, revolves around the way in which consumers may make the best or most well informed choice. Perhaps the most immediately helpful ideas relate to the manner by which self determination may be promoted in the process of discussion. Work should be characterised by openness and honesty on the part of the practitioner, and an emphasis on rational argument. Censorship of information and irrational persuasion are to be avoided if self determination is to be achieved. These quite clearly represent good practice as advocated by many writers for some considerable time.

If we are, therefore, to avoid a situation of confusion, in which a variety of definitions of self determination are presented as characteristic of social work, positive freedom as a concept provides the key. It provides the basis on which to distinguish between authority and non authority roles, and the circumstances under which these roles may be taken. Social workers as care managers are always concerned, within their sphere of responsibility, with promoting rational actions, it is simply that the way in which they are promoted – whether in an authority role or otherwise – varies with circumstances. These circumstances relate closely to definitions about consumer need, and it is to this issue that we shall turn next.

Chapter Seven

Need and care manageme

Care management is centrally concerned with need. Official documents have emphasised this, and the term 'needs led assessments' (rather than service based) have become part of the language of social care. Hence, the Practitioners' guide (Department of Health, 1991) emphasises a 'needs led' approach (p 6) and states that 'if services are to be made more responsive it is necessary to identify the disparity between assessed needs and currently available services' (p 10).

Although need is clearly a central aspect of care management, it is not without question. According to Williams (1974):

> The word 'need' ought to be banished from discussion of public policy, partly because of its ambiguity, but also because...the word is frequently used in...arbitrary senses...in many public discussions it is difficult to tell, when someone says 'society needs'...whether he means society ought to get it, in his opinion, whether a majority of members of society want it, or all of them want it.

Need is, however, widely regarded as fundamental to the social services. These are considered to be large scale experiments in ways of helping those in need (Bradshaw, 1972). Need provides the very definition of the objectives of the services. It is their raison d'etre: 'the definition of need presents a central problem for the social services since this defines the objectives of the services' (Forder, 1974, p 39).

If needs, as a central component of care management, is to be taken seriously, two tasks present themselves. We must understand the nature and validity of the term 'need' and the way (or ways) in which this term is understood in official documents. What, in other words, does it mean to state that care management

...ts social workers to needs led assessments, and is the term ...eed used in just one sense, or in more than one?

'OBJECTIVE-EMPIRICAL' NEEDS

One approach involves an objective definition of need. If needs can be defined neutrally and objectively then the goals of social services can equally be fixed objectively, avoiding messy issues of social and political values. All that is required is the discovery, empirically, of the range of social needs, their specification and their incorporation into the goals of social services. Need definition is an unproblematic empirical act.

There is certainly some evidence of this objective approach. The practitioner's handbook (Department of Health, 1991, p 12) states that 'a needs led approach requires need to be explicitly defined and prioritised in policy statements'. This must be operationalised through guidelines which 'cover all aspects of need'. They recognise that need is not a simple concept and that it is multifaceted. It follows that operationalising need is not a simple matter. It requires detailed classification of the type and range of needs. As a start, however, need is divided into six broad categories, each of which should be covered in a comprehensive assessment: personal/social care, health care, accommodation, finance, education/employment/leisure and transport/access.

Many local authorities have taken up this approach with gusto. Core assessment schedules abound. They offer a number of detailed categories against which need may be assessed. The Devon Core Assessment Guide: Mental Health (circa 1994) divides need into the broad areas defined by the Department of Health, with certain supplementary areas, and provides detailed classifications of each area. Hence the broad area of 'Relationships' is divided into family/partner, others, the carer and social interaction with others. It does not seem to matter if there is some overlap in categorisation. Such classification, with predefined boxes which may be ticked, is heavily weighted in the direction of giving an impression of objectivity. All that is required is for the form to be used fully, for the appropriate boxes to be ticked and – hey presto! we have an objective definition of an individual's needs. Indeed, they go further than this. On the basis of the assessment, the care manager is required to prioritise their level of need. It may be, in descending order of priority: danger of physical/emotional harm, loss of independence and quality of life.

A classification such as this, furthermore, is likely to overwhelm any alternative conception of need. It may not purport to be comprehensive, but it gives an appearance of being so. If a particular facet is on the list it may be counted as a need. If not then it is far less likely to be considered. Hence, these lists not only classify needs but determine the ways in which an individuals circumstances may be defined, largely to the exclusion of alternatives. There is little room for more flexible qualitative assessments of need.

A list such as this is very much the work of the technical expert. Needs are predefined and presented in a number of broad areas. The definition is essentially unproblematic. How far is this unproblematic and objective approach to need possible? on what grounds might we justify it?

According to Miller (1976) an objective approach is most certainly possible: indeed helping define what is distinctive about needs. He distinguishes needs clearly from wants (p 129):

> ...wanting is a psychological state ascribed on the basis of a person's avowals and his behaviour...Needing, on the other hand, is not a psychological state, but rather a condition which is ascribed 'objectively' to the person who is the subject.

This distinction between wants as a psychological state and needs as objectively ascribed is fairly easily presented. We may say of someone in the early stages of cancer that 'they need radiotherapy'. This need is independent of whether or not they want it: its effects are sufficiently unpleasant that someone may, indeed, not want radiotherapy, while recognising their need for it. On the other hand a child may say that they want more sweets, having just finished a bar of chocolates. They hardly need more sweets in the sense that the person with cancer needs radiotherapy. Furthermore, the need for radiotherapy can be externally ascribed, whereas only the subject themselves can say what they want.

Need statements, furthermore, necessarily possess objectives the consequence of which is the alleviation of need. Need is only intelligible in relation to some objective entailing need alleviation. Barry (1965, sec 5 a) has made this clear. He argues that all need statements must conform to the structure 'A needs X *in order to* Y'. Hence, in the above example, the person needs radiotherapy in order to cure their cancer. This contrasts with want statements, which do not require objectives in the same sense. If an adult were to ask the child in the example *why* they wanted more sweets, it would be perfectly intelligible for them to answer that they just do, or because they feel like it. Confusion can arise because in general conversation need statements frequently lack an objective (the person needs radiotherapy) giving the false impression that there is no goal towards which that need is directed, and making it difficult to distinguish them from want statement.

How can we, however, distinguish the kinds of states the alleviation of which create needs? Benn and Peters (1959) note that needs imply a failure to live up to an understood standard, and that standard is one applying to everyone – it is universal (Thompson, 1987). The distinction between wants and needs in this respect, is that of serious harm (Feinberg, 1973, p 111). The implication of the presence of need is that if that need is not satisfied by appropriate action then serious harm of some specified and objective kind will occur. Harm, Feinberg thinks, is any set of circumstances which interferes with or thwarts his interests. Not to satisfy needs, therefore, will be against an individual's objective interests. We can see this, again, clearly in our example. If the individual with cancer does not receive radiotherapy (and in the absence of alternative treatments) they may well die, and certainly suffer further ill health. Furthermore, this statement is applicable, in principle, to anyone in an identical situation, for exactly the same reasons. We can hardly say of the child who wants more sweets that they will suffer significant harm if they do not receive them.

The objectivity and universal nature of need states, furthermore, means that an individual does not necessarily have to be aware of their need for them nonetheless to be in a state of need. The individual may not be aware that they have cancer, yet nonetheless need radiotherapy. This contrasts with wants which are intentional, and depends on how a subject of experience looks upon the world (Griffin, 1986, p 41). You cannot want something of which you have no conception and which you are not in some way trying to get. Want has a core of subjectivity. Of course, it is possible for wants and needs to coincide: a person may be both aware of and desire something they need: for example, if hungry, they may both want and need food. However, it is not necessary for need to be present at the same time as want.

All these aspects could be inherent in Devon's Core Assessment Guide, mentioned earlier. While the classification is broad, the nature of harm arising if no action is taken is quite explicit. The consumer may suffer physical and emotional harm, loss of independence or impairment of quality of life. Indeed this classification helps distinguish the most needy from those with less needs. Those at risk of physical or emotional harm (category A) will be given priority over those with impaired quality of life (category C). The universality of standards, furthermore is implicit. The classification can be applied to everyone, and it is this predefined classification which determines the way in which consumers are viewed. It has implications for services. Resources are likely to be given to those in category A before those in category C. Since care management is centrally about the rational use of resources these classifications are highly significant.

The case for objective needs is, however, not conclusive. There is much scope for individual definitions of need. Some may regard sex as a basic human need, yet a number of individuals consciously choose celibacy (Rensholm, 1977). An individual, furthermore, may not regard an apparently unproblematic outcome, such as death, a matter, for them, of serious harm. This may be the case for the person with cancer, if life holds out nothing for them, and they may choose death in preference to a life with no meaning for them. An individual afflicted by blindness may find other abilities, such as musical talent emerges, in their view, more forcefully, and on reflection consider their blindness a blessing. More generally, different groups or cultures, or those with differing beliefs may actually set different standards for the meeting of human needs. This may be the case with shelter, to which different groups may be committed, but the standards of which, considered to engender serious harm, are variable. Perhaps, then, far from being objective, the concept of need commits us to a wholehearted relativism.

RELATIVISM AND HUMAN NEED

An empirical-objective conception of need does not adequately cover need as expounded in care management. There is, in certain sections of official documents clear evidence of relativism. Need, it is thought, 'is a dynamic concept, the definitions of which will vary over time in accordance with changes in national legislation, changes in local policy, the availability of resources, the patterns of local demand' (Department of Health, 1991, p 12). Need, it is explicitly stated 'is a relative concept' (p 12). It is also a personal concept (p 13):

...no two individuals will perceive or define their needs in exactly the same way. Care management seeks to recognise the individuality of need by challenging practitioners to identify the unique characteristics of each individual's needs and to develop individualised rather than stereotyped responses.

What does this relativism entail, and what is the validity of its claims?

In its strongest form, relativism is the basic conviction that when we turn to issues considered by philosophers to be the most fundamental (reasoning, what counts as knowledge, moral questions, for example) they may be understood as relative to the particular conceptual scheme, theoretical framework, paradigm, and form of life, society or culture. There is no final truth, no single unquestionable form of rationality, no certain moral standards of right or wrong (Bernstein, 1983).

Such truth or moral certainty would, according to Relativists, have to involve universal standards which somehow stand outside and above the competing alternatives. There is, however, a non reducible plurality of schemas, paradigms, and moralities. Where, therefore, a particular view of need or significant harm conflicts with another, we have no way of deciding, objectively, that one is correct and another is not. These views have been fostered in particular by developments in Social Anthropology, the insights from which, many have considered to provide strong support for cultural and moral relativism. For the Relativist, all species of objectivism are almost inevitably the representation of some form of ethnocentrism in which one perception of rationality is legitimated, quite falsely, by claiming for it some unwarranted universality (see eg Winch, 1958, 1964). For Gray (1983, p 182) this means:

> The objective of basic need is delusive. Needs can be given no plausible cross cultural content, but can be seen to vary across different moral traditions. [Perceptions of need] ...generate an illusion of moral agreement where in fact there are profound divergencies of value.

Relativism has become associated, in its broadest sense, with views that perceptions of reality (including standards of rationality and morality) are socially constructed. Two key elements of this approach are evident from Gergen's (1985) analysis: variations according to social and historical context and the social processes by which areas of social life are defined. A wide range of research has shown differences, according to social and historical context, in dominant perspectives of a number of areas of social life closely related to need. There have been variations, according to historical period, in the concept of 'mother love' (Badminter, 1980), the family (Gadlin and Dizard, 1984) and the concept of self (Verhave and Van Hoorn, 1984). In each case constructions of the person and relationships have undergone changes over time, which, according to Gergen (1985) do not appear to reflect alterations in the objects of concern, but rather reflect other historically significant factors.

Cultural differences have been identified by ethnographic studies in areas of personal and social life closely related to perceptions of need. These include accounts of emotion (Lutz, 1982), identity (Lee, 1959), knowledge (Rosalso, 1980) and the self (Smith, J. 1980). If notions such as the family, self, emotion and maternal care – areas of social life closely identified with issues of need – are themselves so variable, need may itself be considered to vary with culture and historical period. Indeed, some have linked conceptions of universal need with power and oppression of one group over another. Those in positions of power, it is argued, can always legitimate its arbitrary exercise through arguing that they know what is in the best interests of the powerless. The preferences of the dominated are downgraded as inferior to their 'real' needs as defined by those in authority (note the close association of this argument with concepts of negative freedom). Human liberation is here equated with reclaiming the right of oppressed groups to determine what preferences they will designate as needs (Rist, 1980).

These insights hold true for the Relativist, for individuals and groups within societies, as well as between cultures. Both Rawls (1972) and Runciman (1966) provide a link between need and equality. The satisfaction of need is the primary aim of Rawl's difference principle in social justice. Where, for example, an individual is in poverty or they have a disability, their needs will be greater than the non poor or able bodied. Needs, in this case are relative, based on a comparison with others. Runciman, however, brings in a clearer subjective dimension. The term Relative Deprivation, he thinks, derives from a familiar truism: that people's attitudes, aspirations and grievances largely depend on the frame of reference within which they are conceived. Relative deprivation should always be understood as a sense (a subjective awareness) of being deprived. This sense occurs, at an individual or group level in the context of reference groups. The sense of deprivation (and hence need) arises because of the comparison with other groups. It is, therefore, inevitably culture based. This sense of deprivation, furthermore seems to vary. Where the reference groups with which individuals compare themselves are not considerably better off, the sense of relative deprivation is likely to be low. Where they are considerably better off the sense of relative deprivation is likely to be high. The sense of deprivation and need is therefore dependent on the choice of reference group.

The social unit defining need may not even have to be the group. Some consider it to be the individual, and a matter of subjective preference. This is a position evident in orthodox welfare economics. Only individuals or groups of individuals can decide those areas of life whose priority they consider to be sufficiently great to attach the label 'need'. Two central principles underlie this approach. The first is the subjective conception of interests. Individuals are the only authority on the correctness of their interests or wants. Note here an echo of the approach to negative freedom. Second, there is a principle of private sovereignty. What is produced (and consumed) should be determined by the preferences of individuals (Penz, 1986). The concept of need is, according to this view, so ambiguous that any attempt to separate it from individual preference is bound to lead to confusion.

The way areas of social life are defined is considered, within Social Constructionist thought, to be a social process. Definitions of social life continually evolve and are free to vary with the predilections of those who use them. Hence Sampson (1983) and Wexler (1983) suggest variations in the way people manage morality in social relationships. Whether an act is defined as envious or just, angry or otherwise, depends on the negotiated understanding of those involved in social life. Indeed, these definitions have consequences for peoples' actions. Descriptions and explanations of the world are significant for laying blame, assigning responsibility, rewarding, censuring and so on.

Smith's (1980) study is particularly important in this context, since it focuses on the interaction of social workers and their clients. Drawing on Berger and Luckman's (1967) phenomenological perspective, he considers need to be the objectification of subjective phenomena. Social need, for Smith, consists in substantial part of the concepts and precepts of professional practitioners who are concerned with the process of

'meeting need'. It also consists of the practical ac\
such concepts the appearance of objective reality to \
them. Need is therefore defined by groups who are in a\
power to make such definitions, yet presented as o\
Definitions of need cannot be viewed as independent of the re\
practices employed by social workers in each case. This make\
situationally defined: it arises in the context of the time and place
where actions occur . Rather than an attribute of the individual,
therefore, need is highly ambiguous and closely dependent on the
concepts and theoretical models employed by social workers.

However, the relativists' position is also flawed. It is, first of all,
self-negating. If there is no truth or moral certainty, if all positions
reflect the cultural milieu from which they arise and are equally
valid, then there can indeed be no universal standards which
somehow stand outside and above the competing alternatives.
However, the claim that there is no single objective truth, but a
non reducible plurality of schemas and paradigms is just such a
claim to a universal standard. In other words, how can we know
that the relativist's position is correct if all views are relative
mere positions. After all, there are no universal and accepted
standards of truth and rationality, but only standards that are
accepted by particular social groups or societies. Relativism cannot
itself claim to be objective truth (Keat and Urry, 1982).

Such relativism leaves us secondly, in a moral vacuum. Yet
need, if it is to have any force, necessarily has moral implications.
Hence as Feyerbend (1978, p 8-9 cf Doyal and Gough, 1991)
comments, a tradition becomes good or bad only when looked at
from the point of view of another tradition. This is a serious
matter:

> Objectively there is not much to choose between anti
> semitism and humanitarianism. Racism will appear
> vicious to a humanitarian while humanitarianism will
> appear vapid to a racist.

Relativism, it transpires, entails in the last analysis indifference
to the behaviour of Nazi Germany's mass extermination of Jews,
Poles, Gypsies and other races. Espousing relativism while
clinging on to the moral content of need appears to be an activity
which even the most accomplished moral contortionist would find
impossible to perform.

Finally, relativism must uphold the utter distinctiveness of
different cultures, coupled with the primacy of culture as a

formative influence. The bite of a relativist doctrine must lie in the view that different cultures shape humans so differently that it is misleading to talk of any human nature common to them all (Trigg, 1982). The cultural expression of this nature varies so widely that there is no way that we can continue to posit it. It appears, however, that it is only on the basis of this that we can move towards an objective understanding of human need. On the wreckage of the relativists' claims, this, perhaps, is the direction that we should proceed.

'CONSENSUS-OBJECTIVE' NEED

Social workers as care managers cannot adequately base their concept of need upon the claims of relativists. However, they do not appear entirely to have done so anyway. While on the one hand proclaiming the relative nature of need quite explicitly in official guidelines, there is also a clearly objectivist dimension, with broad classifications of need enthusiastically seized upon and developed by local authorities. How can we resolve this apparent contradiction between relativist and objectivist conceptions of need? it is in further exploration of the objectivist claims of care management that we shall discover the need assumptions underlying practice. In doing so it is possible to link the need concept underlying care management as social work with positive self determination examined earlier.

The official guidelines show an awareness of a distinction between the relativist approach to need which they propound at some points and more objective notions of need without making this tension explicit. The guidance (Department of Health, 1991) distinguishes between assessment as an instrument of social support and social control: the former 'offers choices... [and] the latter imposes solutions'. Their example of psychotic illness is revealing: 'at a certain threshold of risk or vulnerability [intervention] is likely to tip over into compulsory action' (p 50). Hence we have circumstances in which the presence of psychosis entails involuntary action – the care manger (and others) determine need. This, however, commits them directly to the scientific-objectivist approach underlying mainstream psychiatry. It is furthermore, highly significant for social work. A key dimension of social work practice is the involvement of Approved Social Workers in assessments for compulsory admission to mental hospital. The nature of their involvement necessarily entails commitment to mainstream definitions of psychiatry as well, of course, to the existence of mental illness in the first place (Sheppard, 1990).

At the core of psychiatry lies a distinction between rational and irrational behaviour. The psychotic is an individual whose ideas and behaviour contain profoundly irrational elements. Mental illness, at least in this extreme form, involves those undesirable mental or behavioural deviations which 'involve an extreme and prolonged inability to know and deal in a rational and autonomous way with oneself and one's social and physical environment' (Edwards, 1982).

The distinction between mental health and illness, and the cause of the latter is, in mainstream psychiatry, an issue for science. Buswell (1986, ch 1) calls this the 'liberal scientific' concept of psychiatry and identifies a clear objectivist dimension. Mental illness is viewed as a natural phenomenon, the result of natural processes and hence amenable to natural intervention. Consequently Psychiatry should be based on science. By science, is meant positivist science, that is science in which knowledge is based on empirical observations and logical argument and conforms to the standards of objectivity that have been developed in the natural sciences. There is no place for intuition and metaphysics. Psychiatry is not ideological: notions of sickness and disease are objective and are based on statements of facts not values.

Needs, Drives and Human Nature

One objective approach links needs to human nature through drives. These are a motivational characteristic or property of need states. Hull (1943) suggested that physical deficits instigate the organism to undertake behaviours that result in the 'offset' of those needs. Drives, for Hull, result from physiological disequilibrium and instigate behaviours that return the organism to a state of equilibrium. Hull identified a number of need areas: the need for food (hunger), water (thirst), air, the avoidance of tissue injury (pain), the need for rest (after protracted exertion), the need for sleep (after protracted wakefulness) and so on (Hull, 1943, p 59-60).

Hull's drive theory of need satisfaction was confined to physiological states. Maslow's (1954) rather more famous analysis postulated a hierarchy of need. Rather than proposing one source of motivation, Maslow proposed a multiplicity of need systems.

His hierarchy involved two types of need which are, he felt, qualitatively distinct. Lower needs are deficit (D) values. Attainment of their desired goals produces tension reduction and returns the organism to a state of equilibrium. Hull was exclusively concerned with D values. Maslow, however, also postulated the existence of being (B) values. B values are associated with growth motivation and expanded horizons. These include wholeness, perfection, justice, beauty, creativity and truth. More specifically, Maslow delineated five basic classes of need, which he defined as psychological, safety, love, esteem, and actualisation. Where satisfaction of lower order needs of physiology, such as hunger, is required, the drive to satisfy these will be strongest. As these are satisfied, however, higher order needs will emerge whose satisfaction an individual will be driven to achieve. Finally, a more open ended drive to actualisation appears, whose characteristics involve B values.

These drive conceptions of need, however, can be criticised both for being over-deterministic and reductionist. They confuse constraint with cause. All actions relating to need can, it is suggested, be ultimately explained by our species-genetic inheritance. Hence our actions, which exist in the realm of meaning, understanding and social life are no more than the result of genetics, which occupy a biophysical domain. This reductionism, according to Ryle, involves committing a category error, whereby phenomena in one domain (action) are explained, illegitimately, by reference to phenomena in another domain (physiology). Its determinism, furthermore, neglects the elements of choice in our actions. In an elegant discussion, Midgely (1984) shows that human nature can involve conflicting desires, and that in order to act, a choice must be made between mutually exclusive alternatives. If a parent has strong desires for nurturing, there is no problem until this desire conflicts with a need for employment to pay the bills. At such point choices are required. Furthermore, as Thompson (1987) points out, we are capable of self alteration based upon the accumulation of decisions about how we should act in similar situations. We are not, therefore, the helpless subjects of our drives, but actors who make choices.

Basic Need

This overdeterministic conception of human action does not, however, eliminate human nature as an aspect of need. Taylor's (1973) comments about values – that they would be unintelligible if not related in some sense to human nature – applies equally well to need. This means that, while need is not genetically determined, human nature provides the context for understanding need. A number of writers have pursued this theme in a similar manner (Doyal and Gough, 1991; Plant et al, 1982; Braybrooke, 1987; Thompson, 1987). The two central components of human need, they argue, are survival (or as argued by Doyal and Gough, health) and autonomy. These reflect the fact that we are both living and social beings. They also reflect our self directing, or potentially self directing, nature. Our self directing nature allows us not simply to decide what to do in particular, immediate circumstances. It also involves the development and carrying out of life plans. Survival and autonomy are the preconditions for any act at all by an individual in any culture. These must be satisfied to some degree before individuals can effectively participate in any form of life, and carry out successfully their life plans – for the avoidance of serious harm.

Two senses of autonomy may be identified. The first involves freedom from hindrance . This involves freedom from arbitrary power, whereby one group (or person) is able to control the actions of another. This can arise either from an absence of a framework of social rules or gaps in those rules. The second sense is more akin to positive freedom. It involves the capacity to formulate and follow rules governing one's life. This involves, minimally, the ability to make choices about what should be done and how to go about doing it. An individual's agency is constrained to the extent that they are unable to formulate aims, act on these formulations and evaluate their actions.

Survival is, of course, a prerequisite to any kind of activity at all. However, mere survival, according to Doyal and Gough (1991) is not enough. An individual must do much more than survive to formulate and carry out plans of life. Consider, for example, the position of an individual with serious head injuries and in a coma. To complete a range of practical tasks in everyday life requires abilities with which poor physical health usually interferes. Relativists, however, may object that the biomedical model of health is one adopted by Western medicine, and not transferable across cultures (Morgan et al, 1985). Doyal and Gough, however, using the example of tuberculosis, suggest three reasons for universalism. All individual's whatever their culture, will feel ill. Although different cultures may give the TB bacillus different names and explain its origins differently it is not clear what denying an individual had TB would mean in practice. Finally, the best available technical understanding both dictates the most effective treatments and provides the most complete account of why they work.

Health and autonomy, then, are basic needs. Doyal and Gough (1991) consider it possible from these to develop and operationalise a universal, and hence fully objective, notion of human need. They derive from autonomy and health a range of universal need satisfyer characteristics which enhance physical health and human autonomy in all cultures (Sen, 1984). The capacity to satisfy these needs may vary with, for example, the technology available in the culture, but the principle of their satisfaction is universal. For example, calories per day from foodstuffs have transcultural relevance, as does 'shelter from the elements' (a characteristic of dwellings). They specify precisely which satisfyer characteristics are most important for basic need. Amongst these they include appropriate health care, security in childhood, appropriate education, protective housing, and safe birth control and childbearing.

Social Need

Others draw back from this fully universal position, identifying considerable room for doubt over what will, in fact, satisfy basic needs. Mitchell notes (1971):

> Everyone has a biological need for shelter, but when we campaign for Shelter this is not what we have in mind...we aim to provide...houses where our standards are culturally determined.

Basic needs, according to Plant et al (1982) are always going to be interpreted in a particular society and thus in a sense are going to become social needs. To consider social need can be defined objectively assumes a high degree of consensus: a broad acceptance of the general framework of a society's economic structure, socio political system, distribution of power, status, benefits and burdens. This approach allows for segmentation between groups, but not a high degree of differentiation. Segmentation recognises there will be various groups within the society whose interests may not always converge, but differences in interest would not present a challenge to the norms broadly accepted as fundamental to the society. Differentiation, however, involves considerable differences in interests between groups which make an underlying and fundamental consensus impossible (Strasser, 1976).

This consensus model provides the key to understanding and resolving, the apparently conflicting objectivist and relativist notions of care management. These link to the issue of rationality, autonomy and self determination. Where consensus exists, two approaches are available. Need may first be defined by administrative experts within the broadly accepted values of a society – a largely technocratic exercise. Particular social services may then be set up in response to these expert definitions of need. Such technocratic notions of need are widespread, and associated with the 'end of ideology' view (ie a consensus) propounded by Daniel Bell (1960, 1974). Politics, for him, was, in the post industrial period, a matter of practical compromise within an agreed framework of values. This consensus is often assumed in the lists of social indicators developed by various organisations (Miles, 1985).

The example of psychosis provides a case of need as an imposed definition, a technocratic exercise. In this case there are two critical elements. An individual's autonomy (their basic need) is being 'interfered with' by their mental illness. They cannot, by definition, be autonomous if they are irrational and they are also, by definition, irrational if they have a psychosis. The second element is the 'objective-scientific' approach characterising the definition of mental illness. This perspective does not accept psychiatry as an ideology, but an objective science discovering truths about human nature. It follows that the 'imposition of solutions' entailed in compulsory action involves a situation where need is being objectively ascribed by a technical expert. This objectivism may be considered in one of two ways. Psychiatry may be correct in its claims to make discoveries about human nature and need is based on an objective ascription of need based on this nature. Alternatively, whether or not they are correct, there may be a consensus in society which treats these claims *as if* they were correct. Objective ascription of need, therefore, occurs in circumstances involving the encouragement of rationality amongst the irrational. This is exactly the form of positive self determination discussed in the previous chapter in relation to expectations of 'the reasonable parent' in child care.

The second approach involves a distinction between felt and attributed needs. This allows for a limited relativism as proclaimed in official guides. Felt need, according to Bradshaw (1972, p 641) equates needs with wants. In the case of social care this would involve the views of carers and users rather than those of care managers themselves. However, this equation of needs with wants does not follow once basic needs have been accepted. Needs can only arise out of autonomy and health and of a concept of serious harm which relates to an individual's life plans. Only certain kinds of wants can qualify as needs. This is consistent, in fact with the approach of care management. Here we have the domains of needs pre-defined, either by Department of Health guidelines or through more detailed classification of core assessment schedules, discussed earlier. In these circumstances the relevant areas which may be considered are already determined by the social care agencies, but within this pre-existing framework an individual may define their needs. They may, for example, consider themselves to be in need in the realm of personal/social care, where, for example the care manager did not. Alternatively the level of need they ascribe to themselves may be different from the practitioner. In either case felt and attributed need differ, while the particular condition which may be considered need is predefined.

It is possible, of course, for the views of consumers' definitions of need to be incorporated by involving them in the creation of agency definitions of need. This institutionalisation of consumers' perspectives is evident in areas of the community mental health centre movement where consumers participate in planning and development of services (Grey et al, 1988). It is represented also in elements of the community worker's role. At least part of their job has involved representing the felt need of groups, who might otherwise be ignored, to social services and other agencies. It was the intention of the Gulbenkian Report that this would not represent a challenge to predominant societal norms. Rather the aim was to secure an efficient identification of need within those norms. Hence, community workers should foster local support groups without generating much active opposition either from groups in the area or authorities outside the area. The development of groups furthermore, aimed to emphasis cooperation between people in the belief that they 'grow as persons' in the process. (Thomas, 1983; Popplestone, 1971).

The literature of care management echoes, in part, these proposals. Communication with user or potential user groups is to be improved, dissemination of knowledge about available services is to take place, greater accessibility of services to those in need is to be encouraged. Care management arises in part – in the official line – because of failures in social service provision which were seen in part to be communication gaps. However, neither activity is intended to present a challenge to the existing social and political order. The limited relativism involved here is a relativism available only to the rational consumer. It accepts that there may be different perspectives of needs, but only allows this to those deemed rational. Furthermore, the process assumes that differences, while existing, will not be fundamental – reflecting segmentation but not normative differentiation entailed in consensus models. There is choice, therefore, but it is a choice constrained by definitions of rationality and consensus assumptions. This then is the group for whom some relativism in need definition is possible.

CONCLUSION

Care management documents, while purporting to place need at the centre of practice, remain obscure as to what precisely the term need means. While proclaiming a relativist position, there are also clear objectivist dimensions. The problem has been, therefore, to attempt to understand how it is possible for care managers, at one and the same time to be committed to an objectivist as well as relativist notion of need. The key, as we have seen, is in the capability of the consumer to define their needs in the first place. This involves specific circumstances in which they are or are not considered fully rational.

So there we have it. Care management is, in its own terms of reference, about promoting choice amongst the rational and promoting rationality amongst the irrational. There is, therefore, a close relationship between the concept of self determination and concept of need underlying care management. In so doing, in the last analysis, there is an objectivist core to care management, whatever the protestation, in the official guidelines, that need is a relative concept. There are specific circumstances where need is objectively defined by care managers (and others), most notably in relation to the behaviour of the reasonable parent (towards their child) and the psychotic patient. Rational behaviour (with all its implications for human nature) is something which, in specific circumstances of concern to care management, may be objectively defined. Where certain standards are contravened, a definition of need is imposed upon the consumer. Where they are not, consumers have considerably more latitude, and some scope for a more relativist concept of need is available. However, this also remains constrained by the processes by which need, in individual cases, is likely to be defined.

In order to appreciate the particular senses in which need is used in care management, however, we have had to excavate a specific model of need: what we have called the 'consensus-objective' model. This involves a commitment in care management to an objective conception of basic need and a broad consensus in society as a whole. This, it should be understood, represents the 'assumptive world' of care management. It does not entail an irrefutable argument in favour of consensus objectivism. Conflict models of society, such as Marxist approaches, suggest conflict is endemic in society, and indeed the means by which progressive forces will ultimately overturn Capitalism. Even conflict functionalist approaches (Coser, 1956) accept deep divisions in perspectives and actual interests of different groups in society. This conflict provides the means by which disadvantaged groups, which define their needs and interests in ways fundamentally different from dominant perspectives characterising the status quo, actually achieve changes in the distribution of wealth status and power. Others, however, while accepting these conflict models, suggest an appearance of consensus can be fostered either through the ideological hegemony of powerful groups which creates a 'false consciousness' amongst the suppressed groups (Marcuse, 1964), or by systematically biasing the policy decision making process and 'filtering out' the legitimate claims of these subordinate groups (Bacharach and Baratz, 1970).

It is not, however, the social worker's task as care manager to concern themselves with these more radical perspectives. Because of the centrality of need to the work of care managers, the very definition of their task is underpinned by consensus assumptions. If anyone still held out hopes for the radical potential of social work – so widely held, in academic circles at least, in the 70s – they will be quickly disabused by the close examination of their care management functions.

PART THREE

ASSESSMENT AND THE PROBLEM OF KNOWLEDGE

INTRODUCTION: ASSESSMENT AND THE PROBLEM OF KNOWLEDGE

Part Two has shown that certain quite fundamental developments have occurred with care management. The influence of the New Right can be felt, both in terms of certain neo classical ideas, particularly related to cost-benefit analysis, which have insinuated themselves more directly into the provision of social care, and through the New Managerialism, coming from the same ideological direction. This represents both a high degree of scepticism about the professionalising claims of social work and an attack on traditional notions - particularly those of the public servant - underlying welfare management.

However, notions of empowerment and consumer defined need are also consistent with classical economic ideas that the consumer knows best what they want. Indeed the concern in Economics with wants rather than needs fits neatly with this consumer sovereignty. However, we have also seen that the continued concern of social work with certain areas of social care, such as child protection and mental health, limits this consumer sovereignty, and that this involves state social work in patriarchal actions. More than this, it also implies quite clearly that there is a limit to the kind of relativism espoused in official guides. There is a central core of objectivism which underlies much of social work - and hence care managerial action.

There are, therefore, themes of both continuity and change in the development of care management. There are elements both alien to, and recognisable within, the traditional welfare concerns of social work. The challenge posed to social work is nonetheless real. The central issues involve the extent to which social work can retain areas of social care practice which it has traditionally occupied, or whether these will be taken over by community care workers or other professionals. We have seen that social work has not been particularly successful in pushing forward its professional credentials, and this leaves social workers vulnerable to replacement by others in the new climate of social care. Furthermore, care management, with its emphasis on budget management clearly requires some areas of learning not traditionally involved in the social work curriculum. However, the thrust of chapter five is that this is not a simple matter of learning 'budget management' (whatever that may be), but that social work and care management need build on concepts which will allow them to link the benefits gained from a particular care package with the cost of that package relative to the costs and benefits of alternatives.

Hughes' comment, quoted earlier, that professionals profess, and what they profess is to know more about their areas of interest than others, remains, however, highly relevant. If social work is to survive in some form, it is likely that it will need to demonstrate some level of competence in its areas of concern. Otherwise, care management provides an opportunity for the eclipse of social work. Parts Three and Four will concentrate on key areas of demonstrable competence. It is perhaps worth mentioning to begin with, that certain important areas, such as knowledge of the Law is excluded. This is not because these are unimportant areas - knowledge of the Law is crucial - but because they invoke less controversy. It is, I think, generally accepted both that knowledge of certain areas of the Law is crucial an that it can be successfully taught and learned.

Part Three will concentrate on the issue of the thorny relationship between social science and social work. To a considerable degree social work has relied on social science knowledge as the basis for practice. In this, I am particularly concerned with its importance in relationship to assessment processes. Chapter eight reviews the three positions adopted in relationship to the relevance of social science as a knowledge foundation for social work: the 'Applied Social Science', the Interactionist and the Experientialist approaches. All are found wanting in some respect. Chapter nine presents key elements in the development of the theory of emergent understanding. It is presented as axiomatic that social workers cannot go beyond the bounds of human understanding, and that processes of assessment should reflect this. This entails a focus on the process by which assessment occurs, and a move away from law like propositions which govern a class of people (like the 'causes' of juvenile delinquency) to a case based approach to knowledge application. Crucially it involves two key elements: the application and development of interpretive schemas and a proposition testing approach which seeks always to falsify these propositions. Knowledge is thereby case focused, while incorporating both social science and 'everyday understanding', always provisional and constantly deeply analytical. The approach taken is neither interactionist nor positivist, but realist in orientation. Three key concepts in the use and application of social science knowledge are developed: the approach of reflexive eclecticism, the practice paradigm of social work and the principle of convergence.

However, the difficulties social work has in providing a

convincing professional face are not simply a matter of presentation, about convincing a wider audience about the validity of their professional claims. It goes right to the heart of the knowledge claims of social work, particularly related to social science. Yet this is a realm of knowledge which is riven with dispute. Wherever social work is seen to claim a knowledge base of 'Applied Social Science', or to utilise social research, including that on social work (such as that on permanency or welfare drift) to inform practice, or to use social work theory which refers to social phenomena, it enters into this realm of dispute. Given the importance of these areas, this dispute can hardly be avoided. Yet, this is an issue which lurks below the surface of much social work writing, but which is rarely, if ever, made explicit.

As a prologue to the main aspects of Part Three it is useful to discuss some of these issues. Three are identified: positivism, interpretivism and realism. These, it should be emphasised, do not represent all the possible philosophies of science, which include, for example, intuitionism and conventionalism. However, they are the major themes of social science. Furthermore, there is some degree of diversity within each approach, although the discussion identifies core areas of agreement within each of them.

Positivism

There is a problem right from the start about what actually constitutes knowledge: what counts as knowledge and what does not. Positivism represents a major tradition within the social sciences, although it has many variants (Halfpenny, 1982) and it has tended - perhaps unfairly - to become a term of abuse in recent years. The result is that few people actively espouse a positivist position (Giddens, 1974). The central characteristic of positivism is a belief that knowledge of the external world can only be obtained through 'sense data', by using our senses which tell us of this external world (Bryant, 1985; Fay, 1975; Halfpenny, 1982; Giddens, 1974). It is, to use the jargon, that which is observable. Knowledge of this external world is not, in principle, problematic (the methods for collecting information may be complex), because it is objective. It is 'hard', real and capable of being transmitted in tangible form. The world (and the social world) exists independently of an individual's appreciation of it. It is not something which individuals 'create' (ie by their own conscious processes), it exists 'out there'.

Positivists seek to distinguish between empirically grounded knowledge (that which is gained through the examination of the real world) and mere speculation. There is a strong commitment in positivism to 'facts'. Positivism recognises only two forms of knowledge (Bryant, 1985). The first is analytic truths, that which are true by definition. These are truths which are arrived at because of the logical structure of the case. This is the status, for example, of mathematical truths which do not require recourse to empirical evidence. A syllogism is a logical truth (only men are green; this person is green; therefore this person is a man). Empirically this may not be true but it is true by definition - analytically true. For our purposes, the second form of knowledge: synthetic (or empirical) truths, is more important. These are truths which are gained by the empirical examination of the external world, through our senses. This comes from the philosophical tradition which claimed that all our ideas come, in one way or another, from our sensory experience of the world. Any idea that cannot be derived in this way (such as the idea of God) is not a genuine idea: it is, literally, non-sense. Such a view is dependent on the presumptions [1] that the external world is objective, [2] that it acts on our senses and [3] that the knower contributes little to her own understanding of her experience. In this last respect, the person 'viewing' the world does not impose an interpretive framework on the world, or 'organise' their experiences in a way that leads inevitably to a variety of interpretations each with equal validity. Our understanding of the external world is unproblematic, therefore, in two respects: the external world is objective and 'real' and our apprehension of it is direct and unmediated by any mental processes which may organise it in particular ways.

In Sociology the exemplar of this concern with objective truth lies in Durkheim's (1953) concern with 'social facts'. Durkheim contended that social facts take on the property of 'things' in general. They are external to us, resistant to our wills and constrain us. Social facts are things like the suicide rate or unemployment, external to us as individuals and not reducible to other disciplines such as biology or psychology. They exist in their own right, quite apart from their manifestation in individuals: individuals may commit suicide, but the suicide *rate* indicates a social fact independent of individual suicides.

However, our correct apprehension of the world is dependent on using the appropriate methods for discovery. Science is concerned, first, with describing and classifying (objective) things accurately and second to explain ways in which they were connected, involving a concern with causation. This involves the method of the experiment, since nature and its laws are 'out there' waiting to be discovered. A central element of this is generalisation. The positivist conception of scientific knowledge emphasises observation and empirical method to the relative neglect of theory. Generalisation occurs from particular instances relating together one or more variable. For example, this would be the case if, after intensive studies of samples of families, we found a high positive correlation between the number of siblings in a family and poor educational performance.

These generalisations, involving what is called an 'inductive' method, involve two key elements characteristic of positivism: a concern with regularity and a commitment to verificationism. The inductive method is designed, through the repeated replication of 'experiments' to provide accumulating evidence of the relationship between two or more variables. These may then be formulated into causal 'laws' (such as 'water boils at 100° centigrade at sea level'). These laws serve not simply an explanatory, but also a predictive function. Hence, we not only explain the boiling of the water, we know in future when we may expect it to boil (at 100°). In formulating this approach, positivists are concerned with the unity of science. This involves a commitment to an objective external world, objectively ascertainable, and that knowledge of the social world is to be attained in exactly the same way as knowledge of other aspects of the natural world. This means that there is an explanation of social events which may be attained independently of the views of the subjects involved. Indeed, their views are 'subjective' and are not given the status of objective knowledge in the way characteristic of scientific knowledge. The views of the subjects of research are subjective and partial, and not objective in the way characteristic of the scientific study of their behaviour (Hughes, 1990).

Verification presents positivists with problems recognised as far back as Hume: that is, that we cannot with any certainty predict on the basis of past experience. Because the sun has risen every day for millions of years we cannot say with certainty that it will do so tomorrow. Hume's (1875) answer was to state that past experience was the best we have got so we should stick with it. More recently, however, Popper suggested that although we cannot say with any certainty that a law is correct, we can say with certainty when it is not correct - we can falsify it. His example is of the law 'all swans are white'. No matter how many white swans we see we cannot say with certainty that all swans *are* white. However, if we see one black swan, we can say with certainty that *not* all swans are white (Popper, 1959). Some positivists have, while not abandoning other aspects of their philosophy adopted falsification instead of verification as the key to scientific knowledge (an example from social work is Thyer, 1993). Some indeed, have regarded Popper as a positivist, although he himself maintains he is a philosophical Realist (Popper, 1959), of which more below.

Positivism has been subject to severe criticism within social science circles. From a philosophical perspective, its view of the distinction between true knowledge and other 'knowledge' is considered arbitrary - simply a statement of preference. Neither of the two approaches to knowledge acquisition - analytic or synthetic truths - can establish positivism as the irrefutably correct approach to knowledge acquisition. Ultimately, and ironically, it is metaphysical in origin. Second, and particularly in relation to the social world, we are confronted by what philosophers call an 'open system': a potentially infinite number of relevant variables in explaining any particular social phenomenon (Hughes, 1990). This is unlike the natural sciences, where we can isolate relevant variables and hence be sure of the interaction between them. This undermines the claims to a 'unified science'. The issues of falsification and the open system of social life also undermines claims to predict. This is further undermined by the fact that humans, by their own actions may undermine any predictions. As for an objectivity similar to that of the natural sciences, the capacity of humans to judge themselves about their world and act on these judgements has been considered problematic. What is 'real', it has been claimed, is what people think is real. As Thomas (1982, p 572) stated 'if men [sic] define situations as real, they are real in their consequences'.

Interpretivism

This leads to the central issue which distinguishes positivists from those who may be termed interpretivists: a loose group who are centrally concerned with the issue of meaning. Interpretivism embraces a wide range of thought, including phenomenological, symbolic interactionist and ethnomethodological, which share the common characteristic of attempting to understand and explain the social world primarily from the view of the actors directly involved in the social process (Burrell and Morgan, 1979). Its origins are quite different from positivism, which emphasises the unproblematic nature of facts and 'sense data'. Kant (Schacht, 1984) argued for the existence of *a priori* knowledge: 'in born' organising principles inherent in human beings by which any and all sense data are structured, arranged and understood. We do not simply 'receive' objective sense data. Our minds organise this sense data in a way that allows us to make sense of it, and, indeed, to focus on some things and not others. For Kant our understanding of the world was seen as a product of the mind and the interpretive processes which go on within it.

'Facts' are, therefore, not unproblematic, and we are, when examining the social world, involved in an interpretive process. However, a key element of social understanding - and this is in contrast with the materialist nature of the natural sciences - is the subject status of humans. When studying humans - indeed when interpreting the social world - we must be centrally concerned with the meanings that people attach to their actions. This involves a concern with their subjective experiences. We can understand meaning through the intentions, purposes and reasons which people have for any act they may perform. There is a very close logical relationship between the description of an action and the purpose of that action, or the intention underlying it. If, for example, I raise my glass in a pub, it may be to say hello to someone coming in, to toast someone's success, or even to threaten someone. The same behaviour involves a variety of intentions and hence different actions. One of the major tasks of interpretive social science is to discover the intentions which actors have in doing whatever it is they are doing (Fay, 1975). However, meanings are meanings for *them*, and whether they are meanings for them can ultimately only be told by them. Schutz (1954) has argued that the central aim of Sociology should be the reconstruction of the ways in which agents themselves explain their actions, and that the theoretical concepts of Sociologists should not depart radically from those of the agents.

After Weber (1949), the concern with meaning has been called *Verstehen* explanations. These consist, at the level of individual actions, of demonstrating the reasons why a particular act was performed. Schutz (1967) distinguished two senses in which meaning could be ascribed. The first was the genuine understanding of the other person which could only be achieved in face to face relationships, and is close to empathy. This is the intentional grasping of the experience of the other in a manner akin to looking into the other's stream of consciousness. The second was 'typification': the process whereby interpretive constructs are applied to apprehend what other people do. These constructs are derived from the experience of everyday life. It is through typifications that we classify and organise our everyday reality. For example, I might typify someone as 'caring', 'understanding', 'sexist' and so on. We apply these labels to make sense of the way we perceive people to be.

To understand the reasons why an act is performed, our explanation must include reference to the wider context from which the meaning of the act may be derived. An action is an action only in the context of certain social rules. Thus we can only understand the behaviour of motorists at traffic lights in the context of traffic rules (Hart, 1960). Their actions make sense when we know that motorists are expected to stop when a traffic light is red, to go when it is green etc. It is only because people share certain basic conceptions that there can be certain types of social activity. When we try to explain someone's actions we can do so only by reference to the shared meanings which are encapsulated in the social rules. We know, therefore, what the motorists are doing because we know the rules relating to traffic lights. Hence, an essential part of the interpretivist's position is the importance of shared meaning: that is meaning which is commonly shared by those in society. This allows us to give meaning to our own acts and understand the actions of others. It also shows how acts are incorrigibly social, in so far as they relate to social rules and hence commonly held meanings.

Interpretivists do not go in for external causal explanations. Action is predicated on the idea of an agent - specifically a human agent. An agent differs from a causal process because he or she can be said to make a choice in what they are doing. That is, it is they who decide what it is they are doing and their reasons for doing it. In this respect acts are seen to be voluntary, not externally caused. Hence an explanation of someone running along the road might be that he wanted to catch a bus. This would be the reason they would give for running, and this is quite different from an explanation which emphasised the cause of something, such as bacteria caused a throat infection. Firstly, the person may be said to have acted voluntarily ie they decided to run for the bus. Second, a causal relationship involves the logical independence of the causal factor (eg the bacteria) from its consequence (the throat infection). A very different relationship is posited in interpretivists' explanations. Here, the reason, or motive, for an action and the nature of the action itself, are mutually informing. When we say that someone is running for a bus (an action) we are including the action itself (and our explanation of it), the reason for the action (to catch the bus).

A central issue of explanation by interpretivists is its essential defeasibility, that is that there can always be, in principle, an equally plausible, but different explanation for an action. This is because we can invoke different rules to cover the same behaviour. For example, you might say that I raised my glass to threaten the person next to me, whereas I might contend I merely wished to toast them on their success. Although we each bring forward further information to buttress our contention, in the end, and in principle, the argument may be irresolvable. This means that the choice of interpretations is essentially arbitrary. No one interpretation can claim to be superior to another.

At a cultural level, this leads to relativism in our view of knowledge. This is, indeed, the inevitable 'end point' of interpretivism. Winch's (1958; 1970) view that the criteria of reality, and of rationality, are specific to different forms of life. Hence we can only understand those forms of life by reference to their own beliefs and standards, not by some external means of understanding. The implication is that we can also not judge actions by criteria outside the beliefs and understanding of the culture itself. To quote a topical example, the practice of sexual mutilation of children cannot be judged except by reference to the standards and expectations of the culture in which sexual mutilation takes place (in which, of course, it is approved). This, of course, leads to relativism, since we cannot claim that our understanding of truth is superior to any other. This, however, presents interpretivists with an irresolvable problem - the self refuting nature of relativism. If there are no universal standards of truth and rationality (or indeed morality), simply those standards that are accepted by particular groups or societies, then the general thesis of relativism must be self refuting. This is because it claims that relativism is true, while at the same time denying the existence of universal standards of truth.

Attempts to escape relativism seriously limits the capacity of interpretivists to explain (Hammersley and Atkinson, 1983). In this case interpretivists simply seek to describe how culture members actively construct reality. This restriction to description leads to the rather odd situation whereby interpretivists, who seek to get close to their subject matter, employ quite different methods of understanding from that of their 'subject matter'. Hence while culture members 'freely and legitimately' (Hammersley and Atkinson, 1983, p 17) engage in checking claims against facts and frequently employ causal explanations for actions, the social scientist is debarred from this on the grounds that it would 'distort reality'.

Realism

Realism starts from a 'common sense' position (ontology) in that it takes seriously the things, structures and mechanisms revealed by the sciences at different levels of reality (see Bhaskar, 1978, 1979; Keat and Urry, 1982; Sayer, 1984; Outhwaite, 1987). There is, according to realists an objective external reality. In this sense, it is distinguished from much interpretivist work, which does not assume that we perceive, however partially, some external reality, but that that external reality is a creation of our minds. Hence, 'science is the systematic attempt to express in thought the structures and ways of acting of things that exist and act independently of thought' (Bhaskar, 1978). However, unlike positivists, realists do not confine themselves to that which is observable. The task of science is precisely to explain 'facts' in terms of more fundamental structures, which may not in themselves be observable (an example of this would be the attraction of metal objects, explainable in terms of magnetism, which is not, itself observable).

For the realist, positivists unnecessarily limit the scope of their activity. Bhaskar (1978, 1979) shows that realists take matters beyond the merely observable. He distinguishes three levels. The empirical refers to events which are observable. Beyond this, however, are the 'actual' and the 'real'. The real refers to entities which exists and the interactions between these entities. The actual refers to whether any events are occurring because of these interactions. It is quite possible for entities to exist which are not observable, and of which we can only have some inkling by their observable *effects*. Hence for realist, positivists operate at only one level, and that is the most 'superficial'.

In order to explain these facts, we do need to make (theoretical) interpretations. These interpretations are hypotheses, in the sense that they are potentially corrigible (falsifiable or transcended) by further discoveries. These hypotheses are humanly created descriptions which attempt to represent as adequately as possible the objects which they are trying to describe. Hence we might use the concept (from Freud) of the unconscious to make sense of all sorts of human behaviour, such as anxiety or so called 'Freudian slips'. We cannot 'see' the unconscious, but we can observe its effects (if it exists). However, a future theory or set of hypotheses may falsify or transcend this interpretation. In this sense, realism postulates an objective 'external' reality, but a limited or fallible human understanding of that reality. It is because of this that we have to make hypotheses about that reality.

This points clearly to the provisional nature of our knowledge. Our understanding of reality will always be theory infused because, unlike positivists, realists do not assume that our perception of an observable external reality is unproblematic. What we seek to do when we seek to explain any observable entities (facts) is to explain the mechanisms which give rise to those facts. These mechanisms, which may not themselves be observable (like magnetism), represent theories which enable us to understand the way things in reality occur. This does not prevent us from having some sense of what is true or false. Statements about the world are true if they correspond to the facts of the matter. However, because of the provisional nature of knowledge, we are not confronted with an 'either-or' choice between truth and falsity. There is no truth or falsity in an absolute and timeless sense, but there are relative degrees of truth or falsity.

This becomes clearer when we understand how we may use theory to explain matters. Descriptions of the world will always be, to a greater or lesser extent, theory determined, because we will have partial views of reality, and we will seek to create mechanisms which will serve to explain that reality. This does not, however, mean that one theory or explanation is as good as any other. A theory is better than another if it explains (under its description) most of what the second theory explains (under its description) plus some further things which are not explained by the second theory. This is an argument by Popper which has been widely accepted by realists (Popper, 1963). Just what things require explanation is a matter for the science concerned. Hence, it is no objection to the Marxist theory of Capitalism that it cannot explain, as ethnomethodology can, how to terminate a telephone conversation without offending one's partner (Outhwite, 1987)

Although realists seek to make causal explanations they do not conform to the principles of positivism. We cannot identify causes merely in terms of regularities. What we observe can always be confounded by further factors which make that regularity misleading, or causal mechanisms can neutralise each other in such way that no event takes place. As Outhwaite (1987) points out, the objects on my writing table are all subject to gravitation, but they are all prevented from falling to the ground by the resistance offered by the table. What this means is that we cannot look merely for regularities between different 'variables'. More working class people may vote National Front but this may not be because of class but because working class people in certain areas are more likely to be racist. Realists consider causal explanations should be presented in terms of tendencies, and in terms of generative mechanisms, those interrelated factors which appear to explain matters. These generative mechanisms form aspects of the theory which the realist uses to explain events. These tendencies, in the natural as well as social sciences can make explanations no more than probabilistic.

In the social sciences, like interpretivists, realists are concerned with the issue of human actions and the meanings that are ascribed to them. While in the natural sciences realism considers that things exist and act independently of our (human) descriptions of them this clearly cannot be the case with human actions and social structures, where agents' conceptions are not external to the facts described (Keat and Urry, 1982). For example, a quarrel cannot be adequately described except with reference to the participants' perceptions of their situation. However, this does not mean, as maintained by interpretivists, that our interpretation of situations is essentially arbitrary. There are some effects in society, such as the tendency for the social position of the parents to influence the educational achievements of their children which are as real and general as we could reasonably expect. What is required instead is a means of incorporating the perception of the situation held by actors, including the reasons given for acting, into the overall explanation. An explanation of a quarrel, for example, would have to include the participants' perception of the situation.

What is needed is an understanding of the relationship between human actions and the structures of society. We must first understand that people by their actions, reproduce (sometimes unconsciously) and occasionally transform, the structures of society, such as, for example, class. People do not marry to reproduce the nuclear family or work to sustain the capitalist economy, yet these are the outcomes of their marriage and work. What this means is that social structures do exist, but that they do not exist independently of the actions of people. However, the actions of people also take place within a set of structurally defined positions. Hence when we act we do so in a society where the structures of class, the nuclear family and the capitalist economy are ever present structures (Giddens, 1993). Thus while structures affect peoples' actions, some notion of agency is required to make the structures work. Society is both the ever present condition and the continually produced outcome of human actions (agency).

It is important to understand, furthermore, the influence of these structures on actions. People are dominated in important ways by the structures of social relationships (Keat and Urry, 1982). For any individual such structures have an existence apart from his or her actions, and have a powerful effect on their actions. A poorly educated working class person may become apathetic in looking for a job, because their experiences have led them to be pessimistic about their opportunities and to feel powerless in the face of unemployment. A better educated middle class person may feel more optimistic, and be more successful because their experiences have led them to expect more success. Our explanations of actions, therefore, do not have to rely simply on the agent's reasons for their actions. They can be causal, because their choices are constrained by the circumstances they are in (indeed these circumstances may be causal by giving them opportunities). Explanations may also be considered causal where the agent themselves recognises something as constraining or influencing some action. For example an act of obedience cannot be considered completely non causal because its occurrence depends on their recognising what happened before as a command and acting upon it.

However, there is a connection between explanation and common sense understanding. First, however imperfect they may be, to the extent that they are the perceptions of the agents involved in the situation, they will influence what takes place. Someone may think that they are helping a friend on holiday by taking their suitcase through customs. When customs stop them and find the suitcase stuffed with drugs, they may find instead that they are drug running. However, we cannot explain the situation without reference to what the person *thought* they were doing (helping a friend). Our explanations of actions necessarily must include what the agents themselves thought was happening. Second, common sense descriptions provide a starting point from which we can develop our understanding of the social world.

CONCLUSION

It should be clearly apparent that there are widely divergent views about what actually constitutes knowledge in social science. This is a major problem for a profession whose knowledge focus primarily involves social science. These differences are quite fundamental.

- For the interpretivists the issue of meaning and understanding are central; for the positivist they are at best peripheral; for the realist, they are the *entré* to more profound explanations.
- For the positivist an objective reality exists and it is observable and unproblematic; for the interpretivist all perceptions of the 'world' are interpretive involving active organisation by the mind; for the realist, there is an objective reality, but it is not confined to the observable.
- For the positivist knowledge is objective and cumulative; for the interpretivist it is largely 'created' and merely an interpretation; for the realist it is provisional and theory soaked.
- For the positivist scientific interpretations will provide us with a true representation of reality; for the interpretivist no one form of knowledge is superior to another; for the realist one theory may be better than another if it explains more.
- For the positivist the subject's viewpoint is subjective and secondary to scientific explanation; for the interpretivist the views of the subjects, in social science, are what we aspire to discover; for the realist they are an important factor to be included in our general explanation of social life.

Social work is on dodgy ground where there is so little agreement as to what constitutes knowledge in its knowledge base. Indeed, one group, the interpretivists, deny the possibility of objective knowledge at all. The different commitments entailed in these different 'knowledge positions' involve radically different ways of viewing knowledge in social work, and its use for social work. It has also meant that debates about the status and integrity of knowledge in social work have largely been about an unacknowledged difference in views about what constitutes knowledge in the first place. An example of this is in the next chapter's discussion about the debate between Hardiker and Davies.

Part three of this book concentrates on the consequences for social work of this contentious nature of its knowledge. Chapter eight examines the problems of applying knowledge to social work. Chapter nine, taking into account the difficulties identified in chapter eight, suggests a way out, through the Theory of Emergent Understanding and particularly the practice of 'reflexive eclecticism'. Chapter ten examines the use of knowledge in a way which is consistent with the constraints placed on it by the expectations entailed in the practice of social work.

Chapter Eight

The problem of knowledge

The theory-practice problematic is a perennial one, which has created discussions and debate which, it sometimes seems, has generated more heat than light. This arises from a number of sources. There is considerable pressure (see chapter 4) for social workers aspiring to possess professional credentials, to demonstrate these credentials through a documented and apparently effective knowledge base. This knowledge base need also to be relevant – it should lead to effective practice (whatever that may be) when dealing with areas which are of concern to social workers. Yet there remains considerable scepticism about the validity of any claims by social work in this area.

This scepticism becomes particularly significant with the onset of care management. If social workers cannot demonstrate particular competence in some specific areas of care management – if they cannot establish a niche – then why should social workers be employed at all. It is quite clear (see chapter one) that there is a 'professional' level of care management assessment and if social work is to make a contribution, it is at this level. Why not simply employ 'street wise grannies' (Virginia Bottomley's phrase when Minister of Health), with a concomitant emphasis on life and practical experience. If training is needed, why provide it in Universities? why can it not be on the job? Indeed, why should it be of any length (two years may be considered far too long) and why should it involve what appears to some to be abstract and somewhat esoteric theorising? Could we not, if intelligence is needed, simply employ graduates, and then provide 'on the job' experience? Unless a case can be established for social work, there is no particular reason for its survival in the new care managerial environment.

Yet 'theory for' social work is not an area which has attracted any degree of consensus. 'Theory', as Howe (1987) has pointed out, is generally accepted, rather loosely, as formal knowledge documented in texts and intended for application to practice. Within this broad definition we can identify clear themes in the approach made to the relationship of theory to practice. These themes constitute the content of this chapter.

THEORY AS APPLIED SOCIAL SCIENCE

The theory-practice debate is one which has been dominated, largely implicitly, by a perception of both theory and practice, and in particular a specific kind of relationship between the two, based on separate realms or domains (of theory and practice). Hence Rein and White (1981, p 21) refer to a 'false duality between 'theory' as the task of academics and 'practice' as the task of practitioners' This false duality, they argue comes from an 'objectivist-scientific' approach of a sort associated with positivism that 'science makes knowledge [while] practice uses it' (p 36). Not all writers may be positivist, but they behave in a way consistent with an instrumentalist notion of the use of knowledge for practice. Positivism attaches a particular meaning to 'theory' and 'practice'. Theory is conceived of as a general rule or law (even if for the time being provisional) which is tested against observable evidence. Practice, on the other hand, involves the use of theoretical knowledge, deductively, primarily to control events (Blyth and Hugman, 1982). This approach thus proposes an instrumental engineering conception of the relationship of theory to practice. It involves two key dimensions: (a) the separation out of theory and practice as discrete domains and (b) that the direction of the relationship is one way, from the former to the latter. Not all 'theorists' may sign up to a positivist conception of 'theory' but the theory practice relationship assumes this unidirectional and discrete character. This may be termed the 'Applied Social Science' Model.

This kind of approach is exemplified by Macdonald et al (1992) whose extensive review of a variety of techniques was designed to indicate which should be part of the social work curriculum. It is of the sort of relationship that: if approach A is applied to circumstance B, then outcome C will result. In social work this might apply to the use, for example of cognitive behavioural methods with individuals suffering depression. It involves the use of results from effectiveness studies to indicate methods deemed to be effective in achieving particular goals whose status is deemed to be desirable.

This appeal to universal laws involved in Positivism in principle posits regular relationships between variables held to obtain across all circumstances. However, it is the statistical version of this, whereby the relationships have a high probability of applying across all circumstances, that has generally been adopted by social scientists. We may assume, for example, that people suffering depression and receiving cognitive behavioural therapy, are more likely to improve in their mood, or improve to a greater extent, in a given time period than those not receiving such therapy. Given this model, a premium is placed on the generalisability of findings.

Associated with this is an approach emphasising instrumental reasoning. This refers to areas of social life which are subject to decisions made in correspondence with technical rules. These technical rules are the outcome of particular forms of knowledge generated which may, in principle, be applied to practice. These rules are themselves general, but may be applied to particular situations. The assumption is that although each situation may possess some degree of uniqueness, they are not so unique as to prevent the application of general rules common to these situations. The depressed individual may have particular unique characteristics and circumstances, but they have, in common with others who are depressed, their depression. Indeed, the assumption is further that there are characteristics general to particular situations, no matter how unique they may, on the surface appear to be (Fay, 1975, p 44). Instrumental reason presents an image of rationality and efficiency: rationality, because of the deductive and informed (by knowledge) nature of the application of theory to practice, and efficiency, because such knowledge application is considered to make the achievement of goals more effective than if that knowledge were not used. As Popkewitz (1987, p 11) puts it: 'the language of instrumental reason is important because it projects an image of rational thought and institutional efficiency'.

The outcome is one where the practitioner is seen as, in some respects, a technician. In 'ideal type' technical acts are those actions guided by some pre-arrangement and occur in institutionalised contexts. They contain three key elements. The practitioner follows some prearranged guidelines, ideally rules and regulations so that practice is carried out in a particular and regular way; they require skills rather than the ability to make and justify decisions required by ethical deeds; and they are based on operationalised knowledge (Rotenstreich, 1977). Clearly this approach may apply not only to the relatively sophisticated methods of, for example, cognitive behavioural work, but also to the following of procedures required by the agency (for example in relation to child protection). Obviously the acts of social workers may be more or less technical, and, as Jamous and Peloille (1970) point out for them to become completely technical, where knowledge lacks mystique a degree of uncertainty and judgement in application, this is a recipe for the deprofessionalisation of particular areas of occupational life (see chapter 4).

This concept of the theory practice relationship is one which has been widely canvassed. It has great apparent attractions. Its textual (written) nature allows it to be relatively unproblematically circulated around the professional community and may contribute to a sense of professionally owned knowledge and competence in the wider society. It is one which emphasises theoretical knowledge as 'product', that is knowledge which has been already validated and developed and is ready for application to practice, and which has an inevitably static nature: the particular piece of knowledge is developed and available. This conception of knowledge is one which has been assumed by a wide variety of social work thinkers such as Davies (1986; Sheldon 1979, 1986, 1992, though cf 1983; Sinclair, 1992; Cheetham, 1992; Thyer, 1993). Within this broad church of those committed to 'Applied Social Science' two groups may be discerned. Some embrace the approach wholeheartedly. Thyer (1993) has written enthusiastically about what he calls the 'logical positivist' approach, and even identifies a hierarchy of strategies from empirically based outcome investigations. While they may differ in detail, this enthusiasm for an experimental approach is shared by Sheldon, who seeks to use its results to influence the design of the social work curriculum. Others are more circumspect. There is considerable need for research, but it may be simply investigative rather than experimental in design. A broader term, evaluative research, is used, and Cheetham (1992, p 53) remarks that 'evaluation of social work effectiveness one of the best ways of developing the knowledge base of social work and bridging the gap between theory and practice'. This is well illustrated by Sinclair (1991) who suggests that research can provide social workers with information on the predicaments of their client; it can give useful background information on the effectiveness of services; and it can inform the choices made by social workers, particularly with key decisions (such as those relating to the child's 'journey' through the care system).

This is all very well, but it has failed to convince many and, to a considerable degree lacks conviction within social work as a whole. The technical-applied social science approach has attracted criticism from within its own academic constituency. Davies (1981, 1982; 1986), in particular, in a number of publications has appeared to despair of this approach, though his criticism has focused on social science in general and sociology in particular, rather than specifically social work research. His first criticism is based on the issue of effectiveness. Commenting on an article by Hardiker (1981) espousing the cause of social science application, he stated (1982) that we have no idea whether such knowledge would make social workers better or more effective practitioners, and furthermore, that there is little evidence that social workers ever change individual behaviour, let alone communities. His second concern was that the nature of social work is such that the limits and constraints of the practical circumstances in which social workers find themselves are always bound to exercise more influence on practice than any amount of theory. He commented on three knowledge forms, maternal deprivation, labelling and inequality. We may, he thought, be informed by research on maternal deprivation, but this is of less importance than the intensely practical issue of finding adequate substitute parents for children when required. Because of its agency function social work can only be marginally concerned with inequality as an issue (as a matter of individual poverty, this was a different matter). Labelling, furthermore, is something which social workers themselves do, and its implication, he thinks, is the withdrawal of social work from certain fields of endeavour. His third concern was with the influence of sociology in particular. Its problem, he felt, was that it was permeated by a radical agenda: the logic of many sociologists' arguments would be the abandonment of state sector social work (Davies, 1981). The views of many sociologists about social work were, he considered, 'frankly jaundiced' (1981, p 284) and likely to undermine the morale of social work students. Yet the hopes of 'colonising' state sector social work for a radical agenda were really fantasies.

Davies (1986) own solution was to take refuge in what suspiciously resembles and 'agency apprentice' model. He identified four essential elements to social work knowledge: practice 'know how', legal knowledge, welfare rights knowledge and knowledge of the operation of the local community. In later writing (Davies, 1990) he marginally increased the profile of social science knowledge, suggesting that sociology might examine the function of social work in society, identify what constitutes good practice and discover means by which practitioners may be restricted from pursuing personal goals at the expense of the agency.

Both Howe (1980) and Sheldon (1979) have commented on the steady accumulation of social and psychological theories in an attempt to provide the 'know how' to justify a professional status, none of which seem to have done the trick. The result has been the accumulation of unrelated relics rather than any real knowledge development. Sheldon noted (1979) that this leaves an impossibly wide number of alternatives to apply to different problems. There are, furthermore, no criteria to choose between different approaches, leaving choice as an almost entirely personal matter. In these circumstances there has frequently been a tendency to seek refuge in eclecticism.

While such eclecticism assumes all knowledge is potentially useful, it fails to distinguish the really relevant and useful (if and where it exists) from the irrelevant and useless, and fails to take account of the conflicting assumptions inherent in such theoretical diversity (Howe, 1987). Yet there is a sense of inevitability about such eclecticism because the social sciences are not characterised by consensus and theoretical unity. Indeed, they are characterised by profound and serious conflict at every conceivable level: about what may be said to exist (ontology), what we may actually know (epistemology), theoretical frameworks for understanding humans and society, methodology and findings. These issues are no idle matter: for if the source of knowledge is so uncertain then how can social workers hope to apply it to practice. Stevenson's warning (1971), uttered some time ago, against building the social work house on the shifting sands of social science, may be understood in the light of these conflicts.

Of the two approaches outlined in the Applied Social Science tradition, the positivist approach has come in for particular criticism. (Raynor, 1984; Smith, 1987). Raynor, commenting that 'social workers often experience research as existing on another plane, irrelevant to their real concerns', criticises three assumptions in the empiricist approach. First, there is an implicit underlying determinism, which, he argues, pays insufficient attention to intentions, purposes and reasons for action – the choices people make. Second, an emphasis on 'facts' fails to recognise the 'socially constructed' nature of our perceptions, the product of the interaction of language and experience. Third, there is a concentration on technical issues of how to deal with problems rather than the issues of the purpose of the problem resolution, of means rather than ends of social work.

EXPERIENTIALISM IN SOCIAL WORK

Academic reservations have reflected (and partly arose from) a widespread scepticism in practice about this form of applied knowledge. A number of studies focusing on practitioner accounts of their practice have consistently found a distinct lack of theory use. Social workers do not seek to apply knowledge to practice in the way suggested by the applied social science model (og Carow, 1979, Stevenson and Parsloe, 1978; Corby, 1982). In the absence of any evidence of direct theory use, researchers have been apt to suggests a 'subconscious assimilation' thesis whereby theory informs practice without practitioners being directly aware of it (Paley, 1987). This sounds rather like a pious hope, and anyway the Applied Social Science model certainly implies that theory application would be conscious. Furthermore, the reservations which exist within the academic constituency, can hardly be put down, as suggested by Sheldon (1979) to a simple distinction between the academic and practice subcultures of social work, one emphasising rigorous knowledge development, evaluation and application, and the other the primacy of experience and personal knowledge.

Where the dominant perception of the relationship between theory and practice is the Applied Social Science model, it can be hardly surprising that where it is found wanting, social workers have tended to take refuge in an experiential orientation. Social work knowledge that is distilled from individual experience is generally venerated by social workers and also by some social work teachers. Such knowledge is often regarded (for epistemological reasons which are not generally made explicit) as superior to other ways of knowing the world. Shaw (1975, p 151) observes that 'adhering strongly to a belief in the uniqueness of the individual... [social workers] are reluctant to entertain generalisations... [which are considered] inferior to the warmth and spontaneity of the social worker's relationship with his [sic] client'. There is, of course, with the range of possible explanations and subjective understandings which may be generated, a clear risk of degeneration into solipsism (Hearn, 1982). Of course, some alternative knowledge forms have been advocated, but each tend to feed the importance of personalised experiential knowledge. Hence, for example, we have insights from reading poetry, plays and novels (Valk, 1983; Morns, 1975); insights from direct experience of oppression (Dominelli and McLeod); and extrapolations from life or practice experience (Pratt and Grimshaw, 1985; Carew, 1979).

A directly associated dimension of the occupational community is an oral culture which exists alongside the written texts and journals of social work (Sibeon, 1991). There is, perhaps, a natural concomitant to the frequently noted lack of 'theoretical accounting' in practice (Parsloe and Stevenson, 1978; Carew, 1979; Corby, 1982; Ernstbrunner, 1987). Carew's study, which is typical suggests that social workers rarely draw upon formal academic knowledge derived from written texts. On the job, experientially acquired practice wisdoms are regarded by practitioners as being of far greater importance than written academic or 'professional' knowledge. Practice wisdoms consist of tried and trusted procedures that are passed from practitioner to practitioner and are reinforced by informal discussions and group meetings such as case conferences. Curnock and Hardiker's (1979) observed that practice 'wisdom' remains in social workers' heads and daily activities rather than being formally written down in social work texts. While we are able to read about social science knowledge because it is written down we are unable to learn from (or even understand) practice wisdom. Sheldon (1983) might add that we are unable to evaluate or learn from them, and that such practice 'wisdom' can be pretty primitive stuff. Such haphazard and implicit learning is bound to be problematic for any occupation which seeks to demonstrate professional credentials on the basis of what its members know.

Experientialism also finds its way into academic work. The 'process learning' approach is a feature of professional training for a considerable time and draws upon psychotherapeutic ideas (which have had considerable impact on traditional social work). Advocates of this approach claim emotionally linked experiential discussions in small groups enable students and fieldworkers to understand and work more successfully with the inner experiences of their clients (Greenwell and Howard, 1986; Jones, 1982). This further emphasises the experientialism and cognitive indeterminacy which pervades the wider social work practice culture. It further reinforces the perceptions of uniqueness of individual situations confronting social workers, of the uncertainty pervading practice actions and the personalised-idiosyncratic nature of social work knowledge.

There is considerable evidence, furthermore, from consumer follow up studies of social work education that practice placements, rather than formal teaching in university and college, provides the best learning experience for social work courses (Davies, 1984; Shaw and Walton, 1978; Fairs, 1987). Indeed, a small study of CSS students (formerly the 'under-professional' qualification for social service work) suggested that they tended to learn particularly well through concrete experience (Bradbury, 1984). Evans (1987) argued that it would be possible to build whole qualifying programmes on practice. In the process, he emphasised the importance of building an intake of experienced students who can build on their experience. To be sure, Evans himself (though not some others) is concerned with building on experience through theory to create a new theoretically informed practice. Yet this is nonetheless built on an edifice in which the practice setting and experience provide the undeniable focus.

Perhaps inevitably, the widespread criticism about the use of formal knowledge has led to a rather jaundiced view in certain quarters about the professionalising ambitions of social workers and particularly of the importance of academic knowledge relative to practice 'know how'. Writing about reactions to the development of a stronger agency-practice dimension in the development of the Diploma in Social Work one Director argued that resistance arose from professional self interest, involving 'arguments that concentrated not on clients and their needs but on the extent to which different forms of training might or might not confer higher status on social work' (Harbert, 1985). Another director suggested that 'resistance against reforms emanated from...a shrinking cadre of professionals who were attempting to insulate themselves from the reality of the 1980s [and presumably 1990s] style social services' (Warner, 1986). Such a view expressed by powerful individuals may be interpreted by some as evidence of a strong theme of anti-intellectualism in the practice community (cf

Sheldon, 1979), yet there is a clear logic to it in the light of scepticism about the use of knowledge in the academic community, the apparent pervasiveness of experientialism in practice and the failure of social work to convince a wider society of its professional credentials (see chapter 4).

INTERPRETIVIST APPROACHES

An alternative view, centred around education and learning techniques rather than specifically theory application to practice (but nonetheless with implications for it) emerged during the 1980s: the concept of transfer of learning. This is concerned centrally with the way learning may occur in a manner which allows for 'theoretical thinking' in practice through the generation and application of concepts and ideas which may be used and 'transferred' from case to case and circumstance to circumstance. It operates within an interpretivist paradigm. This broadly emphasises the importance of meaning in the understanding of human affairs (ie how people make sense of their world), stresses that there is not one single view of the world and that individuals and groups may interpret that world in widely differing fashions. Individuals actively 'construct' their view of actions and events and on this basis develop perspectives on their 'world'. All this is underlaid by an emphasis on the subjective nature of human experience and hence the importance of the subject in understanding human beings (Hughes, 1990).

This interpretivist notion of human understanding very much characterised the ways in which Hardiker saw social workers conduct their practice (Curnock and Hardiker, 1979). Adhering implicitly to the 'subconscious assimilation' thesis she argues that social workers operate in their practice with 'practice theories' which are constructs by which they are able to make sense of their clients' situations and act upon them. She (Hardiker, 1981) identified three in particular: a judicial ideology, where social work is seen as part of the institution of justice and an extension of the court system; a community development ideology, where weight is given to resources rather than problems, and where stress is placed on the need to change systems; and a welfare ideology, where social work is a personal service given to individuals and families. These practice theories, however, owe little to textbook learning, but rather reflect the ways in which,

160

and necessity of, making sense of social situations. The result is that practice theories 'remain in the social worker's heads and daily activities rather than finding their way into the literature' (Curnock and Hardiker, p 10).

The outcome is that social science knowledge and social work knowledge differ in that we can all read about and learn from social science because it is written down. However, there is no possibility of learning from practice theories in the same way because they are not written down. Inevitably social workers have to pick up this knowledge as they go along, feeding a tendency both towards experientialism and idiosyncratic personalised knowledge. Of course this hinders continuity and development of knowledge as well as the assessment of which kind of knowledge is most useful in which kind of situation. The result is that each generation of social workers have to work out many of the rules of practice for themselves (Curnock and Hardiker, p 161). Their solution is that the practice theories of social workers should be examined and documented in order that they may contribute to a more generally available knowledge base which is demonstrably that of social work. However, in view of the fact that the methods employed for generating understanding are very much those employed (it is assumed) by people generally, there is no way of saying that these practice theories are any different from the kind of everyday understanding laypeople may use in making sense of the same situations.

Transfer of learning approaches emphasise the way in which learning may be actively constructed by social workers and social work students. It emphasises that it should be practice oriented – that students and practitioners should be able to transfer learning from one area of practice to another and not just from the general to the specific (CCETSW, 1981). As Harris (1983) pointed out, this meant that students would best learn in a controlled environment which as closely as possible resembles the reality of their practice. Of course, this reaffirms that the practice setting itself provides the best focus for learning. It also rests on the assumption that such transfer *could* take place – that experiences and knowledge relevant in one circumstance, case or individual will also be relevant in other areas. Together, these ideas created an image of the active and creative social worker who would be able to analyse situations, draw conclusions from them and recognise other situations where such learning would be relevant. These qualities would be best facilitated by encouraging active rather than passive educational methods, mirroring the processes which are being advocated in practice.

Harris also suggested the need for developing supra-concepts around which new learning may be created and organised. Alternatively social work education could emphasise metatheories, such as Marxist, Systems or Ecological frameworks. The point is that this strategy and the organising concepts can give meaning and coherence to disparate information, not to mention the experience of students in practice. Each practitioner would be, in these circumstances actively 'constructing' their practice in a way which both allows a focus on particular cases, yet allows for learning to be applied 'across' cases. The 'expertise' developed is not in applying given knowledge but in the way in which students and practitioners can examine practice situations.

Gardiner's (1984a and 1984b; 1988; 1989) work extended the ideas developed by Harris. He was concerned particularly with learning styles, and the problems encountered when teachers' teaching did not match student's learning styles. Gardiner emphasised two elements in the transfer of learning: the application of theory to practice and the ability to generate theory from practice experience. The former involves going from the general to the specific and then latter involves generalising from the specific. Of course, one will involve the use of textual knowledge and the other involves everyday or practical experience. The transfer of learning model emphasises that in developing educational techniques we need to understand the ways in which we as human beings make sense of the world, while recognising the active nature of human enquiry, even in everyday situations. Hence we will not learn primarily by 'passive absorption' of a given body of knowledge which is then applied to appropriate circumstances. Learning must recognise the more active creative nature of human learning and assessment.

Learning occurs in a cycle. This involves a number of elements. We have an experience and in this experience we recognise (or more properly construct) that which is salient from it. We may notice that where behavioural problems are present in a child that the mother frequently oscillates between anger and apathy and has low self esteem. We build up patterns which help us explain the occurrence of these various salient aspects. The pattern may be explained by depression. We make further patterns of the patterns we have identified. We recognise these characteristics in other cases, for example where a partner has just 'walked out' on someone. From this we can develop a notion of loss being the characteristic in both cases: a sense of loss of independence (indeed engulfment) for the mother caring for the child and the loss of the partner for the other individual. These then become generalisations which can be applied to other situations, where we make use of our experiences.

More recent developments in Enquiry and Action Learning (EAL) represent practical methods for encouraging individual learning and transfer of learning, based on similar insights about adult learning methods (Burgess, 1992; Burgess and Jackson, 1990; Taylor, 1993). This approach involves the presentation of a particular practice problem which is then used as the basis for group discussion and reflection. The group becomes the context for identifying key elements in the situation, and the means by which appropriate responses may be identified. It involves the use and application to the situation of both formal learned knowledge and that based on experience. It is based on the premise that people learn best when that learning involves them actively, rather than passively as recipient of given knowledge, and involves also a considerable value being placed on experiential as well as more formally learned knowledge. The process of identifying the problem, salient issues and appropriate responses, represents, in effect, a group 'construction' of the situation as the basis for intervention. While this approach is deemed to facilitate theory practice integration and mobilise effectively the processes by which adults learn, there is no indication of the way in which one form of knowledge may be chosen as against another in a particular circumstance, nor of the weight that may be given to experiential as opposed to formal written knowledge.

CONCLUSION

Clearly there is no consensus about the status of knowledge in social work, or the appropriate relationship between theory and practice. The different positions reflect both different assumptions about the nature of social science knowledge and the degree of optimism or pessimism about its application. There are certainly grave reservations amongst many about the Applied Social Science model, and of course the experiential orientation gives primacy to practice and life experience.

163

Although the transfer of learning is based on a more interpretivist approach, it is subject to the relativism which is its inevitable accompaniment. There is really no guidance as to which theories, whether experientially developed or selected from formal knowledge, are to be considered in relation to any particular practice situation, nor any indication of which approach may be taken in any particular circumstance. In these conditions, there may, in principle, be as many interpretations as people involved in making assessments. Furthermore, as Badger (1985) pointed out, there is no acknowledgement that there may be conflicting conceptual frameworks available, nor that any two social work educators or practitioners may not agree as to which concepts are essential.

Indeed, this approach, while recognising the usefulness of both experiential and theoretical knowledge, does not indicate which should get priority. Should experiential knowledge only be used when theoretical knowledge relevant to the case is not available? or is it in some circumstances to be preferred to formal theoretical knowledge? indeed, should the relevance of theoretical versus experiential knowledge be entirely a personal matter? Gardiner (1987, p 49-50) has certainly come close to preferring a personalised non textual form of knowledge when he argued that 'competent' professional social work knowledge is so individualised that it cannot be communicated to another. Anything that can be communicated is a form of knowledge that is 'relatively inconsequential'.

The overall impression is that the transfer of learning gives knowledge in social work a rather uncertain status. Certainly its strength lies in its flexibility, its focus on practice and its emphasis on the practitioner as active analyser. However, it provides no way of indicating whether or not any particular construction in a particular circumstance is the right one. Indeed, its relativism suggests that there is no one right construction, just number of alternatives which may be used in any particular situation. Yet we know, from the point of view of social work responsibilities, that there can be wrong constructions. Where a child dies when being supervised by a social worker who, however understandably, did not take action to prevent the death, and where this arises from a misreading of the situation, the social worker has clearly interpreted the situation wrongly. Furthermore, as a mode of learning it encourages a more individualised and creative approach which is practically bound to lead to idiosyncratic practice and which does little to help professional community wide, and hence more permanent, text based knowledge.

All three approaches, Applied Social Science, Experientialism and Interactionist, therefore, have major difficulties. In pursuing a solution to the problems presented, the kind of emphasis on characteristic ways in which humans make sense of the social world which appears in interactionist approaches appears a fruitful way to proceed. However, the interactionist, transfer of learning approach concentrates too much on the construction of ways of understanding and too little on the degree of accuracy this provides in relation to any particular practice situation. We may also learn, therefore, from certain aspects of the Applied Social Science model, in particular the process of hypothesis testing which characterises much of its work. However, this is presented as a case focused approach, rather than the formulation of general rules which are applicable across all cases of a particular type. This is a retroductive activity in which a concern with the avoidance of error is of central importance. This case focused approach helps social workers manage the issues of uncertainty outlined in chapter 5. It is in the synthesis of the active interpretation of situations by practitioners and hypothesis testing that we can move forward in understanding and developing a theory-practice relationship appropriate for social work and care management. However, a third element is also significant: we cannot consider the approach to knowledge without considering what it is for – social work. Hence the kind of constraints outlined in Parts One and Two of this book – what might be termed the 'world of the social worker qua social worker' – need to be incorporated into any theoretical schema. These relate in particular to the core of objectivism and consensus assumptions which pervade those specific areas of social concern with which social workers are involved.

Chapter Nine

Towards the theory of emergent understanding

It is a truism to state that in pursuing social research we cannot go beyond the limits to human understanding. The content of the knowledge generated no doubt goes well beyond that which we as individuals could harvest from everyday experience. The process by which this may take place owes much to the processes we use to make sense in everyday life. A number of writers have commented on similarities between 'common sense' understanding and the kinds of understanding achieved by social science knowledge. Common sense can refer to at least two things (Fletcher, 1984). It is first about content: it involves a set of shared assumptions about the nature of the social and physical world, as well as shared beliefs about its workings. Examples might include notions that the world exists independently of our perception of it, that other people possess conscious awareness, that the cause of crime resides in unemployment or individual personality. It is second about process: here it refers to a way of thinking about the social and physical world. These are tacitly known mental processes involved in explaining, interpreting and understanding the behaviour of self and others. Essentially this concerns aspects of lay cognition and the way in which people process information about their world.

Some 'hard' scientists, for example, have been quite convinced that all science -particularly the process of achieving scientific understanding - is just common sense. Huxley, wrote in 1902 (p 42) that 'science is nothing but trained and organised common sense, differing from the latter only as a veteran may differ from a raw recruit'. Medawar (1979) also commented that while few people other than lab scientists use laboratory experiments, the general device of experimentation is widespread. The qualitative methods of social scientists some have suggested (Sheppard, 1995; Hammersley and Atkinson, 1983) are no more than refinements or developments of those used in everyday life. The market research interview, journalistic interview and social research interview may have distinctive purposes, but they are overlapping varieties of the same interactional format. Rock (1979) suggests that many ideas of deviance represent part of the common stock of everyday language; it is only the esoteric nature of academic formulation which separates the academic from everyday life.

This does not mean that social science and everyday formulations are equivalents. Wallace and Bruce (1983) identified three key ways in which social science knowledge transcends everyday information:

1. social scientists are more routinely and professionally concerned with explanation than most lay people (though arguably not more than social workers);
2. common sense formulations are more superficial and more easily satisfied;
3. common sense explanations are more concerned with the personal than the general. What distinguishes social science and common sense is rigour. Wallace and Bruce (1983) conclude that sociology and its methods are 'more systematic forms(s) of common sense'.

While social science and common sense knowledge are not equivalents, this does begin to account for the difficulty encountered by those who seek to justify a formal social science knowledge base for social work. On the one hand, it may be the very similarity of the processes of generating common sense and social science knowledge which makes the former appear attractive. This is emphasised by the necessary contextual relevance of common sense knowledge when applied to a specific social work problem, a relevance not always possessed by social science. Furthermore, the Applied Social Science model, with its emphasis on law-like application, seems to 'sideline' processes which social workers experience as significant in making sense of practice situations. Little mention is made of the processual nature of understanding, of its contextual dimension, and of the significance of reflexivity.

It is the contention of this chapter that the development of a knowledge base for social work requires, at least in part, a focus on the processes by which humans explain and make sense of situations. While, as Huxley and others have suggested, this requires an understanding of common sense ways in which we explain situations, this is insufficient in itself for the purposes of social work. The greater rigour which should mark out social work from the layperson in conducting analyses of practice situations leads us to examine the more rigorous approaches involved in the pursuit of explanation in social research. This will lead us to develop the concept of *Reflexive Eclecticism* to characterise competent practice in social work.

MEANING AND UNDERSTANDING

Making sense of the world is a not a straightforward matter. The search for meaning lies at the heart of the attempt to make sense, and as such is as much a part of social work assessments as it is of common sense and social science understanding (Rickman, 1967). *Verstehen*, the theoretic interest of understanding or interpreting meaningfulness, was an absolutely crucial dimension, according to Weber (1969) in the understanding of social life. *Verstehen* is, so to speak, about understanding peoples' understanding, of making sense of the way they make sense. For Weber, the explanation of social affairs has to be adequate at the level of meaning, and the essential purpose of social science is interpretive, ie to understand the subjective meaning of social action. If we do not understand the meanings social groups place on their circumstances and actions we cannot understand fully their actions, or their perspectives on their circumstances. It is this emphasis on meaning which distinguishes the social from the natural sciences. The contrast between the natural and social sciences occurs because, in the latter, human beings are both the subject and object of enquiry, which means that knowledge of society is a form of self knowledge. *Verstehen* (interpretive understanding) gives social observers a method of investigating social phenomena in a way that does not distort the social world of those being studied. Since the essence of social interaction lies in the meaning agents give to their actions and environment, all valid social analysis should refer back to these.

What does this entail? Meaning is about understanding the wishes feelings, hopes and concerns of other persons or groups (and indeed oneself). It relates to their purposes, intentions and feelings that relate to their purposes. We can only understand the disappointment of a woman whose pregnancy test proves negative if we know she desperately wishes to have children. We can only understand the joy of another woman at the same result if we know that she wishes to pursue a career and pregnancy has no part in her current plans. We must have the capacity to 'pick up' or receive this information, which is a complex task (Brown, 1973). We are all, therefore, in a sense, social observers, while being participants in that same interaction. Our observation and understanding of these women is based on an understanding of the meaning of the event of pregnancy for them, and a response consistent with that meaning is dependent upon picking up the appropriate understanding. *Verstehen* is, therefore, as important for everyday life as it is for social research. Indeed, if humans were constitutionally incapable of ascribing meaning in this way, then social life would be fundamentally altered and social research - if it could exist - would also be incapable of incorporating meaning. Social work practitioners would also be incapable of ascribing meaning . Both practice and social research therefore are, in the capacity to ascribe meaning, dependent on a constitutional capacity in humans to ascribe meaning. What is true, furthermore, for understanding individuals is at least equally true in relation to the understanding of groups or societies.

Making sense involves at least three key human capacities: intuition, the capacity to impute motives and intentions, and the capacity to follow and understand rules. England (1986, p 28) refers to the intuitive capacity of individuals to understand others and considers this the central characteristic of social work. For him reference to personal experience is the key to understanding. The worker 'knows about the client's meaning because the worker's own human nature tells him...he only knows the character of his client's meaning because he himself knows, in general, what it is to experience mental or emotional states and can extrapolate from them'. We can only know what it is like to experience sadness because we ourselves have experienced sadness. It may not be about the same thing (we may be sad because of a marital separation, an elderly client may be sad because of the death of their pet dog) but the emotion is the same (or similar). We understand others, he thinks, by this essential and spontaneous reference to experience, a capacity which we all as human beings possess. For England this intuitive ability of understanding others, and of others experiencing themselves as understood is the key element of social work. While this is an ordinary ability, in the sense that human beings generally possess this capacity, it is the degree of reliability with which it is manifested that marks out social work from ordinary understanding.

Beyond this, however, and when ascribing meaning, we do so on the assumption that the actions we are describing are those of a subject who has motives, intentions and so on. In describing actions we are unavoidably involved in imputing motives of one sort or another: in order to give an account of a particular action we need to know what that particular kind might be, and that requires us to understand the motives, intentions and so on of the actor. It is through understanding the actor's motives and intentions that we are able to make sense of those actions. Hence we have different classes of acts according to the different types of motives and intentions which my be imputed from that act. This 'internal understanding' - imputing reasons, motives and intentions to acts - forms a *necessarily* core element to social work practice. How, for example, are we to make sense of a parent's beating of a child, which leaves severe bruising, without imputing motives? in itself the bruising and act of hitting tells us little. Their intention may have been to discipline their child, arising from a belief in the value of corporal punishment as a deterrent; it may have been the frustrated act of a parent at the end of their tether, whose 'intention' was to alleviate frustration by forcing the child to behave; or it may have been the malevolent act of a parent who delights in causing the child pain and the power they have over them. The act and its consequences are the same; the intentions are quite different. The concerns and response of the social workers, furthermore, (one would hope) would also be quite different.

Motives, intentions and reasons direct attention to an internal 'psychological' dimension of meaning. These, in turn occur within a social context. The notion of rules is used to help understand social conduct because they are part of the system of meaning actors use to make sense of their situation. Rules relate to norms, to expectations of behaviour in particular social situations. It is only by reference to such norms that we are able to make sense of situations.

Rules relate primarily to roles, and are sometimes referred to as 'role expectations', attached to the incumbent of a particular position within a network of social relationships (Emmet, 1966; Emmet and MacIntyre, 1970). They guide appropriate modes of behaviour for someone in these positions. They are, so to speak, external to the individual and exist prior to an individual occupying a particular position. This provides us with the ability to contextualise behaviour, to view it as situated activity (Layder, 1990). The same activities carried out in different contexts will carry quite different meanings. An individual with his head down and on his knees in a church is likely to be praying; the same activity in front of a monarch would probably indicate that he is being 'knighted'; the same activity on a busy highway might be regarded as incomprehensible and possibly an indication of mental illness.

It is possible to make sense of actions, in part, because similar rules apply to the same positions: managers as a group are all subject to much the same kind of expectations, as are mothers, fathers and so on. Of course, there may not always be normative consensus about particular roles, or all aspects of them, and these role expectations may change over time. This is evident in both cases with, for example, variations between traditional and non traditional role stereotypes of women, particularly as mothers (Wilson, 1974; Douglas, 1971; Hughes, 1990). It is, of course, perfectly possible for an individual to be aware of different expectations, and adjust their interpretation of behaviour accordingly. Where, by the standards of traditional role stereotypes, the woman who went to work four days per week, leaving their child at a nursery may be considered a 'bad mother' this is not likely to be so with non traditional role stereotypes. The meaning of these acts is, therefore, dependent on the specific rules constituting role expectations which are adopted by the individual concerned (Sheppard, 1993). The issue of traditional versus non traditional role stereotypes in motherhood is one that is widely known to social workers, reflecting awareness of the different rules attached to these differing conceptions.

However, it is important to appreciate that social rules do not dictate or determine behaviour. Humans are not the helpless actors of particular rules required within specific roles (Rawls, 1955; Coulter, 1973). Rules are instead used by humans. They (generally) know what they are and know what is expected of them. They therefore can be used to guide behaviour in particular circumstances, but also to give them some idea of how others will react to them if they do not follow the expectations inherent in the rules. Humans remain, however, rule using analysts (of social situations) rather than being governed by rules (Payne et al, 1981). The notion of rules enables humans to evaluate what is being done, to attribute fault, to be subject to criticism. Invoking rules is a way of depicting actions, of pointing out what it is we are doing, of making our actions accountable (Doyal and Harris, 1986). Used in this way rules are part of our resources for making the world understandable.

SOCIAL INTERACTION AND REFLEXIVITY

We may take this further, however, by examining the implications for social work of humans as 'rule using analysts'. The centrality of meaning comes in Weber's well known analysis of social action and interaction. An action is social when a social actor assigns a certain meaning to his or her conduct, and, by this meaning, is related to the behaviour of others (Weber, 1969). Such an action may be the raising of a hand in the classroom. As a pupil I raise my hand because I wish to draw the teacher's attention to me in order that I can say something or indicate something. I do this on the assumption that they know what I am trying to do, that is that they know the meaning of my act, otherwise it would be pointless my doing it. Social interaction occurs where actions are reciprocally oriented towards the actions of others. In a social work interview, a consumer may disclose that they are in despair about the behaviour of their teenage son, with no idea how to deal with it. They may bury their head in their hands and become tearful. The social worker may then reach out and hold the hand of the consumer, with the intent of showing that they understand and sympathise with their distress. This reciprocity indicates social interaction, and, as a requirement for its occurrence, necessitates that both parties are able to understand the meaning of the communication of the other, either in word or action.

All social work intervention necessarily involves social interaction. The reciprocal orientation, however, is not simply a matter of recognising and responding to the meanings given by another in communication (recognising distress and so on). Any interaction is set in a particular context and this provides a critical dimension to the meaning of any particular action. The context in which the consumer's distress is to be understood may involve various factors, but is likely to include, for example, the role (or perceived role) of the social worker and consumer and the relationship between them, the understanding the participating individuals have of the situation and its purpose, the power each exercises in the situation and the feelings and trust each have for the other (and particularly the consumer has for the social worker). This by no means exhausts the list. If we take just one of these factors as an example, it is evident that the distress shown by a consumer who expresses this distress to someone they consider to be a caring and helpful individual is not the same as that expressed by the desperate parent pleading with a powerful authority figure not to 'take their children away'. One scenario involves the actions of a consumer towards someone seen as kind hearted and helpful, the other that of (possibly) a hard hearted (or someone perceived as such) authority figure whom the consumer could not wait to see the back of.

Making sense, therefore, in social situations, and particularly where social work is involved, means unravelling potentially high degrees of ambiguity. Interpreting the acts of others always contains the potential for ambiguity, but this is perhaps greater with social work than, for example, communication between friends. Where friends are likely to know each other, to have a 'history' and to know something about each other's biography, emphasised by (frequently) a preparedness to disclose personal information to each other, this will often not be the case with social work, particularly at the beginning of intervention. This is essentially a meeting of strangers, in which the consumer may have unclear notions of the nature and purpose of social work, of the reasons for a social worker's involvement in this particular instance, in which there is no necessary initial reason to trust the practitioner sufficiently to disclose personal information and so on. All this may develop with time, but it will do so only within the interactional format of the professional-client relationship, which is not the same as friendship (Perlman, 1979).

An important theme in qualitative sociology, one which is of major significance to social work, is that of *reflexivity,* through which an understanding of social situations and phenomena may emerge. Reflexivity refers to capacities which we as human beings 'naturally' possess, and frequently use in everyday life, and which is utilised by social scientists in the processes of research (Steier, 1991; Woolgar, 1988). It is a form of self reflection; of other reflection; and a processual way of making sense of social circumstances and social life. It is, at least in part, this to which Payne et al (1981) are referring when they call humans 'rule using analysts'. It recognises our own and others situated place in social life. It involves three things: reflection on ourselves (including our thinking) and others (including their intentions and motivations):

monitoring the acts of ourselves and others: and the creation of ways of explaining situations in which we are involved or social phenomena in which we are interested. It is, therefore, a (1) process of monitoring, (2) reflection and (3) explanation, or making sense. Such reflexivity is always contextual: the process of 'making sense' is undertaken always taking into account the situation with which the subject is concerned (indeed defining that situation is part of the reflexive process). It is not, therefore, to be mistaken for mere reflection, which constitutes only part of reflexivity and which denudes it of its processual quality and the emergent nature of consequent understanding.

Such reflexivity is frequently associated with constructionist modes of explanation, but it is also central to Realist conceptions of social science (Keat and Urry, 1982; Bhaskar, 1978). Reflexivity very much emphasises the process of making sense rather than its content or outcome. Atkinson (1980) has described it in research, from an interactionist perspective:

> The actor engages in the process and flux of the natural and social world and, through his or her acts, negotiates the world and the self. Through a constantly developing series of transactions with the world, the social actor creates and recreates social worlds and social meanings...in this manner [too] the ethnographer navigates and explores the varied surface of diverse social scenes.

Reflexivity occurs in social interaction because of the inherent ambiguity of that social interaction. If a woman becomes pregnant we may not be sure whether to congratulate or commiserate with her because we do not know if the pregnancy fits in with her expectations. Our response - its appropriateness - is dependent upon our capacity to ask ourselves: how does she feel about the pregnancy? do I need to explore further to find out the extent to which this fits in with (indeed defines) her life purposes? All this, of course, depends on our capacity to know, or imagine, that different responses may occur according to the life plans of the woman.

Barnes and Todd (1977) identified a number of aspects to the use of reflexivity in a group educational setting. The participants showed an ability to reflect on their own thinking; they showed a capacity to monitor speech and thought strategies; a capacity to understand and interrelate alternative viewpoints; a capacity to evaluate their own and other's performance (does their explanation of something make sense? is it a good or bad explanation?); a capacity to set up hypotheses - presenting ideas which might explain something about which they were concerned; and a capacity to use evidence to support their own, or evaluate others' arguments. Barnes and Todd emphasised that such reflexivity was not used all the time, but individuals did show, from time to time, a capacity for its use.

Hammersley's analysis (1983) identifies three dimensions in the researcher's use of reflexivity which apply equally to social work practice. It suggests that the researcher's (and social worker's) own actions are open to analysis in the same terms as the other participants'. Just as others are trying to 'make sense' of situations, to negotiate them and pursue goals, so is the researcher and social worker. Second, the researcher (and social worker) is obliged to be aware of the decisions they are making and the motives that underlie them. Social workers may bring 'personal baggage' with them. How far will an investigation into possible sexual abuse be affected by the fact that a close friend of the social worker was abused as a child? does this provide a deeper understanding or a predisposition to assume guilt and judgemental attitudes? The social worker's role will also affect situations. Their authority role in child protection investigations may affect the content of parental responses to questions: is their hostility to the social worker reflective of a 'short fuse' or simply anger at the investigation taking place? Finally account should be taken of the actions of the researcher (and social worker). How far were the responses of consumers (say, again, the angry responses of an individual subject to child protection investigations) the result of insensitive, hamfisted or less than honest approaches by the social worker?

CATEGORIES AND INTERPRETIVE SCHEMAS

Reflexivity emphasises that the interpretation of the social world is no straightforward matter. It is not, as Positivist orthodoxy might have us believe, simply a matter of a sufficiently attentive gaze of the observer upon an unproblematic reality. In any situation we are bombarded by innumerable sensations, only some of which we are able to attend to. This is widely appreciated. We know, for example, that we can sit in a room deep in conversation, while the television is on. At the end of the conversation, despite the television being clearly audible, we can remember nothing of its broadcast. Our attention is on the conversation and, in effect, we have heard nothing of the broadcast. As with reflexivity, the notion of purposeful action - this time our own - is crucial. Our purpose has been to carry out a conversation and the result has been that we have not 'heard' the broadcast.

Purpose, then, is crucial to our own actions. When our purpose is to make sense of people and situations we do so, to a considerable degree, through interpretive schemas and categories. These concepts allow us to take the issue of reflexivity further, because it is our own purposes, categories and schemas that provide the backdrop for our reflexivity. A schema is a 'naive theory about a certain class of stimuli' (Berkowitz, 1986, p 82) or a 'cognitive structure that represents knowledge about a concept or type of stimulus including its attributes and the relations among these attributes' (Fiske and Taylor, p 98; cf Brewer and Nakamura, 1984; Taylor and Crocker, 1981). Schemas are a critical dimension of our everyday understanding and serve largely the same purpose that theories do in social research: they organise various aspects of data in a way which helps us make sense or explain particular phenomena. In this sense we are all active theorisers about social reality. As structured knowledge that we bring to everyday perceptions schemas emphasise our active construction of reality. These schemas are brought to bear on particular circumstances and provide a means by which sense is made of those circumstances. As human's theories and concepts about the world, schemas are concerned with the general case, abstract, generic knowledge that holds across many particular instances.

Categories are the 'building blocks' for the application of schematic knowledge to social perception. Categories provide the means for identification. When we enter a social situation we require some means for identifying it (in terms of generic qualities). Hence we can use particular situational facets to categorise someone. A petrol station attendant for example may be identified by attributes such as wearing overalls, use of the cash till and presence at the petrol station. Such characteristics might also be evident in a thief stealing from the petrol station, emphasising the ambiguity in social situations. We identify people in terms of particular categories and this provides a guide to subsequent expectations. The person may be expected to fill up your petrol tank and collect your money (or if you have got it wrong, to threaten you with a baseball bat in order to get away). Categories, then, provide the means by which we can interpret situations and make certain 'predictions' about them. They identify stable and repeated qualities in social situations. They allow us to negotiate social situations in a reasonably routine manner.

The process by which categories and schemas are applied to social situations is encoding. Encoding represents the classification of particular situations in terms of certain generic qualities which recur in other situations. Someone may be old or young, intelligent or stupid, caring or unconcerned and so on. Particular qualities are ascribed to each category and it is these qualities that are used in social situations to cue relevant categories. If someone reacts to another person's distress by attentive listening, appropriate sympathetic remarks and even gently holding their hand we may then consider them caring. Interestingly, age and sex seem to be the main categories initially used by people in classifying situations, from which other categories are generated (Brewer and Lui, 1989).

Categories and interpretive schemas are crucial in the conduct of social work practice. Where we undertake an assessment of someone with reference to their mental health, child protection or offending behaviour, we are asking ourselves: what is going on here? what is the nature of the actions that an individual is performing? how can I explain or make sense of these actions? Where, for example, we visit a family on a child protection investigation, we might well look at the way the mother, or father, and child relate to each other. Is the child comfortable in the parent's presence? does she sit in a corner avoiding going near the parent? do they go and sit on the knee of the parent while the interview is taking place? Each of these actions invite a defining category through which we may make sense. The child may be 'withdrawn' or 'preoccupied', and the mother may be 'caring'. Each of these terms carry stable qualities which are used to define the person and situation. If we decide the mother is caring we may no longer be concerned for the child's welfare (although no doubt more information would be required by the social worker). If we consider the child withdrawn we may investigate further: is the mother 'cold'? is she 'aggressive' in her relationship with her child? does this represent inadequate attachment and a failure at bonding? Each of these categories represent an interpretation of the situation. It involves focusing on specific aspects of the situation to the exclusion of other aspects (the television may again be on), and defining it in such a way as to represent a theory about the situation. In all this, it should be noted, the focus of the social worker, the definition of the situation and hence the categories and schemas generated, are all related to the social worker's purpose: in this case child protection.

This encoding, then, is not some neutral activity, but heavily influenced by the particular concerns of an individual. Frequently activated ideas 'come to mind' in social situations more easily than ideas that have not been activated. This is referred to as 'priming'. Because much social information is inherently ambiguous, social perception is heavily influenced by the accessibility of relevant categories: categories that are easily activated given the perceiver's current goals needs and expectations (Bruner, 1957, 1958). Where particular categories are considered more important, more easily and typically accessible, individuals are more likely to remember and describe others in those terms (Higgins and King, 1981; Borgh and Thien, 1985). Dimensions that are frequently accessed may become central aspects of an individuals construction of interpretive schemas. Such dimensions will allow more immediate coding of individuals and situations in terms of those dimensions than other dimensions.

This priming can affect both the speed with which judgements are made and the nature of those judgements. People may start with an effortful use of general rules that are independent of specific settings, but can make speedy, even 'automatic' judgements about frequently encountered stimuli. For example, if a probation officer over time judges hundreds of instances of behaviour as honest or dishonest, some of the repeated inferences (eg shoplifting as dishonest) will become faster and easier over time (Smith, 1984). These 'instant judgments' also affect social interactions. Smith (1989) suggests well practiced judgments will preempt equally reasonable but less practiced judgements . For example, a teacher who is used to judging intelligence may view positively a person who is intelligent but unsociable, whereas a sales supervisor emphasising sociability may view them negatively.

Priming, then, has a high degree of significance in social work. The kinds of judgements made and the ways in which situations are interpreted will be considerably influenced by the nature, range and frequency of categories and schemas used. It is through the categories and schemas used that social workers may draw upon three sources of knowledge which may be related to practice: that gained from experience of everyday life, that gained from practice experience and that gained from more academic or formal knowledge. It is important to realise, first, therefore, the essentially contextually based nature of knowledge use. Knowledge, whether experiential or academic, is employed at the point of social interaction with the consumer. These situations inevitably possess some complexity and the uniqueness of the situation may be tempered by the generic categories and schemas employed to interpret or make sense of those situations.

The ultimate justification for the employment of formal knowledge in social work, therefore, lies in its capacity for use in the very specific interactional contexts of practice. Whether it adds to experiential knowledge or renders social workers more effective, while arguably being important issues, is secondary: we could not even consider these issues if it could not be used in the first place. Formal knowledge, however, can have a distinctive place in practice. Brown and Harris's (1978) work points to the importance of three children aged under 14 as creating a vulnerability for depression in women. Such knowledge may provide a 'cue' for social workers to detect the presence of depression. The theory informed practitioner, in these circumstances, may well consider the possibility of depression as a factor in the care of the children. It is quite possible for the practitioner without this knowledge, to define the mother a 'non coper' (Rees, 1978; Sheppard, 1993), a category which has serious stigmatising and labelling effects and could have considerable practical implications (if she cannot cope, is accommodation the appropriate response?). The practitioner who is 'primed' to consider this regularly is more likely to pick this issue up more quickly and it will hence influence their practice more deeply and pervasively. Those who think entirely in experiential, rather than theoretical, terms are less likely to pick this up and categorise in different ways. Priming, then, helps begin to explain two significant aspects of practice. The first is the capacity of practitioners to judge situations more quickly (whether they do this better than inexperienced practitioners may depend on other factors). The second is the impact of theory on practice. Whether consciously or subconsciously used, the frequency of its use is likely profoundly to influence their practice. The more it is used, the more theory oriented the practitioner becomes. Of course the reverse is the case with those who rely on experience.

HYPOTHESES

It is important to realise that encoding occurs from the earliest moment of perception. Such categories as age, race, sex attractiveness and so on are instantly used to form impressions. This is particularly apparent with stereotyped perceptions: white individuals may recognise positive stereotypical words (intelligent, ambitious, clean and so on) faster when preceded by the words 'white' than the word 'black' (Gaertner and McLaughlin, 1983). Furthermore various dispositional inferences are frequently made virtually immediately as first steps in encoding information about others. Individuals may rapidly identify others as angry instead of afraid, kind instead of cruel and so on. Social perceivers characterise each other in relatively automatic ways and they may or may not reconsider what they have done (Fiske and Taylor, 1991). Gilbert et al (1990) suggests two steps are necessary to maximise accuracy in making sense, and not always taken. The initial event of comprehending (categorising an action) causes an individual to accept provisionally the proposition as true (eg some behaviour - listening attentively - does reflect a disposition - such as to be kind). This is relatively automatic and spontaneous. However, rejecting or refuting takes an extra step (situational correction). This, second step is both optional and deliberate. This has, potentially, huge implications for social work.

These steps represent the formulation of hypotheses. It is in the nature of reflexivity and human's status as rule using analysts that they are constantly making hypotheses. When we provide an initial category or interpretive schema with which to characterise a particular person or situation, we are presenting a hypothesis that this schema or category accurately reflects the situation. The hypothetical nature of categories and schemas is well represented by the earlier example of the petrol pump attendant. We might initially hypothesise that the individual was a petrol pump attendant, and only when we are threatened as the person tries to make their 'getaway' do we revise our view, providing a more adequate category for him (thief) and interpretive schema for the situation (robbery).

The example also illustrates the contextual and analytical nature of our judgment. Our initial judgement is made on the basis of cues: wearing a boiler suit, the setting of the petrol station and the appearance that he is working there. We ascribe a role to him - petrol pump attendant - and intentions - to collect money from customers and fill up petrol tanks. Our revision arises because the actions of the individual, in making his getaway, are no longer consistent with our initial hypothesis. The revision provides an interpretive schema (a robbery) whose adequacy of fit with the situation is greater than the first schema.

The revision and new hypothesis is, perhaps, glaringly obvious. The example nonetheless illustrates that making sense of situations is, or frequently can be, a processual matter. It is only through a process of analysis and hypothesis testing that we come to the most adequate 'fit' of interpretive schema with situation. It is, furthermore, an example of everyday understanding involving the actions of the naive scientist. Some situations will be relatively straightforward and our initial schemas will be adequate. No revision will be required. Other situations, as we have seen, are filled with ambiguity and the capacity adequately to interpret them involves this process of hypothesis testing. Situations subject to social work assessments are frequently complex and laden with ambiguity. They are also subject to change, requiring development of further hypotheses. The capacity, therefore of social workers to analyse situations and to revise hypotheses is quite central to social work. In complex situations, the good social worker has to be the good analyst. This is a cognitive ability of some difficulty.

Social workers who are to be good analysts need to be good 'scientists of human life'. Analytic rigour is an enormous virtue in good practice, as it is in social research. Hanson (1958) refers to the retroductive nature of rigorous methodology for discovery and explanation. This provides a systematic method for conducting assessment, bringing together both observation and interpretation, through which 'sense' is made of the observations. Hanson emphasises that theories are developed both inductively and deductively. Concepts are not just developed out of observations, but neither are they imposed *a priori* categories. Rather, their use is justified in terms of their context in a particular theory and particular observations which the theory seeks to explain. While this last statement holds true of the use of interpretive schemas and using formal knowledge to make sense in social work, the schemas and categories used are generally available prior to the situation to which they are applied. In our example the category of robbery was a concept already known which was applied by the observers to make sense of the situation.

There is a constant interplay between observations of reality and the concepts (or categories) and theories (or schemas) which seek to make sense of these observations. The genesis of any theory is best described as a reciprocal development of observational sophistication and theoretical precision (Bulmer, 1979). The logic of such a procedure may be formalised through which the form of inference is:

1. Some phenomenon P is observed.
2. P would be explicable as a matter of course if hypothesis H were true.
3. Hence we have reason to think H is true.

This would provide the initial conditions for an interpretive schema which might provisionally explain a situation. However, as emphasised by Popper (1963) and various writers on analytic induction (a qualitative method of sociological analysis which employs a retroductive technique), if we seek to obtain the most adequate representation of the observed phenomenon, we should actively seek to falsify our hypothesis (Znaniecki, 1934; Lindesmith, 1968; Robinson, 1951). We should, in other words, constantly be on the look out for elements in the situation which casts doubt on the efficacy of the schema as an explanation for our observation. We should also seek to identify (or develop) a schema or theory which provides a more adequate 'fit' with our observations ie incorporates those elements which do not fit with the original schema.

This, of course, in a very obvious situation, describes the process undertaken by the observer of the robbery at the petrol station. With more complex situations, frequently confronted by social workers, the process is more difficult and complicated, but the 'principles for discovery' remain the same. In the example of the child protection assessment given earlier, we may initially hypothesise tentatively that the child who is withdrawn is the victim of physical or emotional abuse. However, further enquiries may cast doubt on this: her school work is fine, for example, and she presents no behavioural difficulties. We may discover that her withdrawn behaviour is simply the result of a 'telling off' she has recently received and that this does not generally characterise her behaviour or her relationship with her parents.

The process, furthermore, does not have to end with a revised hypothesis. This may itself not prove fully adequate and need further revision. Complex situations may require a number of revisions and refinements of hypotheses in order to achieve the most adequate interpretation. Likewise situations may themselves change requiring revision of hypotheses. Two critical dimensions of assessment emerge from this:

- Any interpretation must always be regarded as provisional. Social workers should always be prepared to revise their interpretation.
- Social workers should always be on the look out for observations or evidence which falsify the schema or interpretation used.

This is by no means as straightforward as it appears. Psychologists have been long aware of the phenomenon of 'confirmation bias' in the way humans seek to interpret social situations. Rather than seek to question whether or not the initial interpretation made is the most accurate, people tend actively to seek out information which confirms their initial interpretation. In the process they have a tendency to ignore observations and evidence which might disconfirm or falsify their interpretation. Thought patterns tend to shape ambiguous information in accordance with these schemas and lead us to search for supporting evidence. This is facilitated when the observed encounter is relatively complex and rich in details, exactly the kind of situation frequently confronting social workers (Ross and Anderson, 1982; Daley and Gross, 1983). Where evidence is inconsistent with schema there is a good chance that this information will be ignored or little attention given to it (Eber and Fiske, 1984). Alternatively, if it cannot be ignored it may be resisted, and the information discredited. Information challenging a conception to which the individual is committed can be dismissed as 'implausible' or 'untrustworthy' or otherwise not worthy of attention (Lord et al, 1979). Furthermore, schemas affect memory. People tend to remember schema relevant information and forget other information. Memory, in effect, filters out factors which might cause us to question our initial schemas, and even assumptions (Cohen, 1981). Continuous exposure to a situation will not therefore automatically lead us to question our initial impressions - rather the opposite, it will tend to reinforce them.

Snyder and his colleagues (Snyder, 1984; Snyder and Swan, 1978; Snyder and Campbell, 1980) have carried out a series of studies focusing on the development and examination of schemas. They concluded that humans generally carry out a biased search, primarily attempting to find information that will uphold existing beliefs. This is reflected in characteristic lines of questioning used when examining our schemas against our observations. For example, when individuals were told that someone was introverted and asked to investigate matters further they did not try to discover whether the individual had ever acted extrovertly, which would have provided disconfirming evidence. They preferred to investigate further the introverted nature of his or her behaviour. The kind of question asked was 'what factors make it hard for you to really open up to people?'. Of course, such questions assume introvertedness and are likely to lead to evidence in line with the schema. The result of this is a one sided search in which individuals tend to behave as if their initial schemas and categories are valid.

This problem is exacerbated by time constraints. Our tendency to confirm initial impressions means that more time is required to digest and accept alternative points of view as compared with confirmatory evidence (Kruglanski and Freund, 1983). The kinds of time pressures which effect busy social workers are likely provide an inhospitable environment for undertaking the kinds of thought processing required to combat confirmation bias.

All this is bad news for social work. The tendency to confirmation bias might lead to erroneous interpretations; it is more likely to occur in complex situations (which characterise the more difficult and potentially tragic cases); time constraints only serve to emphasise further confirmation bias; and memory serves to confirm rather than question. Sheldon (1987) indeed has argued that confirmation bias is consistent with child abuse fatalities where, with hindsight, the pointers to tragedy seem obvious. The problem seems to have been, for example, in the cases of Maria Colwell and Jasmine Beckford (DHSS, 1974; Blum Cooper, 1985), that the professionals involved appear to have been 'blind' to the indications that these children were at serious risk of death. This suggests practitioners possessed schemas which were not sufficiently accurate, they focused on the wrong sorts of things and they were oblivious to, or discounted, events which would cast doubt on their judgements. They were, in short, busy confirming their particular theories. We may understand this in the light of human constitutional frailties biasing them in favour of verification. We may recognise that the situations (perhaps inevitably) were complex, and that the practitioners (certainly inevitably) were busy. We may sympathise with them because this certainly exacerbated the situation. *But the fact is two children died*. They died because (among other things) social workers missed crucial clues which would have prevented their death, and which with hindsight appear obvious.

Child abuse fatalities highlight the dangers of confirmation bias. But we should not assume that this bias does not occur in less dramatic circumstances. Rather, they are less obvious because they have not been put under the spotlight as have child fatalities. Indeed, it may even be impossible to spot them because the interpretation becomes the 'accepted wisdom' of a case. The notion of the mother as 'non coper' will be continually confirmed because the social worker seeks to confirm this interpretation, despite the fact that she is really depressed, that her problems coping are related to the depression, and that with appropriate action the depression is preventable. Indeed the actions of the practitioner can create a self fulfilling prophecy (Snyder, 1984). By behaving in ways which assume the woman is a non coper she remains a non coper. The child may, for example, be taken into accommodation, emphasising her failures and feeding her low self esteem. The low self esteem reinforces (indeed is a characteristic of) the depression which in turn further makes coping difficult.

The point is: social workers would not be human if they did not make these mistakes. Well maybe. The problem is surely that they are utilising only those common sense processes of understanding which are used in everyday life. While we cannot ignore these processes, it is their lack of rigour which is problematic (and seems sometimes to be fatal). Some research examining work by social workers in child care and education welfare teams show them to have relied on experience, to have used pretty primitive ways of explaining situations and to have been almost completely unreflexive (Corby, 1982; Pratt and Grimshaw, 1985). The very best that could be said of this common sense approach - and this is extremely charitable - is that they were descriptive rather than analytic. There are two processes which would, on this analysis, reflect poor practice, and one which would represent good practice. Poor practice involves:

- First, making an initial hypothesis and simply sticking to it, regardless of any further evidence that came along. It involves no further analysis following the initial interpretation. It is an approach which involves the least use of cognitive faculties. It is an approach to which those who rely on intuition and experience are particularly vulnerable. If, as England (1986) (approvingly) suggests, social workers have recourse to the statement 'it just felt that way', then we would legitimately suspect that, rather than having some 'privileged' direct understanding of the situation, the practitioner is involved in a primitive unreflexive exercise in prejudice. The same kind of situation may arise with the practitioner who relies on experience, and who says 'my experience tells me' that such and such is the case.

- The second form of poor practice involves confirmation bias. At least in this case the practitioner is acting analytically - they are making a stab at analysing the situation, rather than prejudice. However, the kinds of questions asked would only serve to confirm existing hypotheses, in which the possibility of a child protection fatality remains. However, this does not mean we should not ever engage in the kinds of questioning which characterises confirmation bias. Where we wish to explore further particular facets of a situation then these kinds of questions are important. If we wish to examine further why someone lacks confidence in child care, for example, we might look at particular facets of child care which they find difficult. This could be undertaken in preparation for a parenting skills programme designed to increase their competence and confidence in relevant areas.

Good practice, on the other hand, involves the retroductive process outlined in which the active search for disconfirming information plays a significant part. It involves developing new hypotheses or interpretive schemas when disconfirming information is identified and when another schema provides a more adequate 'fit' with the evidence. This, it should be emphasised, is no easy matter. Clearly it is not a 'natural', or at least predominant, process for humans in making sense of situations. It relies on common human attributes, but is not a matter of mere common sense. Yet the failure to undertake this process clearly has serious consequences. Its use, however, demonstrably shows that social work cannot be a matter of mere common sense.

CONCLUSION

From our analysis it is possible to generate a new concept: that of *Reflexive Eclecticism* to characterise the level of competence required by social workers. This incorporates a number of elements:

- The generation and incorporation of a wide range of schemas of potential relevance to practice situations.

- The use of a retroductive approach to the process of analysis involving high levels of sensitivity to disconfirming evidence.
- A case based focus for knowledge for practice in which the 'adequacy of fit' of the schema or theory in relation to observations is the test of appropriateness.

This approach accepts the existence of an external reality 'out there' to which humans can constitutionally give limited attention and of which they have limited grasp, but against which they are able to assess and adjust their schemas or theories about their cases. This is neither Interactionist nor Positivist, but Realist in orientation.

Some situations confronted by practitioners are relatively straightforward. Where an elderly person is alone, physically disabled and wishes to go into residential care, it will be a relatively easy process to interpret their situation appropriately (we may, however, be aware that they might suffer sense of loss when leaving a home they had lived in for decades). But this is not the only kind of situation confronting social workers, and even this may become more complex (where, for example, further consideration of the matter increases their ambivalence about residential care in the light of their impending feelings of loss). Furthermore, the retroductive, falsifying process, when it is undertaken, will be easier in some circumstances than others. The example of the petrol station robbery is one extreme (of straightforwardness) in this respect. At another extreme lies child protection issues.

Clearly, the position of social workers as care managers lies at the 'professional' end of the scale identified in official guides (see chapter one). If social workers are to justify their status as 'experts' or 'professionals' then they must build on and transcend these common sense processes. This requires three elements:

- Creating the widest possible range of interpretive schemas with which to examine situations for which their work gives them responsibility. While this can be achieved in a number of ways, this would include the examination of concepts, theories and evidence in social science.
- Developing precision and clarity in the understanding of the content, application and use of concepts and theories, categories and schemas.
- An awareness of the process of making sense and explaining situations and becoming continually sensitive to disconfirming

information. This involves an acute awareness that any interpretation can at all times only be provisional and an active awareness of falsifying information.

Social work cannot, in short, be a matter of common sense, even though it relies to some degree on our common sense ways of understanding.

Social work, furthermore, is a high level cognitive activity which requires considerable analytical ability. This comment may not be popular in some quarters, where the emphasis is on intuitive understanding or life experience, yet it is difficult to see how complex cases can be competently managed without these high level abilities. To the extent that these analytic abilities define what is generally considered to be 'intelligence', social work requires individuals who are highly intelligent. Intelligence is, in terms used by philosophers, no doubt not a *sufficient condition* for good practice, but it is a *necessary condition*. To the extent that social workers are not highly intelligent, or are unable to apply their intelligence in a practical way to the problems of social work, the levels of competence in practice are reduced. Recruitment should be in the business of highlighting the potential analytic abilities of aspiring practitioners (and student social workers). Education and training should foster analytic capacities and the capacity to falsify. The capacities shown in higher education, to perform well in academic assignments have considerable relevance for the abilities of individuals as practitioners. The 'streetwise grannies' of Virginia Bottomley's (one time Minister of Health) social work fantasies, are out of the question.

This processual model of assessment has implications for the relationship between formal knowledge and practice. It, first, indicates the case based nature of the 'knowledge for practice' formulation. Knowledge relevant for practice is not simply applied in some law like manner, but emerges in a retroductive process in which there is an interplay between theory (or schema) and practice in a search for the most adequate 'fit'. It does so on the basis of the identification of the most salient characteristics in a situation - which in turn derives from the definition of the problem - which provide the cues for the identification of the relevant knowledge.

The case based focus and processual orientation has further implications for theory use. In everyday life we do not worry about living in a multiparadigmatic reality. The same individuals are able happily to explain social actions and events in terms both of reasons and intentions *and* causes (Buss, 1978), alternative explanations which generate such conflicting debate in social science (Doyal and Harris, 1986)[1]. The concern expressed by some authors (eg Sheldon, 1978) to erect a consistent, widely accepted knowledge base for social work rather misses the point. It focuses on some monolithic notion of 'theory' which is then capable of application to practice. By focusing instead on the individual situations confronted by social workers, emphasising reflexivity and adequacy of fit, we are able to compare, and even develop, theories and schemas in terms of adequacy of fit.

To take this approach is not simply to reflect the complexity and individuality of practice situations, nor only the gaps in formal knowledge relevant for practice. It reflects the necessarily limited and partial nature of human understanding which results in competing and conflicting theories and schemas. Sufficiently astute analysis may allow us to develop adequately fitting explanations for particular situations. The development of a 'Grand Theory' of social life which provides consistent explanations of the variety of circumstances encountered in practice is - as the history of social science demonstrates - clearly beyond us.

This analysis further shows the ways in which the social worker will, perhaps inevitably, rely on schemas as well as theories - on knowledge built on the process of everyday understanding as well as social research. To rely on experience alone is to run the risk of solipsism. As remarked earlier, some schemas based on experience are pretty primitive. Formal knowledge is likely to be more rigorously developed and widely empirically examined. On the other hand, formal knowledge may be insufficiently focused on the specific problem at hand to be helpful. While, therefore a general preference for formal knowledge characterises the reflexive approach to emergent understanding, reliance on experientially derived categories and schemas is frequently inevitable. However, even where this is the case the retroductive disconfirming approach to analysis characterising emergent understanding provides for greater rigour and the potential for greater accuracy of fit between schema and situation than is possible using common sense approaches characterised by confirmation bias.

We may finally characterise this approach to social work in the form of a 'T' shape, in which the horizontal axis refers to theories and schemas and the vertical axis to the level of analysis. Social science may contribute to social work by extending the range of explanations available and making the nature and definition more rigorous. This is about breadth of understanding. It can, through the processes by which explanation is achieved, create a greater depth of analysis. In practice, there is something to be learned here from the methods of qualitative social research (Sheppard, 1995). It is, then, in these two respects, breadth of understanding and depth of analysis, that social workers can establish their credentials in care management.

1. The issue of cause is an interesting one, and, of course, is inconsistent with an explanation which relies solely on an agent's reasons for their actions. However, we do ascribe cause to human action in everyday life, and this seems to occur when we are dissatisfied with an explanation based on intention or reasons of the agent. For example, where someone is considered mentally ill, we may ascribe their behaviour to some causal factor - the illness. When we do so this is because their actions are deemed unintelligible or irrational (Coulter, 1973; Smith, 1978). Interestingly, Fisher et al's (1984) study of mental health social work showed social workers themselves used the criterion of intelligibility to decide about the presence of mental illness. Of course this everyday sense of intelligibility or irrationality is related to the nature of rules, discussed in the section on meaning. Nonetheless, the issue of meaning and making sense is central to our everyday method of ascribing cause in relation to mental illness. It is only when we consider an action unintelligible, ie it does not make sense, that we look for some explanation which does not include intention.

   Peters (1960 p 10) suggests we are likely to give a causal account of action when something has gone wrong: 'where there is some kind of deviation from the purposive rule-following model; when people, as it were, get it wrong'. Also we tend to give causal explanations of action where the actor's choice or responsibility is minimal. We might do this, for example, when a third party is persuaded to do something the true consequences of which they were unaware. Such would be the case where someone was asked to take a suitcase through customs, without the carrier knowing it contained drugs.

Chapter Ten

Assessment and the use of social work knowledge

The assessment role of the care manager-social worker is very much one of 'making sense' as a basis on which to act. The previous chapter has indicated that understanding this involves, first and foremost, recognising it as a process. This is not, however, enough. Where social science knowledge forms such a central part of the curriculum, we need to examine the knowledge 'product' which may be used in the process of assessment.

The notion that social workers should somehow be applying social science knowledge to practice has probably had as much to do with the drive to professionalisation as a demonstrable link between competence in practice and the use of social science knowledge (Lerghinger, 1978; Heraud, 1981). One key problem is that social science is characterised by considerable paradigmatic and theoretical diversity. The attempt to apply social science immediately prompts the question: exactly which social science is to be applied to practice (and with what justification)? Even within Sociology the range of alternative perspectives is impressive. Sibeon (1982), for example, distinguishes between structuralist sociology - which may or may not be radical - symbolic interactionism and phenomenology as well as a long British tradition of empirical sociology. These approaches possess fundamentally different assumptions, not simply about the nature of social reality, but what counts as knowledge in the first place. A commitment to one approach (say, phenomenology) entails rejection of alternative approaches (eg structural functionalism).

Fortunately the way in which the task of social work has been socially defined commits social workers *qua* social workers to particular positions in relation to the validity of different forms of knowledge. Drawing, therefore on earlier chapters which have examined key aspects of the social work orientation, we shall develop what I have called the 'practice paradigm' of social work - which acts as a kind of 'statute of limitations' on knowledge use - and develop this in terms of criteria for use of knowledge, and the characteristics possessed by different forms of knowledge which make them more or less useful for practice.

PRACTICE LED THEORY

Practice-Led Versus Theory Driven Approaches

It is important first to establish social work has, implicitly or explicitly, a particular position in relation to the use of social science knowledge. One central problem underlying the use of theory for practice lies in the direction of this relationship. Problems in the use of social science have arisen to a considerable degree because of an emphasis on a 'theory driven' rather than 'practice led' approach to knowledge for social work. Theory driven approaches are based on an image of social work, and prescriptions for practice, derived from theory. This is the kind of relationship which broadly exists, for example, between psychology and the practice of psychologists.

To presuppose a similar theory-practice relationship for social work contains two fundamental errors. The first is that the practice of social work and acceptance of its role arises from a pre-existing knowledge base, the application of which is widely regarded both as necessary to a certain area of welfare work *and* defines its terrain. Social work, however, as a *state occupation*, arose as a job whose task was to deal with certain areas of social life. The state, then, largely defined the social work task. Attempts to develop knowledge for social work, therefore have largely occurred for a pre-existing occupation and in response to a perceived need for this knowledge to carry out the social work task.

Second, and in view of the paradigmatic and theoretical diversity of the social sciences, where practice is theory driven, there is no reason to prefer one theory or paradigm as against another. Theory, in this case does not simply seek to make social work more effective but also to define its very nature. Social work becomes the prisoner of particular partisan perspectives. For example, Corrigan and Leonard's (1978) Marxist approach created an image of social workers as political revolutionaries whose ultimate focus was at the level of social structure. The result was a social work 'theory' which as a prescription for practice, was of little use to social workers, and which the passage of time has emphasised was a radical fantasy.

For social science to have any use for social work it must be led by practice. This does not mean that the work of practitioners is ahead of or somehow better than theory. Rather, a practice led approach entails that the social science knowledge used is consistent with the nature and limits of social work.

The Practice Paradigm of Social Work

The practice of social work may be understood in terms of state delegated authority. Social workers have powers, are enabled to act, and have limitations to their powers prescribed by the state. This is, metaphorically, a straightjacket because there are certain general assumptions underlying state social work practice which broadly speaking commits social workers to a particular view of the social world. The term 'paradigm' is generally used in relation to academic discourse, but it can equally well be applied to this set of practice assumptions (Kuhn, 1970). This term, in a social work context, emphasises the commonality of perspective which binds the group of practitioners together in such a way that they may be regarded as approaching practice within the same problematic. It does not imply complete unity of thought, and allows for the fact that within the paradigm (and hence the profession) there can be debate between different practitioners (and theorists) who adopt different standpoints. It does, however, have an underlying unity in terms of its basic and often 'taken for granted' assumptions.

This social work paradigm may be expressed in terms of three areas: the definition of phenomena with which its deals (needs or problems); the perception of human nature and explanation of behaviour; and the appropriate social focus of practice.

Definition of phenomena

The official purpose of social work as care management is the alleviation of need. This is nothing new and has been considered a focus for social work for some time (Sheppard, 1991). The preceding discussion on need and self determination has shown that there is a core of objectivism, and limited relativism in social work practice. Objectivism postulates that the social world is a real one: it exists independently of the individual perceiving it. This contrasts with a subjectivist view that our perceptions of the world are no more than that, subjective perceptions. This objectivism means that, for example, mental illness or child abuse have an objective reality. They are not matters which are purely the creation of the human mind: child abuse is not a mere social construction. There may be some debate about the 'threshold' distinguishing abuse from non abuse, but the fact of its real existence is not, for the objectivist, disputable.

This assumption of objectivism underlying social work practice has even been accepted by those working from within a phenomenological viewpoint, one which ascribes a high place to subjective perceptions and which sees social reality as 'socially constructed' (Smith, 1980). Indeed, Smith goes so far as to castigate social workers for their commitment to objectivism where, in his view, they are merely 'socially constructing' clients. To regard need as 'independent...is a feature of members' accounting practices' with the result that it is given 'the appearance of objective reality' (Smith, 1980, p 67 and 68).

However, it is important to recognise that while this objectivism is at the core of social work there is some scope for some variation in interpretation of the same reality. Outside those areas, such as definition of mental health needs in relation to compulsory admission and child abuse where social workers are deemed to possess 'cognitive superiority' over their clients, care management allows for some differences of perspective, and that both users and carers, as well as care managers may identify different types of need (although nonetheless constrained in ways outlined in chapter seven). Along with the core of objectivism, therefore, goes a limited relativism.

Perception of human nature and explanation of behaviour

Alongside, and closely related to this is the extent to which human actions are considered voluntary or caused. At one extreme we can consider humans to be completely autonomous and free willed (the voluntarist view). Here we look no further for the explanation of action than to the reasons an individual has for that action, and within that the meaning they ascribe to the situation - their perspective of it. At the other extreme actions may be perceived to be caused in some way, for example by biology, psychological factors or environment. Such action will be considered involuntary.

The official position of social workers as care managers, evident both from their responsibilities and official care management literature is one of 'limited voluntarism': a view of human action that is voluntary except where circumstances indicate some 'external' cause. There are certain circumstances when actions are assumed in some way to have been caused rather than voluntary. Such is the case with the above example of compulsory admission with mental illness. According to Peters (1960), in everyday life we generally assume actions are voluntary. However, we are likely to give a causal account of action where there is some kind of deviation from a purposive, rule following model, where actions appear considerably at odds with normative expectations.

There appears to be three circumstances in social work where causal accounts may be provided. Actions may be considered involuntary, first, where an individual did not understand what they were doing. For example, they may view their mode of disciplining a child to be legitimate punishment where it is 'really' (ie officially defined by the agency) child abuse. The second case of involuntary behaviour would be where an individual did not *really* want to do what they did. This has been discussed in the chapter on self determination and relates to the difference between life plans and immediate actions. A parent may wish to care adequately for their child but, because of stress or some other factor, excessively hit the child, an act which they may later be horrified about and seek help to prevent a recurrence. Finally, an action may be considered involuntary where the act is simply incomprehensible. This, as Fisher et al (1984) have shown, is the main way social workers distinguish individuals who are mentally ill from those who are not.

Social workers as care managers, like others in everyday life, do not entrench themselves in single positions, that human action is either voluntary or involuntary, in the way frequently evident in the somewhat artificial debates in the social sciences. However, the logic of their responsibilities at times commits them to causal explanations of behaviour, and these arise, for example, with mental health and child abuse. The 'objective' distinction between mental health and mental illness is associated with an equivalent distinction between voluntary and caused behaviour. Care management as social work therefore, is characterised by a limited voluntarism.

The appropriate social focus for practice

The final area involves a position which is closest, in academic terms, to what Burrell and Morgan (1979) term the Sociology of

Regulation. Social work is subject to major structural constraints on its practice. These structural constraints leave it as an individualised and personalised service rather than one which is concerned with social change. This reflects an emphasis on social need, as it concerns care managers, as a residual issue for society. The structural constraints are evident in the social organisation of social work. Social workers are only able to practice under delegated authority (Sheppard, 1990). For the most part social workers' authority is derived from their status as agency functionaries (Howe, 1979) although with compulsory admission assessments their authority is derived direct from the state (Sheppard, 1990).

Social workers, for example, in the realm of juvenile justice do not have a responsibility for affecting those aspects of society which, according to a radical theory, might explain young offending. These might be apparent in models of radical non intervention, where social workers (and others) should simply not be involved with offenders for fear of turning them into long term criminals through a labelling process (Schur, 1973). Likewise, if inequalities are considered part of the problem, it is not social workers' responsibility somehow to alleviate these inequalities (Taylor, Walton and Young, 1973). Their role in juvenile justice is to focus on the individual offender and their family. They may have a supervision order or they may be involved in intermediate treatment. In either case the focus is on the individual offender, rather than society or social institutions.

The practice paradigm characterising social work as care management, therefore, is that involving a core of objectivism, limited voluntarism and an individualised-personalised service. It is easy to understand, once this paradigm is grasped, why Marxism provided so few recipes for the conduct of practice. It quite simply directed social workers to practice outside domains which were consistent with this paradigm. It is also interesting to note however, that other approaches, if taken *in toto*, are also inconsistent with this paradigm. An exclusively phenomenological approach, for example, demands that social work concerns be always a matter of social construction and hence disputable. However, it is clear that there is an objective dimension to practice inconsistent with phenomenology's subjectivism. We may learn, from phenomenological research on child abuse practices, about different perceptions of parenting behaviour which have been considered to be abusive by social service authorities. This can inform us both that different perspectives exist and what these perspectives are. However, if we then go on to take a phenomenological perspective that child abuse is no more than a social construct, this does violence to the objectivist core of social work. Phenomenological research, in other words, may provide useful information, but it does not follow that in using that research social workers should take on a phenomenological perspective.

This does not mean that these theories have no place in social work as care management. What must be understood, however, is that *in the use of theories, concepts and evidence, the practice paradigm of social work provides the framework through which these approaches should be viewed.* Hence, from the practice paradigm perspective phenomenology has a limited value insofar as it is exclusively subjectivist and voluntarist in its approach. However, unlike Marxism, it is unconcerned with wider social structures.

There appear to be two central considerations when using social science knowledge as 'theory for practice' and in a way consistent with the structural constraints entailed in a practice led approach. The knowledge or theories used should either be consistent with the individualised nature and domain of social work practice or they should be used in ways which conform to these constraints. An example of the first is Attachment theory. This is a theory of psychological development (and well being) which is individualist and so does not direct social work attention away from its structurally constrained domain. An example of the second is Labelling theory. Labelling theory may be used as a rationale for radical non intervention (Schur, 1973). This is because social work involvement in the justice system, by labelling someone as an offender, is deemed to 'confirm' the individual in their deviant identity. That is they change from a person who happens to have offended to someone who identifies themselves as an offender, and thus 'solidifies' their offending behaviour. This would entail social work withdrawing entirely, for example, from the juvenile justice system (together, it should be noted with the police and courts) (Cohen, 1975). This quite simply conflicts with the role prescribed for social work by the state. However, labelling theory can serve to remind social workers of unnecessarily labelling clients. It has a precautionary function.

This approach to social science is one which sees social workers using aspects of it as may be helpful for practice, but only in a way that is guided by, or viewed through the framework of the practice paradigm. This approach requires a clear understanding on the part of the practitioner, and the social work student. Only if the clarity of understanding, together with a confidence in this paradigm is achieved can social workers and social work students hope to negotiate the conflicting social science approaches. It is only through a thoroughgoing practice led approach that students and practitioners will avoid becoming seduced into choosing a particular theoretical approach and hence becoming theory-driven. From the social workers' point of view the role of social science knowledge is one determined by social work, not the reverse.

CRITERIA FOR CHOICE OF KNOWLEDGE

Having established clearly what it means to be 'practice led' and that a practice paradigm exists which limits the freedom with which social workers may choose and apply knowledge, we can further explicate the processes by which choice may be made, and through which we can maximise the relevance of social science knowledge to social work. This involves, in the first instance, a number of relatively straightforward distinctions which nonetheless help in the conduct of practice.

Background Knowledge

The first is a distinction between *Foreground* and *Background* knowledge. Foreground knowledge may be distinguished as forms of knowledge which in any particular instance, are of direct relevance to the understanding of the particular problems, needs or issues of a case. This will be considered in more detail below. Background knowledge is concerned with the nature, limits and context of social work practice. It forms a backdrop to the consideration of practice in all cases. Three forms of background knowledge can be distinguished. First there is knowledge which helps in our understanding of the nature of, and limits to, social work itself. Hence, knowing that social work practice is structurally constrained forms one part of background knowledge. Our perspective on this may vary, as, for example, between Marxist and Functionalist explanations. A Marxist approach may make us critical of the position of social workers in a way that a Functionalist approach would not. This cannot, of course, alter the restrictions placed on social work or the realities of the practice paradigm. A social worker may have a personal commitment to some form of Marxist perspective, but there are considerable limitations on the extent to which this may directly determine the conduct of practice. It is certainly the case that anyone committed to such a perspective (and who is not deluding themselves) will have to compromise in their principles in order to be a practitioner.

The second area of background knowledge is an understanding of the broad issues of social science knowledge. Hence social workers may know the distinction between the sociology of regulation and radical change and the emphasis on a subjective versus objective understanding of human actions or behaviour. This knowledge is necessary to inform social workers understanding both of the practice paradigm of social work and of the orientation associated with any particular explanation of the issues with which social work is concerned.

The third relates to broad issues of social concern whose solution resides at the level of social policy rather than social work practice. The most obvious of these is the problem of inequality and poverty. There can be little doubt that poverty and associated problems of lack of job opportunities, poor housing and so on are issues for many - indeed the majority - of social work consumers. At the level of the individual case the social worker may attempt to alleviate the impact of poverty: they may attempt to obtain new housing for an inadequately housed family; they may rehearse interviewing with an individual who has lost confidence because of unemployment; they may attempt to reduce conflict in a family where it arises because of poverty related stress. But the issue of poverty as a society wide problem is not one about which the social worker *qua* social worker can do anything. It is a necessary background to the understanding of many cases. An understanding of the structural basis of inequality may frequently prevent social workers making the error of blaming the victim - as clearly arguably happened in late 1993 with the Conservative government's 'discovery' of the relationship between single parenthood and all kinds of social problems (many of these problems would probably reduce if single parents were not so frequently disadvantaged and unsupported). As such, it provides an important backdrop to the understanding of their cases. But the concern of social work cannot be with equality *per se* (as opposed to the problems of poverty *for this particular consumer*) because of the structural constraints preventing them operating at the level of social policy. Social workers' task is to implement social policy, not to make it.

Background knowledge, therefore, is concerned (a) with an understanding of the nature and position of social work (b) with a proper understanding of the theory which is available to inform practice and (c) issues of social concern whose solution resides at the level of social policy.

Foreground Knowledge

Foreground knowledge is knowledge which in any particular case, is of direct relevance to the understanding and management of that case. In order to determine the kinds of knowledge most suitable as foreground knowledge, it is necessary further to conceptualise the links between social science and practice. The relevance of social science for assessment lies in its ability to help define, make sense of, and direct practice. A key dimension of this lies in the possibility of *congruence* and *specificity* between the knowledge form chosen and the practice in any particular case. Congruence and specificity is established through the problem as it is defined in the case. Thus, for example, if the problem is one of offending behaviour on the part of an adolescent (the consumer is a young offender) the knowledge form adopted, if consistent with the principles of congruence and specificity, would be research and theory on juvenile delinquency. It is congruent because both practice and social science knowledge is concerned with adolescent offending, and it is specific in so far as the concern is specifically with young offending, rather than, say a general theory or paradigm, such as an interactionist perspective. In practice, the practice problem is likely to be based on some case definition (such as child abuse) or identification of a primary need. On this basis, the task of those concerned with education and training would be to seek out those areas of knowledge the central concerns of which are precisely the same as the range of problems which are the concern of social work. These might include, for example, knowledge relating to child abuse, offending behaviour, or specific mental health problems such as depression or schizophrenia.

We can develop a matrix by which theoretical preference can be developed in line with the principles of congruence and specificity. One dimension of this matrix involves a distinction between those forms of knowledge which are congruent with the particular concerns of social work and those forms of knowledge which are general theories or paradigms. Hence we could distinguish between social control theory (Hirtschi, 1969) - the concern of which is with juvenile delinquency, and which is hence congruent with cases where the problem is of a young offender - and a broader interactionist perspective which represents a way of looking at social phenomena. The second dimension of this matrix relates to the degree of evidence which exists in support of the particular theory or hypothesis. Those theories or hypotheses which have been the subject of research, the concern of which is directly to determine their validity are to be preferred to those where no such research has been undertaken and hence no support exists. These two elements: congruence and research validity measure what may be called the *Convergence* of theory and practice.

These dimensions could be presented in the following diagram:

Research Validity	Theory Specificity	
	Congruent	General
Support	A	B
No Support	C	D

This is, of course, somewhat schematic, and designed to bring out clearly the significance of the points made. We are, in fact, likely to encounter theories or hypotheses with variable degrees of support, from, at one extreme, those which have been subject to little or no research, and which hence have little support, to those which have been extensively researched. If, however, we do not distinguish between theories or hypotheses for which little support exists from that where extensive support exists then the social work knowledge base will amount to little more than the 'taking up of positions'. It is likely to reflect the preferences of the individuals involved, rather than a hard headed examination of the validity of these preferences. At a time when social work has been accused of being 'too ideological' and suffering from a surfeit of 'political correctness' it is important that social work has some rational means for choosing between more or less valid forms of knowledge.

In terms of this matrix it is possible to identify, an order of preference in relation to any particular problem of available forms of knowledge. The preferred position would be position A (high convergence). If such a knowledge form exists it is to be preferred to others. Failing this, positions B or C are to be preferred, with position D being chosen in the absence of any alternative (low convergence).

This approach helps us take account of the issue of applicability of social science knowledge. It helps us distinguish the most applicable (the high convergence, congruent-specific) from less directly applicable. It also takes account of the essentially provisional and emergent nature of our knowledge of social phenomena. There are limits to the extent to which social science knowledge exists which will inform practice. These limits should be recognised, but rather than abandoning social science knowledge it is better to develop means by which the best use may be made of what we have got.

Social science based assessment schedules present ways of more directly applying the product of the endeavours of social scientists to social work. These are schedules which embody the main dimensions of a particular area of knowledge which is operationalised in such a way that practitioners may use these schedules directly with clients. They embody the principle of convergence. They are, therefore, on the one hand grounded in social science, on the other hand directly usable in practice. An example of such a schedule is the Compulsory Admissions Assessment Schedule, which I developed for approved social workers for compulsory admission assessments (Sheppard, 1990). This was grounded on a combination of a theoretical understanding of approved social work, a conceptual framework based on risk analysis, applied to the arena of mental health, and the detailed results of a research programme. All these came together to produce an assessment schedule which was subsequently evaluated in practice. Another schedule developed is the Assessment Schedule on Social Support of Mothers At Risk For Depression (Sheppard, 1994). This was based on a combination of a conceptual analysis of social support, together with a wide ranging review of findings of research in this area. The result was an assessment schedule which can be used in practice, grounded in the extensive theoretical and empirical endeavours of social science. Both CASH and the Social Support schedule are highly convergent (in the technical sense defined here) because they work with a knowledge form whose definition of the problem is precisely that used in practice (compulsory admission assessment and social support) and because they bring to bear research evidence in support of their use. Although by no means providing an answer to all the problems of 'theory-practice integration', social science based assessment schedules present one way forward, and embody a high convergence rating.

Foreground Knowledge and the Process of Assessment

The second dimension of foreground knowledge is that relating to the processes involved in conducting assessment. There are three main areas residing in this dimension: issues of problem definition, issues of meaning and issues of explanation. These are three, conceptually identifiable, if not entirely conceptually distinct, key issue for those seeking to use theory in the form of social science knowledge, in the conduct of assessments.

The problem of definition as part of the assessment process is different from that relating to social work-social science congruence and specificity. In the case of congruence, it is a principle which seeks to link problem definition in social work to problem definition in social science. In relation to the process of assessment, it involves, in relation to the particular case with which the social worker is concerned, the issue of identifying what exactly the problem is. This requires that, in advance of assessing this particular case, we are both clear about the range of problems (as defined in social work) which are the concern of social work and the social science knowledge which is directly concerned with the same range of issues. As practitioner, the social worker is confronted with the question: what exactly is the problem or need in this particular case? This is a central consideration to assessment and a necessary prerequisite to informed intervention. The identification of a problem in any particular case involves the capacity to recognise it in the first place. The role of social science in this respect is to aid the process of recognition on the basis of being 'theory informed'. A good example of the potential role of such knowledge is the extent to which the issue of depression in child care cases is so variably identified by different social workers.

Issues of meaning are significant, although their significance varies according to the nature of the problem. Meaning relates centrally to the way in which the consumer defines their circumstances. It is 'their story', and consumers do not necessarily agree with practitioners. There appears to be two sources of relevant social science knowledge. Client perspective studies can inform practitioners about consumers' experience of social work intervention and hence the meaning they attach to their encounter with the social worker. What do they expect when they approach social services? Is it a relationship they consider helpful? are they ashamed - do they feel stigmatised? The second source is that of social science studies whose central concern is the explication of meaning in individuals defined in certain kinds of ways. How do young offenders make sense of what they are about? how does it feel for an individual who has just been diagnosed as suffering from a life threatening disease such as cancer?

Where social workers are not in the business of regulating behaviour, as with child protection or offending behaviour, the capacity to understand consumer meaning allows them to define more effectively the needs and circumstances of the consumer in a way that is consistent with the consumer's understanding of their need. This is a necessary prerequisite to encouraging consumer choice. Where they are regulating behaviour understanding consumer meaning helps practitioners understand and anticipate consumers' reaction to social work definitions and actions. To state the obvious, a recognition that different groups may define adequate parenting differently helps the social worker understand that their definition of some behaviour as abusive may be seen by parents as legitimate punishment, and help them also anticipate their likely reactions.

The third 'process issue' is that of explanation. This is about understanding the cause or reason for behaviour in any particular case. Indeed, it is important to distinguish circumstances where external causes are ascribed from that where the problem arises from intentional acts. We may understand offending behaviour in terms of involvement with a delinquent peer group (subculture) (Matza, 1990); because, at an individual level the young person steals to obtain goods that they could not otherwise afford because of poverty (linking inequality and anomie) (Merton, 1968) or because of familial problems preventing (West, 1990) them developing a commitment to conventional (legal) rules.

GENERALITY AND ADEQUACY OF FIT

One argument frequently presented by those who perceive a theory-practice gap relates to the generality of social science knowledge, which makes it, it is suggested, ill suited as a knowledge base for social work (Sheldon, 1978). Practitioners, it is said, are concerned with specific situations involving particular individuals who have particular problems or needs. Those who practice are inevitably acutely aware of the complexity and uniqueness of these individual situations. Theory, operates at a level of generality which does little justice to the rich complexity of real life situations. This criticism, frequently levelled at quantitative, particularly positivist, research, has its mirror image in relation to qualitative research. Much qualitative research derives from the study of the single setting, a school, community, gang or whatever (Rist, 1984). For many, this reliance on single case research poses a problem of how far it is possible to generalise the results of such research. Many qualitative researchers themselves display an unease about the extent to which it is possible to generalise the results of such research (Bulmer, 1986).

However, there are particular advantages held by social research which make it preferable to experiential knowledge. Experiential knowledge is idiosyncratic, subjectivist, and when promoted as the form of knowledge appropriate for practice, creates an inevitable drift towards solipsism. When an individual's experience is all that matters there can be no higher arbiter of the validity of a position than individual experience. Yet the variability of experience, and the variability of its interpretation allows, potentially, for as many views as there are individuals presenting them. It is relativism in a very clear form. However, this is not the only reason for preferring formal knowledge to experience.

The processes of social research are subject to critical analysis and comment through the process of peer review. This both encourages, as a matter of course, greater rigour in the conduct of research, and subsequently leaves that research subject to critical scrutiny from the academic community (rather than being a localised matter). This is undertaken in the open, frequently through publications. The result is that both the knowledge 'product' and the process of reaching that product is in the public domain, and hence widely known. As Hammersley (1992, p 91) states:

> This process is at the heart of the justification of research as a source of knowledge... [which] rests on the claim that research based knowledge is less likely to be in error than information from other sources because it is subjected to scrutiny in terms of higher levels of routine scepticism than is common outside the academic community...it is

this rather than any appeal to a concept of brute data...that is the major rationale for the intellectual authority of research.

It is, then the greater level of rigour and routine scepticism which lies at the heart of the greater robustness of research findings. However, the high levels of rigour characteristic of academic work are equally important for social work practice. This must be the case in an occupation where the realm of uncertainty remains considerable and where the consequences, at times, of making errors are quite appalling. While, therefore, Reflexive Eclecticism emphasises an enhancement of rigour in the conduct of practice, an emphasis on social research is quite consistent with this enhanced rigour.

Arguments bemoaning the over-generality or over-specificity of social research, furthermore, display a 'theory centred' rather than case or situation centred approach to theory practice relations. This involves examining them (theory and practice) as separate entities and lamenting an apparent lack of fit between the two in this more abstract rarefied relationship. The case centred approach characterising the theory of emergent understanding emphasises understanding theory's relevance 'at the coal face' of the particular practice situations confronting the practitioner. Incorporation of theory happens (or should happen) at the 'coal face': incorporation occurs in the process of making sense in a reflexive manner. To this has been added the principle of convergence by which that formal knowledge characterised by high convergence (high theoretical specificity and research validity) is to be preferred to less convergent theory. This further emphasises the case centred nature of theory practice incorporation because of its emphasis on congruence and specificity. It does so while recognising that a significant contribution of formal knowledge lies in its capacity to transcend the idiosyncratic perspectives of individuals through its emphasis on research validity.

No-one, presumably, considers that 'proper' theory-practice incorporation involves some unproblematic direct application of social science to practice without serious consideration by the practitioner of the extent to which it is applicable and useful in the particular circumstances for which it is being considered. Reflexivity emphasises that formal knowledge provides the practitioner with some idea of the kind of factors (s)he could look for and also those which are, on available evidence likely to have a bearing on the case at hand. The practitioner is likely to be aware of factors in the situation other than those in the particular knowledge they are using, which are of interest to them in this particular case. They are, however, engaged in the exercise of judgement: what does theory have to tell us about this particular situation? how accurately does it represent this situation? what other factors might be playing a part? and so on. Social work practitioners are not involved in some rigid process of knowledge application. They are engaged in a creative reflexive exercise in which judgement about adequacy of fit is of considerable significance. This allows us to take advantage of the merits of formal knowledge while recognising the specificity of individual situations.

The argument - based on its generality - about the appropriateness of social science knowledge, therefore, rather misses the point: that we can only judge its use in the manner by which it becomes relevant. This can only be achieved reflexively in a case based manner in terms of its adequacy of fit. Its manner of application, furthermore, depends on the forms of knowledge being utilised, since different forms have different qualities. Reflexivity in knowledge use involves taking account of its particular characteristics. Social research generally appears in conceptual (and theoretical), qualitative and quantitative forms. While, of course, they are not discrete elements (concepts appear in empirical work), these different forms can be considered in terms of their use for reflexive practice.

Concepts

Concepts serve two key purposes: they are central to the process of making sense in the analysis of social data and they have the capacity for transfer - reflexively - from one situation to another. Probably the most widely quoted example is that of loss. Loss is a concept which may help us make sense of situations as diverse as recent unemployment, bereavement and a willing choice of an older person to enter residential care. Other concepts which may be used in this way include, for example, role and reference group. The point about such concepts is that they may help us to understand and explain situations - to make sense - and hence carry out more informed interventions. Indeed, they may at times be crucial. Without concepts like role or reference group it is difficult to see how ideas challenging traditional role stereotypes could be developed This is an important part, for example, of our understanding of depression in women (Corob, 1987).

The usefulness of concepts arises from their nature. Concepts provide, according to Bulmer (1979) a means for summarising and classifying the formless mass of social data. They are the social science equivalent of categories. They are according to Myrdall (1961) 'the spaces into which social reality is fitted by analysis'. Where, however, do they fit into our schema of useful knowledge? They may, in fact, fit into any one of the four dimensions, and where they fit depends upon the concept used. For example, considerable general evidence exists about the concept of reference groups and the use of this concept may most frequently be placed in dimension B (general theoretical specificity with research support). A concept such as expressed emotion may be placed in dimensions A, B, or C. Expressed emotion (EE) refers to the emotion expressed in the familial situation by relatives of people diagnosed as suffering schizophrenia (Leff and Vaughn, 1984). It has three main elements: hostility, over involvement and critical comments, of which the last is the most significant. In brief, the complex findings of research show that high levels of EE together with lengthy face to face contact between the person diagnosed as suffering schizophrenia makes relapse considerably more likely. If used in relation to intervention with a person suffering schizophrenia, then it is a concept which is both congruent with the problem confronted by the social worker and it possesses research validity - it is in dimension A. However, it also presents a useful organising concept for considering relationships between family members. We may, for example, think about using it in relation to intra familial problems in the area of child and family care. Now we have no idea about the precise nature of its impact on these situations, because no research specifically examining expressed emotion has been undertaken (of course we do know about areas of family life related to expressed emotion). However, it may provide a concept which is useful in relation to the particular case with which this social worker is concerned. In this case it would appear in dimension C (congruent in theoretical specificity but lacking direct research support).

The use of concepts in this way reflects an important truth about our social science knowledge: that it is limited. There will be times when we are unable to apply directly congruent research based knowledge to practice. However, the social worker cannot simply state, as might the academic, that we have no knowledge in a particular area. Social workers are practitioners: they must *do* something. This practice imperative requires they make the best use they can of available knowledge. Transferring concepts from situation one to situation two may be helpful, even in the absence of supporting research specific to situation two. However, this does not mean they should become ideologues for particular positions. This involves the degree of convergence, in which dimension A comes at the top and dimension D at the bottom. If social workers are to choose relevant forms of knowledge in any particular situation - if they are to be informed professionals - they must have the capacity to recognise preferred forms of knowledge.

Ethnographic Work

We may take further the usefulness of research by examining qualitative and quantitative research findings. Ethnographic research is an approach which seeks to describe and analyse qualitatively and in detail a particular area of social life, drawing extensively on the perspectives of the subjects being studied (Hammersley, 1992; Burgess, 1984). From a social work perspective this information can be useful. These works are immersed in the culture of those groups who are studied. The active recreation, through description, of the perspectives of subjects can sensitise practitioners to the fact that there are a range of different ways of perceiving the world, and not therefore, to take for granted that their own 'world view' is shared by consumers. They facilitate reflexivity. The social worker might 'see' the world as one of opportunity where others only see thwarted hopes and dominant groups (amongst whom social workers might be included).

In a more specific way, social workers may gain a greater understanding of the actual perspectives of particular groups with whom they are concerned. Hence, they can gain a greater understanding of the world of the young offender, the mentally ill patient and social service clients (the experience of receiving social service support) in general (Rock, 1973; Fisher, 1983). This can undeniably constitute a professional knowledge base, information which may be taken with the practitioner when making assessments and trying to make sense in the particular circumstances of individual cases. It may also considerably aid the capacity to empathise with clients. Understanding is, in relation to empathy, not on its own sufficient; this understanding must be effectively transmitted back to the consumer who is thereby able to 'feel understood'. However, understanding is a necessary prerequisite to empathy. There is considerable evidence that empathy plays a significant part in facilitating the helping process, both in counselling in general and social work in particular (Truax and Carkhuff, 1967; Sheppard, 1991; 1992; 1993)

However, it is important to understand that much ethnographic research is characterised by an interpretivist approach. There may be a tendency to accept the views of subjects as of equal validity to all other views. Indeed, all views may be treated as equally valid. There is, then, a thoroughgoing relativism which contrasts with the core of objectivism characterising social work's practice paradigm. Approved social workers do not, in fact, treat the views of individuals assessed for compulsory admission as equal to those of professionals undertaking the assessment. Likewise, where social services professionals, having gone through the appropriate processes, have decided that a particular case is one of child abuse, and where the courts agree, a protest by the parent that this was simply legitimate punishment will not be treated equally.

Social workers using this literature need guard against the implicit relativism contained within such ethnographic work. As shown earlier they need remain practice led, rather than theory driven. An approved social worker who failed to compulsorily admit an individual where they believed this to be the proper course of action would be open to having acted with bad faith or without reasonable care, as required by the Mental Health Act. No amount of protesting, derived from an interpretivist position (which would be theory driven), that all views are of equal validity would provide protection against such accusations. Social workers must remain practice led and this involves using helpful ethnographic material, but only within the constraints of the practice paradigm.

Quantitative-Descriptive and Empirical Generalisations
Quantitative approaches may be divided into quantitative-descriptive and empirical generalisations. Descriptive quantitative data is the kind of data through which, for example, large numbers of cases might be classified and intervention processes counted. Hence we would know, respectively, how many cases were in the realm of child care, adult services and services for older people. It is a numbers game, one which has been important in identifying the nature and range of social work practice as it is conducted (Goldberg and Wharburton, 1979). Descriptive-quantitative approaches are, as defined by Merton (1967), post-factum

interpretations. Basically, these involve the collection of data which are only subsequently subject to interpretation: descriptive statistics. This approach, he thinks, provides less robust conclusions than hypothesis testing. This is because interpretations are found which 'fit the facts'. Should a subsequent study be undertaken throwing up different 'facts' an alternative, equally plausible, interpretation may be presented. This is unlike hypothesis testing where we may seek to discover the circumstances - where data from different studies diverge - in which the hypothesis is shown to be supported or not supported by the evidence.

Much social work research entails interpretation of descriptive statistics. One example from my own research relates to communication between general practitioners and a social services department (Sheppard, 1985). This allowed certain information to be gleaned, for example, that where GPs had a poor view of social workers they tended not to refer, and that when they did, neither GP nor social worker tended to contact each other. This was interpreted as a technique of 'avoidance' to prevent unpleasant clashes. Another study, by contrast, was in the form of proposition testing. In a comparison of GPs who had had experience of social workers attached to their practice with those who did not, no difference was found between these two groups in their views of social workers, even controlling for age, the contemporary nature of the attachment, sex and recency of qualification. (Sheppard, 1987). This overturned propositions that the 'attachment' group would be more positive than the 'non attachment' group. This also overturned some widely held assumptions in social work. For our purposes it illustrates that particular facets of the social world can, under this approach, be supported or undermined by the data.

Empirical generalisations according to Merton (1967) are isolated propositions summarising observed uniformities of relationships between two or more variables. An example from the work of Brown can illustrate their significance. His pathfinding study of depression (Brown and Harris, 1978) has shown that it is vastly more common (indeed an epidemic) amongst urban working class than middle class women, and that women with three or more children aged under 14 are (amongst others) particularly vulnerable for depression. Such information can help social workers target high risk groups and engage in preventive measures which may alleviate depression, support the woman through it, and even prevent accommodation of children by the local authority (Sheppard, 1990; Sheppard, 1993).

These approaches are often considered by social workers and social work students, more captivated by humanist approaches, to be somewhat arid and uninteresting. However, to state this is not also to state that they are unimportant or not useful. Knowing, for example, that avoidance is a common means of preventing conflict between GPs and social workers allows social workers better to manage situations where involvement of GPs is particularly important, such as child abuse case conferences. It helps them interpret GPs behaviour and develop strategies to achieve their ends. To discard important approaches because they are uninteresting can hardly be considered professional, and indeed does a disservice both to the profession of social work and its consumers. Where these approaches can be problematic is when they fail to take account of meaning - the understanding the subjects of the study have of their situation. However, there is no reason why quantitative research cannot incorporate meaning (Marsh, 1982) and, indeed, this is exactly the approach of Brown and his colleagues to depression.

The issue of the relative merits of inductive and deductive approaches may be - certainly from the social work point of view - less important than Merton considers. Hanson's approach emphasises that the process of knowledge production is both inductive and deductive (retroductive) and both approaches provide information which transcends the merely idiosyncratic nature if individual everyday knowledge. Using social science knowledge anyway involves recognising its provisional nature - that new interpretations may be developed which provide more convincing accounts or explanations of social phenomena. It is also - and this is particularly the case with quantitative data - probabilistic. We are really in the business of identifying tendencies or likely outcomes. Social research cannot endow social work decisions with certainty in relation to outcome (or indeed interpretation). This sits easily however, with the case centred reflexive approach of emergent understanding. The constant examination, checking and adjusting of interpretations which occurs in the specific circumstances of practice situations is appropriate where knowledge, even where convergent, can only be probabilistic and provisional. The theory practice integration occurs in the practice situation, not outside it, although we can identify - indeed we have identified - salient characteristics contributing towards this integration.

CONCLUSION

This chapter has extended our understanding of theory use by developing key concepts by which suitable knowledge forms may be chosen and used for practice, and considering how, through the reflexive approach social science knowledge need not be too general (nor specific) for social work.

The concern frequently expressed about the contradictory and conflicting nature of social science paradigms, theories and explanations is not one, after all, that need worry us. It is something we must accept but it is something we can work with. It is, indeed, only to be expected where human understanding is itself limited. The rejection of eclecticism seems to involve a search for consistency for its own sake. For social scientists in the pursuit of ideas and evidence this may be highly desirable, although instead of producing inconsistencies within individual thinkers, it simply produces conflicts between different schools of thought. Why in practice, social workers should worry about the availability of inconsistent alternative approaches is not entirely clear. It is not the job of the social worker to generate elegant and consistent theories, but to generate, from potentially conflicting explanations, the one that actually fits best.

To suggest, furthermore, that social science produces over generalised knowledge is itself to generalise. We are forced to ask: exactly which knowledge is the individual referring to? There are, as we have seen, areas of social research which may quite precisely fit areas of concern in social work. Research on offending behaviour performs that task as does information on Expressed Emotion. Social science knowledge is not thank, goodness, all a matter of Grand Theory: attempts to explain all areas of social life. Indeed different forms of knowledge may have different characteristics, and fully reflexive practice involves taking into account those characteristics when using it for practice.

We have, therefore, to recognise that the user of the knowledge is the person who is themselves socially located in the practice situation. They are, so to speak, looking out from (as well as looking into) this situation when they are seeking to use social science knowledge. The practice paradigm ensures that their use of knowledge is consistent with assumptions inherent in the nature of social work. It is, in this respect, practice led. The principle of convergence provides a means by which we can identify that information which is most validly used in practice situations. All this nonetheless involves reckoning with the variable forms and contents of social science knowledge. Using social science knowledge cannot, then, go without taking into account the nature of social work (ie what it is being used for) and the nature of social science (what is being used). Only once this is recognised can a fully productive relationship between the two be sustained.

PART FOUR

THE USE OF
SOCIAL WORK THEORY

INTRODUCTION: THE USE OF SOCIAL WORK THEORY

Part Four of this book examines three conventional areas of social work theory which are of particular importance in the conduct of care management: interpersonal skills, social networks and social supports, and task centred practice. They are particularly important because they are both relevant to the specific and stated concerns in official documents on care management and because each area has a substantial formal knowledge base which considerably enhances the claims of social work to have a place at the professional level of care management. It will become apparent that each of these areas involves complex forms of knowledge which are consistent with the kinds of education and training available to social workers. Both interpersonal skills and social support assessments and development are specifically identified in government publications as key areas of care management (Dept of Health, 1991a and 1991b; Smale et al, 1993). Task centred practice represents a process of practice which has many similarities to the process of care management, but whose rigour is such that it would considerably enhance the care management process. It is suggested that social work courses which seek to prepare students for care management should give precedence to these approaches over alternative social work methods. Qualifying social workers should be proficient in all three methods.

Part Four seeks not simply to describe these approaches, but to explain their intellectual origins. In so doing their connection with certain fundamental aspects of social work, identified in Chapter 3, will become apparent. Interpersonal skills emphasise the consumer as subject: social support and network emphasises that humans are social beings and the interactionist focus of social work; and task centred practice emphasises that consumers are capable of purposive actions to ameliorate or resolve their problems. In these key respects, therefore, care management is closely linked to social work. Social work practice involves working with consumers who are considered to be subjects, who are social beings and are capable, in general, of purposive actions.

Chapter Eleven

Care management and interpersonal skills

The emphasis, in care management, on the importance of interpersonal skills, is one that sits easily with a central and traditional preoccupation of social work education and training. Skills training forms a significant proportion of the curriculum and its traditional importance for practice has been reaffirmed in the most recent requirements issued by CCETSW for Diploma in Social Work courses. The importance of interpersonal skills is based on two key considerations. The first is that social work is in the 'people business' (the latter word being particularly apposite in view of the new managerialism characterising social care) – that its central concerns are with people and their problems or needs. The second is that the capacity of individuals to work constructively with people with problems and needs, can be (considerably) enhanced by the development of capacities (such as the ability to empathise and listen). Their *possession*, at varying levels, is generally considered innate to human beings. However, the skill and sensitivity with which they are used – the ability purposefully to *direct* these skills – can be created, or developed to a much higher level, by training in interpersonal skills. It is interesting that this belief, so pervasive that it enters advisory government documents practically as an article of faith, has been so little subject to empirical scrutiny. Questions such as: how effective are interpersonal skills in the conduct of practice? and to what extent does training in interpersonal skills change an individuals capacity to practice? have rarely been subject to rigorous research, in the British context at any rate (Sheppard, 1992, 1993).

At a theoretical level, the importance of interpersonal skills is based on the considerable influence of humanism on both the definition, and perceptions of the appropriate conduct, of social work. It reflects a key, but not exclusive, element of the way in which human beings are viewed in social work. It represents a very axiom of the nature of human beings: that they are 'subjects'. Clark and Asquith (1985), for example, comment that social work is 'profoundly humanist', while Brandon and Jordan (1979) state that 'humanity is the essential stuff of which social work is made'. The extent to which humanism has exclusively influenced an individual's practice has depended to a great deal upon their particular stance. Hence, the influence of humanism on the practice of those guided by the work of Rogers or Kelly will be greater than its influence on those who practice behaviourally. Nonetheless, few would dispute its importance as the bedrock of practice whichever of these alternatives are chosen. Even behavioural practice requires good communication (indeed clarity and precision are at the heart of behavioural practice) (Hudson and Macdonald, 1986), and interpersonal skills provide the bedrock on which all aspects of practice are built.

The importance of interpersonal skills is based on at least three premises:

- The first is the recognition of humans as conscious sentient beings who construct meanings – reach their own understanding – of the world about them. This is at the heart of humanist thought, and is consistent with the limited voluntarism characteristic of the social work paradigm. Voluntarism entails the capacity to understand and direct one's life, and this would not be possible if we were not conscious of the world about us, able to make sense of it and to found our decisions on this understanding.

- The second is a recognition there is, in addition to a conscious dimension to the human condition, the realm of the unconscious or preconscious of which we are largely unaware. This arose in the first instance, through the influence of psychoanalysis, but is now, implicitly or explicitly, widely prevalent in practice. This is again consistent with limited voluntarism, since, if we are, at times, unaware of our true motivations we cannot be considered to be entirely self directing.

- The third is that for consumers, and humans generally, coming to an awareness of what we really want (encouraging active willing choice) can be at times a difficult and painful task, the encouragement of which requires delicacy and sensitivity on the part of the social worker or care manager.

This third point is not simply about unconscious or preconscious blocks to the opportunity for active willing choice. It is also about awareness of available alternatives, and in the light of these helping the consumer to make that choice in the most informed way possible.

The forum for the conduct of interpersonal skills is social interaction, between the social worker and others. Social interaction, it will be recalled, occurs where one or more persons' actions are reciprocally oriented towards the actions of others. This reciprocal orientation involves the use of reflexivity, as discussed earlier, and the conduct of interpersonal skills necessarily entails the capacity, on the part of the social worker, to be reflexive. Reflexivity, then, is central to interpersonal skills. If interpersonal skills are considered to be pretty well ever present in work with consumers, then it follows that reflexivity also need be ever present.

MEANING AND CONSCIOUS PURPOSES

This reflexivity involves the same kind of emphasis on meaning identified earlier. Human beings are, within this perspective considered to possess 'essential properties' which distinguish them from other creatures. These properties include consciousness, reason, compassion, responsibility and choice. Human beings, in pursuit of their own, willed ends, to a considerable degree, 'make their own history' (Rojek et al, 1988). In the social sciences this outlook has frequently been considered to distinguish the social from the natural sciences. A central element of this is the notion of *verstehen*, or understanding (Weber, 1949). This, as we have seen, involves the social scientist as investigator who seeks to understand the reasons, purposes and perspectives of human beings, their inner minds and feelings and the way these are expressed in their outward actions and achievements. This is quite consistent with pretty well universally accepted approaches to social work, and is encapsulated in the phrase 'starting where the client is'. To start where the client (or now, consumer) is, involves being clear about the way the world, and in particular their situation, is viewed by the individual consumer.

Such understanding is necessary because interpretation of the social world is far from unproblematic. Where there is scope for interpretation we need ways of understanding others in order to communicate meaningfully with them. If I, as a care manager, am to work with and for a consumer, it is important that I know their purposes (which in due course I may influence) and their perspectives on their situation. In this we are seeking to achieve, in Schutz's (1967) words 'genuine understanding'. Genuine understanding means the intentional grasping of the experience of others, in a manner akin to looking into their stream of consciousness. It reflects the true comprehension of subjective meaning. Genuine understanding is possible in face to face 'we' relations. It depends on direct exchange and interaction. As we pass from these situations of direct interaction to modes of indirect experience of others, we have to resort to more and more abstract conceptualisations.

This 'genuine understanding' involves a constant jockeying, adjustment and readjustment of our perceptions of an individual's communication. A consumer (say, a parent whose child is the subject of a Child Assessment Order investigation) may, after a number of visits, apparently welcome the social worker into their home, saying that they are pleased to see them. They may, however, sit down, crossing and uncrossing their legs, and gripping their armchair, when they are not fidgeting. Understanding how a consumer feels involves not necessarily treating the initial statement at face value, but in interpreting the statement in the light of other aspects of the interaction, linguistic and non linguistic. Their body movements may suggest that, far from being pleased, the parent is rather anxious and fearful. The practitioner may form an hypothesis (that they are really anxious but they are trying not to show it) against which they can check out other salient aspects which emerge during the interview. Does the parent retain a friendly attitude? do they relax during the interview? is there an 'edge' to statements they make and so on. They may be informed by considering how they (the practitioner) might feel in the same situation (the skill of 'tuning in'). Their considerations involve an awareness of self (the parent may have begun by being pleased to see the practitioner, having reconciled herself to the CAO, but the practitioner's manner may itself be confrontational). The essential reflexivity involved in the use of interpersonal skills entails a recognition of the socially situated interaction of which both social worker and consumer will be consciously aware and which constitutes a key element to the social interaction. It is this which is central to the reciprocal orientation of the social interaction and the adept use of interpersonal skills. The skilful conduct of the interaction involves the three key aspects of meaning outlined earlier: a recognition of the socially situated nature of meaning; the intuitive grasp of feelings, based on our having experienced similar feelings; and the awareness (and search for) the intentions, purposes and reasons for the consumer's acts, including what they say.

It should be noted that understanding does not necessarily mean agreement. We may fully understand a consumer's perspective and still consider it wrong. Indeed, the core of objectivism characterising the social work paradigm means we may, at times, consider their perspectives to be objectively wrong. Such is the case where someone is considered to suffer delusions or hallucinations – where we consider them insane. In such a case we are likely immediately to seek some cause for their problem, rather than take their perspectives at face value and consider them to be of equal validity to that of the practitioner.

CONSCIOUS, UNCONSCIOUS AND PRECONSCIOUS

While the humanist dimension to social work addresses itself to the conscious self, it is assumed that clients are to *varying degrees* conscious of their wishes and purposes. Some might be quite clear about what they want, why they want it and how they are pursuing it. Others my only be dimly aware of their true purposes in pursuing particular goals by particular forms of action. In such cases, their behaviour may be considered to have unconscious or preconscious purposes. This is clear in a statement by Goldstein (1981, p 438). Social work is directed towards:

> ...changing personal or shared misconceptions of reality that obstruct healthy adaptation and problem solving. The individual may be hampered by the lack of proper knowledge or may unwittingly misunderstand himself, others, or conditions in his environment. It is possible that his reasoning is confused, resulting in personal meanings that tend to distort reality in unhelpful ways.

This provides a further dimension of the reflexivity involved in interpersonal skills. If we consider that humans are frequently unconsciously motivated – they are unaware of why they are doing certain things – then this must enter into the reflexive conduct of interpersonal skills. This unconscious motivation constitutes a form of causal attribution identified earlier. It involves being aware of the possibility that an individual genuinely believes that they are motivated in one way while their actions are more consistent with a different motivation. An individual, for example, in a group therapy session may accuse others of being difficult and argumentative. However, arguments may arise as a result of the continual tendency of the accusing individual to make statements dismissive of others in the group, or with no sensitivity to others feelings, or challenging what they are saying. Their argumentative response may simply be an understandable reaction to that individual's own behaviour. That individual's accusations might be interpreted, in psychoanalytic terms, as a form of projection, where their own behaviour is projected on to others

To mention the unconscious is inevitably to invoke the influence of psychoanalysis on social work. The widespread recognition of unconscious purposes which at times characterise consumers' actions is a testimony not only to the continuing influence of this school of thought, but that certain elements, such as the unconscious, exercise a general influence on social work beyond those who consider themselves guided primarily by psychoanalytic thought. As Howe (1988) points out, people often distort reality in ways which, given the circumstances, do not appear to make sense. They may over react to an apparently innocuous statement, respond angrily to someone who appears to have behaved quite reasonably or deny an important factor in their situation which seems obviously relevant to the outsider. In these cases, psychological defence mechanisms are working, with the purpose of warding off anxiety invoked by the particular issue raised. Defence mechanisms are those unconscious strategies designed to protect individuals from pain and anxiety which they cannot handle in real world terms. If challenged an individual will not accept that they are acting defensively. They may, for example, 'project' on to someone else their unwanted feelings, or they may dissociate themselves from these feelings, intellectualising on them in a dispassionate way, as if it were not themselves they were talking about. The point is that, by definition, unconscious acts are those whose true purposes the individual is unaware of.

A further dimension, identified by Hollis (1970) is that of the 'preconscious'. The distinction between preconscious and unconscious according to Hollis is one of accessibility. Preconscious material is that of which we may not be fully aware, but which can, compared with unconscious material, be relatively easily recalled. Unconscious material, however, consists of all that which cannot be recalled 'at will', and cannot be recovered except through special means such as 'free association' or hypnosis. Unconscious memories are those which are actively repressed. Hollis considers casework, when used therapeutically, is concerned with the preconscious rather than unconscious: it promotes the emergence of the less accessible parts of the preconscious. The caseworker does not use free association, hypnosis or drugs but she does have clients talk about matters of which they have been previously unaware, and of which, Hollis thinks, they presumably could not have been conscious without the intervention of the caseworker.

It should be noted that in the quote from Goldstein and the subsequent discussion on unconscious and preconscious purposes, there is an assumption of an objective social reality which is shared by all rational people, and which it is possible for the social worker to apprehend. Where unconscious drives are 'distorting' behaviour, it is the social worker or care manager who is assumed to have an objective grasp on reality and the consumer who does not. There exists, within the social work paradigm, limits to the extent to which all interpretations of reality may be considered equally valid. This is, in part, reflected in the inclusion of the ideas of the unconscious and preconscious in the reflexive conduct of practice.

ENCOURAGING ACTIVE WILLING CHOICE

Much, though not all, of the purpose of interpersonal skills amounts, consistent with the aims of care management, to the encouragement of the exercise of choice. There are, of course limits to this, examined in detail on the chapter on consumer choice and user self determination, and encapsulated in a phrase I used earlier, that the purpose of care management is to encourage choice amongst the rational and rationality amongst the irrational.

However, the encouragement of choice (and certainly rational behaviour) is not a straightforward matter. The first problem arises in fully understanding where the consumer is coming from – understanding their perceptions of their situation and how this relates to their purposes and aims in relation to the care management process. The care manager's understanding of the consumer's situation and purposes is bound to be patchy at the outset since frequently they will have never met the person before. Their rich personal biography, upon which their current aims and purposes are founded, is something of which the practitioner has practically no knowledge. Yet it is only in terms of a more detailed understanding of this than they can possibly hope to gain from a referral, that real choice for the consumer – a choice which represents their preferences rather than those imposed on them by the practitioner – is possible. Even where the care manager has had previous contact with the consumer, they will be initially unaware of changes which may have occurred in their lives in the intervening period.

Where, furthermore, there is some scope for interpretation, for variations in perspectives, then understanding the particular interpretation of their situation held by the consumer becomes an important prerequisite to encouraging choice. Indeed, there is evidence that without this professionals can stereotype consumers. 'Typifications' refers to categories developed by professionals which relate to their practical concerns (Robinson, 1983). Rather than responding to people as 'unique whole individuals' these involve suggestions about what ought to be done 'under these circumstances with someone like this'. For example evidence exists from routine ante natal clinics that doctors typified their major problems as 'worrying mothers' and responded with routine medical reassurances, rather than to the specific circumstances of mother and child (Davis and Strong, 1976).

Both these require skills in communication, through which the practitioner may be able to discover what the consumer thinks and feels. A further element in encouraging choice involves the consumer's awareness of the range of available alternatives. Indeed, consistent with care management's resolve to respond creatively to need – to be needs led – the range of potential alternatives, not just those currently in existence should be creatively considered. This has been discussed earlier, and this awareness is certainly crucial to the exercise of consumer choice. It is fairly obvious why: if they are not fully aware of the alternatives then how may they be expected to exercise choice between them? Again, however, communication skills become necessary, particularly where the capacity to understand the choices, what they mean for the consumer and their implications are to be maximally understood.

A final element in the relationship between interpersonal skills and the exercise of choice involves working through ambivalence or motivations of which the consumer may not be clearly aware. It is in this – encouraging active willing choice – that interpersonal skills most obviously drift into psychotherapy, of which more will be discussed below. The ambivalence may be fairly obvious. Where an older person is considering the option of going into residential care compared with remaining in their own home, this may raise all kinds of emotional issues which have to be worked through before a final decision may be made. They may have come to the conclusion that, given their physical state, it is not viable for them to remain in their own home, yet, having lived in their home for many years, feel a great sense of loss. Indeed, the apparent finality of the move into residential care may well engender thoughts about their own mortality, confronting them with further difficulties. Until these conflicting impulses are resolved a real choice is not possible.

An individual may be less immediately aware of their purposes – in Hollis's terms these reside in the area of the preconscious. Ragg (1977) provides an example in this respect of a woman with two children who, finding life at home and her relationship with her husband intolerable, walks out. She phones her two young sons daily, saying she will return soon, and tells her husband that she is seeking 'time out'. It is not obvious that she has left her husband or that she sees herself as having done so. The role of the practitioner, in these circumstances, is to facilitate an accurate description by the woman, so that, through this process, she realises what she was actually trying to do. An ultimate decision to separate makes manifest what was latent in her actions (of course this may not always occur as in this case example) and draws to the surface the actual purposes motivating these actions.

Keith-Lucas (1972) describes this as a process of moving from a position of non choice – being overwhelmed by, or evading, reality – to one of choice. Active and willing choice is where the individual as a whole person chooses a course having weighed up clearly the implications of the alternatives. It involves a commitment to the decision to take one course rather than another, to do something destructive or constructive, to come to terms with life or to struggle against it. For Keith-Lucas (p 44) it is the choice between growth and refusal to grow, life or the negation of life.

The process of encouraging choice is a reflexive one, and can be so in the most detailed of ways. The earlier example of the anxious parent subject to a Child Assessment Order and the individual projecting their argumentativeness on to others illustrates how, throughout the process of intervention, the alert practitioner will be reflexing on the situation. In more general terms, the process of understanding others involves the kinds of attempts to make sense outlined in chapter 10. Hence the capacity to consider intuitive, intentional and normative aspects of meaning, the capacity to use categories and schemas (and concepts and theories) and the ability to hypothesise all form central elements of the process of understanding others.

In the previous example (Ragg's), we have the case of a woman who apparently starts in a state of ambivalence: while having left her husband and children, it appears she has not made a decision whether this is a temporary or permanent situation. This attribution of ambivalence represents an hypothesis. It might be right or wrong. We might subsequently discover that what appeared ambivalent was already, in fact, a firm decision. Our attribution of ambivalence may have occurred because of the way the woman presented the situation rather than the content of what she said. Perhaps her case was presented in a diffident or sad manner, reflecting her sense of loss having made the decision, leading the practitioner incorrectly to consider her ambivalent. On the other hand her behaviour may have reflected a real ambivalence. Either way, the hypothesis of ambivalence is open to refutation.

The term ambivalence, furthermore, represents a category or schema with which we make sense of the specific situation using generic terms. Ambivalence means being unsure, as between different courses of action, about which to choose. In the case of separation it is likely to be emotionally 'loaded'. The sense of loss of relationship, the possibility of loss of the children, or alternatively of having to care for them as a single parent, foreboding about the future, might generally be included. However, additionally, the frustrations of the relationship, anger at the partner, weariness about constant arguments, provide further elements. Added to this may be a concern about the well being of the children: would they be better off if both parents stayed together or if they separated and the children did not see the parents argue any more.

Ambivalence, then, is a complex category which is situation specific and which is seeped in reflexive potential. Intuitive dimensions of meaning apprehension include knowing the woman feels sad or anxious and knowing how that feels, regardless of whether the practitioner has themselves been separated, because they too have felt sadness or anxiety. Intentions and motives are implicit within this ambivalence: what the woman intends is the problem, though the reasons for her ambivalence may be clear. The 'social location' of the woman in this context is rooted in the role of the parent and partner/wife, and, indeed, the possible rejection of these roles. Feelings of guilt may make sense in the light of the role expectations of parents (to nurture) and the likely effects of separation on the children.

Our understanding of her feelings, views and ambivalence are dependent upon our understanding of the kinds of meanings which may be present. However, we cannot be sure we have got it right. Does the woman, for example, really have a sense of foreboding about the future, or is she quite confident that she could manage on her own, if that was the outcome? does she really have a sense of loss, or is her anger so great that it is difficult to look into the past with fond memories? is she actually much bothered about her children's feelings, or do the onerous tasks of child care form one aspect of her desire to escape from the relationship?

Providing the foundations for the exercise of choice, therefore, requires an understanding of the woman's position, which involves a high degree of reflexivity, of an ability to hypothesise and alter one's hypotheses to attain a more accurate view of the situation. It is on these foundations that working through the ambivalence becomes possible, of helping the woman examine the consequences of choosing a particular alternative from the different choices in a way which suits her best. This involves generating the salient characteristics of each of the alternatives.

OPERATIONALISING INTERPERSONAL SKILLS

The social work literature has a great deal to say about interpersonal skills and the way they should look in practice. This reflects their core place in the education and training of social workers. In this respect – and it is a major one – social work training already prepares practitioners for care management. This, furthermore, should not be lightly dismissed. Training in interpersonal skills seems to be a complex process. One study has demonstrated that the theory, operationalisation and practice of interpersonal skills by social workers stood out by comparison with community psychiatric nurses, a group who are themselves subject to a minimum three year training in an area closely related to social work (Sheppard, 1991).

The skills are founded, by general consent, on two key element in the social work process, the importance of the relationship and of communication. Hence, Haines (1981, p 130) comments that 'skills in relationships permeate the whole of social work practice, and are one of the essential attributes of the social worker'. Likewise social work authors have traditionally emphasised the central importance of good communication in the social work process (Compton and Galloway, 1979; Brown, 1973). The operationalisation of interpersonal skills can be divided into two loose groups, which, while possessing a certain degree of distinctiveness, in practice merge into each other at the margins. These are, first, relationship qualities which are an attribute of the person, an element of their essential 'humanness'. These include empathy, genuineness, authenticity and so on. Second they are expert skills, which are knowledge based: therapeutic skills, provider of information and advice and so on. These are loose divisions, and it should be remembered that expert skills require human qualities and relationship qualities, if manifested competently, require considerable skill. The classification of these skills is, in effect, a classification of reflexive actions available to the practitioner. Of course, they may be undertaken appropriately or inappropriately, well or badly, but they are, when performed well, central aspects of the reflexive process in practice.

RELATIONSHIP QUALITIES

Commitment, care and concern for others is extensively discussed in social work. It involves 'a sincere interest in the client and his predicament' (Kadushin, 1983, p 56), that one cares about the person's hurt and the consequences of their behaviour, whether for themselves or others (Perlman, 1979). It involves support and a sense of obligation: an awareness by the consumer that the practitioner will not give up on them, or desert them because of some disappointment (Keith Lucas, 1972). Care and concern can obviously occur in normal social circumstances, but according to Haines (1981) , they can become high level skills. Pippin (1980) believes they are largely transmitted non verbally: the tone of voice, the facial expression, gestures used, body posture and so on.

Acceptance, and its associated value of being non judgemental is a core relationship quality widely examined in social work

(Kadushin, 1983; Pippin, 1980). It involves respect, concern and a belief in the individual worth of human beings. It leaves the relationship non blaming and non censorious, according to Perlman (1979), that 'I accept you but not (necessarily) your acts'. It implies commitment to the consumer on the part of the worker: although the practitioner may disapprove of the consumer's behaviour, the relationship will continue as far as the practitioner is concerned (Moffett, 1968).

Empathy, listening and individualising are another closely related cluster of qualities. Empathy is perhaps the most widely discussed element. Empathy is presented in a range of similar ways: it is imaginatively understanding, or getting on the same wavelength, as others (Haines 1981); it is putting one's self in another's shoes (Biestek, 1957); it is 'controlled emotional involvement' (Compton and Galloway, 1979). It involves an intuitive dimension (Jordan, 1979), but also a cognitive element through which we are able to get a mental representation of others (Collins and Collins, 1981). However, it is not enough to understand; that understanding must be accurate and it must be conveyed so that the consumer *knows* the practitioner understands (Epstein, 1985).

Listening is a prerequisite to accurate empathy. Listening is not a passive activity: it is an active search for meaning and an active understanding of the consumer's communication (Compton and Galloway, 1979). It is, in England's (1986, p 23) words to 'listen and know what I mean'. It also has a positive element: encouraging the consumer to express themselves. Individualisation is also closely related to empathy: to empathise is to do so with an individual who has unique qualities (Kadushin, 1983) . It involves recognising the individual as the possessor of a personal biography, involving a past, a present and future actions, the perceptions of which contribute to personal identity (Ragg, 1977).

A fourth set of relationship qualities are authenticity, genuineness and openness. Authenticity requires the practitioner to be real and human in the interview, implying spontaneity and the willingness to share one's own feelings and reactions. Authenticity involves being open and honest about the reality of the practitioner's position: that the practitioner's powers and limitations are stated where appropriate (Kadushin, 1983, p 65). Authenticity and openness, therefore, involve being authentic as a professional and not just a private person. However, it is the synthesis of the personal and the professional which is significant. The practitioner should not pretend that they are a friend and only a friend, because they are not. Equally they should not take on an 'air of professionalism' involving a guardedness and loss of spontaneity (Pippin, 1980). This is only possible with a high degree of self understanding: as Perlman (1979) states it involves being:

> ...free of pretension...to have a sense of wholeness...of knowing who and what one is, what one's guiding values are...being on fairly good terms with oneself.

EXPERT SKILLS

One cluster of expert skills is the provision of information, advice and social skills education. Anderson (1988) considers the provision of information to be ubiquitous in social work practice. Middleman and Goldberg (1974) consider it may occur at all points in the social work process and can cover a wide range of activities: facts, opinions, increasing knowledge of situations and events. Advice is closely related. It may relate to practical issues, enabling the consumer to carry out tasks or go beyond this to emotional issues. Hence Haines (1981) considers advice to be about the best way to achieve an object or interpersonal advice about a particular approach to resolving difficulties. Education in social skills of everyday life are concerned with learning how to live, with learning how to plan for the future where appropriate to consumer needs. As Germain and Gitterman (1980) comment (p 53):

> The social worker carries out the function of teaching adaptive skills through clarifying perceptions...offering advice and suggestions...modelling desired behaviour, and teaching the steps of problem solving.

Therapeutic skills are a group broadly designed to develop insight in consumers and to release feelings which enable them to function better. They may be divided into three. Clarification skills involve a process whereby the consumer is able to reorder their thinking about themselves and their situation (Haines, 1981). They can involve elaboration: where client's presentation of their situation is fragmentary and which focus questions to help consumers elaborate and clarify specific concerns. They can involve also putting consumer's (dimly appreciated) feelings into words, which according to Shulman 'gives permission' to the consumer to discuss their own feelings about themselves (Shulman, 1984).

Promotion of self understanding is a second therapeutic skill. This is about insight development, considered an essential part of 'emotional health'. Siporin (1975, p 299) considers it not simply to be an enhancement of understanding, but it should help him/her to change, thus helping them 'to discover and actualise their creative powers, to realise [their] capacities for personal change and growth'. A third group of therapeutic skills may be broadly described as enabling skills. These are designed to help the consumer to become better able to manage their life and their problems. It involves a release of feelings which clients should feel safe and free to express (Hollis, 1970) . Sustainment or encouragement are also enabling skills are designed to support, reassure and help individuals feel better about themselves. Confrontation or challenge may occur where information is skewed or contradictory (as, for example, between verbal and non verbal information). Challenge can help remove obstacles to work by preventing discussion of necessary concerns (Anderson, 1988)

A third group of expert skills are those most directly reflecting care management and involve the process of intervention. These may be broadly termed analytic processes, which refers to the step by step process of rational analysis. These steps generally involve assessment, planning and goal setting, intervention tasks and ending and evaluation. It demands the maximum degree of collaboration and mutual understanding between consumer and practitioner. It is most closely associated with Task Centred practice (Reid, 1978). This is so closely reflected in the care management process that discussion need not detain us here.

THE DRIFT INTO THERAPY

Official literature on care management is not entirely clear about why interpersonal skills are required, just that they are. They seem, implicitly at least, to be important because they provide – metaphorically – the oil which lubricates the engine of the care management process through which needs may be met. Interpersonal skills are important because without them the care manager would be less effective in encouraging the consumer, in discovering what they want, in communicating with them and so on.

231

However, there is another dimension to interpersonal skills – that is that they may be therapeutic in themselves. When initially used for care management purposes, interpersonal skills may blend imperceptibly at their margins into counselling and psychotherapy. The relationship may be of major importance *itself* in achieving change. However, psychotherapy and counselling are, of themselves, provider tasks. It is perfectly consistent with care management that the care manager should purchase the services of a therapist. Indeed, the purchaser-provider split suggests this should be the case. However, the reality of practice is such that there is a constant potential when conducting interpersonal skills for care management purposes for a drift in (and possibly out) of therapeutic relationships. This is unsurprising given the close relationship between interpersonal skills and psychotherapy and the centrality of the relationship to therapeutic work. Care management also requires a relationship.

This is most apparent in the work of Rogers (1951). His client centred approach, which has exercised considerable influence on social work, testifies to the all important position of the relationship. Consumers with problems are often trying to make active sense of their experiences. The central task of the practitioner is to establish a climate of trust and warmth – agape if you like – in which the consumer feels safe and is able to face up to the consequences of his or her actions or make difficult decisions about their future. This environment is fundamentally enabling. It helps them either to recover true control of their lives (where they have found facing up to life's problems to be very hard) or to make difficult decisions (such as whether or not to enter a residential home for the elderly) which have major implications for their future lives.

This is not itself straightforward. The practitioner has to attempt to understand the consumer's meanings, the way they view their world and the feelings they have about it. Subjective states need to be open and shared. This process requires careful and sensitive listening and responses which demonstrate to the consumer that the practitioner has listened and understood. These qualities are key elements of interpersonal skills, and hence, when practice is conducted competently are necessarily incorporated into the care management process. However, where the impact of the relationship is so pervasive, interpersonal skills have something of an internal dynamic where the boundaries between care management and out and out therapy are likely to be crossed. Where, furthermore, the relationship is of such importance, it may, at times be difficult to see how care managers who may, in the care management process, have developed a good relationship and begun the therapeutic process, are acting in the consumer' best interests by then purchasing a therapist to continue (or more likely recommence) this process. Indeed, the consumer's first choice may well be for the care manager to continue the therapeutic process. There is, then an implicit tension between the institutional atrophy of the care management and provision distinction, and the overt claim made for care management that it increases consumer choice.

This is evident, unsurprisingly, from practice, as well as a logical consequence, in theory, of the relationship. This is well illustrated by Fisher (1991). The social work in partnership study found that where care management operates social workers fight to retain the casework model of the relationship as the major vehicle of therapeutic impact on the client. In the United States early guides to case management clearly saw it as an extension of social work counselling. O'Connor (1988) claimed that case management was a 'general form of social casework' and 'one of social work's core technologies'.

However, this observation calls into question the ease with which care management and provision may be divided and separated. Some local authorities have created an institutional division between care management and provision by the creation of teams whose specific purpose is one or the other. This is further encouraged by an expectation – in adult services at least – that the provider sector should be 'floated off' and provider work overwhelmingly undertaken by voluntary and private enterprise rather than by the public sector through local authority employees. Yet it is local authority employees who will be care managers. What begins as essentially an *intellectual* distinction between the care management and provider tasks, appears to be atrophying into an organisational distinction which is in some tension with the reality of social care.

CONCLUSION

Interpersonal skills are clearly an aspect of the overall reflexive approach of the practitioner. By providing a commitment to the use of interpersonal skills, official documents are, in effect, making a commitment to reflexivity, in at least one aspect of practice. This is a significant commitment, since whatever stage in the care management process is being undertaken, it is expected that interpersonal skills should be appropriately used. They are expected to be a more or less ever present aspect of practice when it is conducted competently.

The commitment, in official documents, to interpersonal skills as an aspect of the care management process makes a great deal of sense when examined in some detail. However, the attempt to restrict the role of interpersonal skills to that of facilitating the care management process is problematic in view of a 'natural dynamic' towards a therapeutic process. The division between care management and care provision entails an unduly restrictive role for interpersonal skills which will, if adhered to, almost inevitably lead to an arbitrary division of labour. This may neither correspond with the consumer's wishes nor their best interests.

Interpersonal skills form a core element of social work training. Such evidence as exists suggests that they are not easy to acquire nor are they easily manifested in practice (Sheppard, 1992; 1993). If government agencies are serious about the importance of interpersonal skill in the care management process then training for care management would need to emphasise training in, and possession of, interpersonal skills at least as great as that evident from current social work training and practice. We should not assume that such skills are universally available or even available in other welfare or health professions. Such evidence as exists suggests that social workers possess these skills to a greater extent than, for example, community psychiatric nurses (Sheppard, 1991). Social work training in this respect – and it is an important one – is therefore a prerequisite to competent care management.

Chapter Twelve

The assessment and use of social support

It is arguable that all aspects of the care management process are in some way connected with the provision of social support. An individual may receive the help of a family aide, of domiciliary support, day care, residential care, help with playgroup fees or an introduction to a support group. Assessment is undertaken in order to identify which supports are required to match the needs of the consumer concerned. Even where, in the end, for whatever reason, they do not receive support, consideration is given about the possible supports available or required.

The reason for this is fairly straightforward. The terms social support is itself a ubiquitous concept It provides a generic term capable of subsuming all aspects of that which the care management process provides. It has, however, a wider importance in social work. Social support, social networks and support networks are terms which have been used interchangeably with the specific purpose of transcending social work's more traditional therapeutic concerns for their clients. As Garbarino (1983) pointed out, in North America (and Britain too) practitioners have typically seen the solution to social problems in terms of dyads, or at most the nuclear family, and 'cures' have been sought through individual rehabilitation and therapy. Social support, or social networks, have been presented as a way of helping clients without relying primarily on the direct actions of the individual practitioner and therapist, but rather by utilising the resources which may reside in the community. However, social support may be provided by individuals as well as in group contexts.

It is this which makes this form of practice of particular relevance to care management. The central concern of care management with need, and of the management of resources (human and material) to alleviate that need, means that care managers are legitimately concerned with a wide range of potential providers. The term 'manager' has quite clear implications: the practitioner is a manager of resources. It is not the care manager alone who provides the help the consumer needs; indeed, given the split between management and provision, it may be inappropriate that the care manager provides directly any help (we should, of course take on board the qualifications to this offered in the previous chapter). The resources are significant to the extent that they are able to alleviate identified need. Social support provides us with a way of bringing together, conceptually, the range of services provided and a focus for that which it is the care manger's concern to manage. It is, in a sense, the flip side of need. The care manager assesses and identifies need; it is her responsibility then to provide support the purpose of which is to alleviate that need.

HUMAN CHARACTERISTICS: PEOPLE AS SOCIAL BEINGS

The importance of rooting practice in social systems, networks and supports, reflects the notion of humans as social beings and is predicated broadly, on three dimensions of human characteristics. The first is a need for attachment or affiliation. Attachment is an emotional bond between two or more people lasting over time and may occur in adult-adult as well as parent-child relationships. Attachment theory indicates that the binding of individuals together arises through biological determination (Hinde, 1982). It is considered innate, and linked to species evolution, arising, according to Henderson (1977) because of preferential selection for the capacity for human bonds because this would facilitate group survival. Two types of attachment, or social bond, have generally been identified. Attachments can occur between two people, and are evident according to Weiss, in close dyadic relationships. They are particularly strong emotional bonds. Affiliation, a second form of social bond, is less intense, but involves shared interests which provide for mutual loyalty and a sense of community. This is characteristic of friendships and other consistent 'non partner' relationships (Weiss, 1974, 1978; Bee and Mitchell, 1984).

A second dimension of group cohesion relates to the concept of social integration. Durkheim emphasised the importance of shared expectations or norms in preventing a sense of individual futility and meaninglessness - of 'knowing one's place' (Durkheim, 1897, 1947; Wright Mills, 1960). Anomie develops where poor integration exists. Anomie can be a state characterising the group or an individual characteristic. Anomie develops where poor social integration exists. At an individual level this refers to a state of futility and meaninglessness associated with normlessness: a psychological state, anomia. Srole (1976) conceptualised anomia as a continuum of 'self to other belongingness' and 'self to other distance' or 'self to other alienation'. McIver (1950) similarly identifies it as the breakdown of an individual's attachment to society and Laswell (1952) characterises it as a state of feeling alone, cut off, unwanted unloved and undervalued. McClosky and Schaar (1965) suggest the core concept is a feeling of moral emptiness, while Meir and Bell (1959) suggest this includes despair, hopelessness, discouragement, demoralisation. Poor social integration has consequences. In anomia we have its psychic correlate.

A third dimension relates to an individuals sense of control over their life. This is often discussed in terms of 'locus of control' (Rotter, 1966). An internal locus of control refers to a perception of events being a consequence of one's own actions and thereby potentially under personal control. Alternatively, an external locus of control refers to the perception of events as being unrelated to one's own behaviour. It is, then, about a feeling of being in control and able to direct the course of one's own life. This can, of course, be an entirely realistic assessment. Some disadvantaged groups experience lack of control of their lives, and their fatalistic external control beliefs match the reality of their situation (Lefcourt et al, 1984).

These three concepts - attachment, integration and control locus - clearly do not provide a comprehensive theoretical basis for understanding humans' social nature. However, they are key human characteristics assumed in an emphasis on systems analysis, social networks and supports. They help make sense of much of the literature. Systems analysis stresses the importance of an individual's place in relation to others, and the interactions between self and others. Social network analysis emphasises aspects of social integration (through number of network members, frequency of interaction etc). Social support emphasises the importance of emotional support, which may be related to attachment and affiliation. It also emphasises the importance of practical support, such as helping parents with childcare, or lending financial help when individuals are in debt. Such circumstances are consistent with being (and feeling) out of control of one's situation.

Systems Analysis

Systems analysis, was initially developed by Von Bertalanffy as a means for conducting the study of biology but was increasingly presented as a General Theory which would have application to a variety of fields of study, including the social sciences and social work. Its purpose was to develop broad, overarching concepts applicable to all fields (Lilienfield, 1975). In social work the main interest in systems analysis developed in the 1970s. The terms 'systems theory', 'systems analysis' and 'systems models' are variously used in relation to this approach. However, as Roberts (1981) points out, it does not provide explanations of situations and hence has little prescriptive capacity. It primarily provides a framework for examining complex situations. It appears, therefore, that systems analysis is the most helpful term for describing this approach.

Various definitions of a system have been presented. Von Bertalanffy (1973) considers it a 'set of units with relationships among them', while Buckley (1968 p xvii) identified three further definitions: 'a totality of elements in interaction', the dynamic interrelatedness of components' or 'a whole which functions as a whole by virtue of the interdependence of its parts'. In the kind of analysis relevant for social work, a family would be a system, the components of which are the individual family members. The family itself is part of a wider system, the local community, where individuals and families have some relationship with each other. Within the local community, schools would constitute systems, and these systems would have a relationship with the family systems where a member of the family is a pupil at the school. Indeed, each individual may, themselves be considered a (biological) system. Systems analysis, therefore, is concerned with the relationships between these components.

Part of the difficulty of systems analysis is its use of obscure language and its confusion of analogy with reality. Thus, for example, society is seen as an organism (rather than *like* an organism) and there is a notion that the relationship between the components of a system involves the transfer of energy or matter from one component to another. For social work, there are a number of key dimensions to systems analysis (see Davies, 1977; Pincus and Minahen, 1973):

- The first is that social workers are dealing with 'open systems'. An open system is a system in exchange of matter with its environment, importing and exporting energy, building up and breaking down its component parts (Von Bertalanffy, L. (1973). Hence we cannot isolate an individual from the various effects of interaction with his social environment, upon which he, in turn, will act and interact.
- The notion of input, or importation of energy, is also important. Individuals receive inputs from various sources, such as stimulation from education and socialisation agents.
- Output, a third important concept, is, in an open system, energy of any kind generated from within the system as a result of the system's reaction to energy input. The energy output may in turn constitute potential energy inputs for other systems. In the welfare sector this is complex because many of the input-output relationships are indirect. Some recipients of aid, for example, can offer only the fact of their survival or gratitude as outputs in exchange for inputs.
- Feedback is the response of the initiating system to the response of the system upon whom the action was originally initiated. For example, a consumer may request help because of disability. The practitioner may make a particular suggestion (such as home care) and request that the consumer tell them the extent to which this alleviates their need.

This is not a comprehensive list of concepts, but gives a clear indication of the social interactive emphasis of systems analysis. As Davies (1977) points out, one of the main attractions of systems analysis is its apparent recognition of the confused realities of social life and its willingness to incorporate essentially unpredictable elements. This is not inconsistent with care management, which allows for the review and evaluation of the effects of particular courses of action, which may not in the first instant have been entirely predictable. However, it does so in a way which allows wider social consideration beyond the person to be taken into account.

Social Network and Social Support

Social network develops the ideas of systems analysis in a way more directly applicable to social phenomena. According to Scott (1991, p 2) social networks are about relations. These are the 'contacts ties and connections, the group attachments and meetings which relate one agent to another, and so cannot be reduced to the properties of the individual themselves'. The study of social networks has a long sociological tradition. Much of the work originated in the thirties and forties in Chicago and Harvard. Warner was particularly influential. He emphasised the stability, cohesion and integration fostered by social networks in communities. He identified two forms of social configuration: relatively stable social institutions such as the family, the church, classes and associations; and community subgroups he called cliques (Warner and Lunt, 1941). These were (non-kin) informal associations of people among whom there was a degree of group feeling and intimacy and in which group norms have been established. These would be referred to by members as 'our crowd', 'our circle'. Warner argued that people were integrated into communities by informal and personal relations of family and clique membership, not simply through the formal relations of the economic and political system.

Homans (1951) centred his interests around the interaction of these group members with each other. The internal structure of the group was presented as a system with interactions which varied in their frequency, duration and direction. He set up various hypotheses about the internal system: such as those who interact frequently with each other will tend to like each other and that, as the frequency of their interaction increases, so the degree of their liking for each other will increase.

Work by Barnes and Mitchell extended further this understanding of internal network structure. Barnes (1954) distinguished informal networks - the informal sphere of interpersonal relations - from the total network of the whole of social life. The former was a 'partial network' of this 'total network'. Mitchell (1969) called this sphere of interpersonal relations the personal order: the pattern of links individuals have with a set of people and the links these people have in turn among themselves. Mitchell presented a number of concepts through which this structure of interpersonal relations can be examined:

- Relations could be distinguished by their reciprocity: the extent to which the transaction or orientation from one person to another is reciprocated. Person A may consider person B a friend. If person B considers person A a friend there is reciprocity, if not it is unreciprocated.
- Durability is a measure of how enduring the relationship is: from the transient relationship of a single interaction to the enduring one often associated with kinship.
- Intensity refers to the strength of obligations involved in a relationship.
- Density refers to the completeness of a network, the extent to which all members of an individual network have a relationship with each other.
- Finally reachability refers to how easy it is for all people to contact one another through a limited number of steps.

These concepts allow the identification of the structure of social relations, where systems concepts allow the identification of the processes through which interaction may occur and provides a situational base on which to locate an individual.

Social support provides a further dimension to our understanding of an individual's social location. Pierce et al (1990) define support as social transactions which facilitate coping in everyday life and which are perceived as such by the recipients. In Weiss's (1974) terms it involves provisions of social relationships. Social support, therefore, is a provision arising from the social system or social network of an individual.

Its utility is identified in diverse findings. It is reported as a buffer against work stress (House, 1981; Marcelesson et al, 1988), heart disease and cancer (Waltz et al, 1988; Funch and Mettlin, 1982), it reduces pregnancy complications (Nuckols et al, 1972; Norbeck and Tildon, 1983), and mental illness or psychological distress in general (Miller and Ingham, 1976).

This generally accepted relationship between social support and health and social functioning is not entirely straightforward. It is important to separate structural properties (presented above as social network) from functional properties (what that network provides) (Cohen and Syme, 1985). It is, furthermore, unclear whether social support has a direct effect (the absence of social support is associated with, for example, poor health) or a buffering effect, preventing deterioration in the face of life stress (Henderson, 1984). It may be both. Others emphasise the importance of meaning, or cognitive appraisal, in the effectiveness of social support. It depends on how the subject interprets actions (is this a helpful act or the work of an interfering busybody?) as to whether the actions may be considered supportive (Pierce et al, 1990; Wilcox and Vernberg, 1985) Finally, the way in which social support affects different conditions, such as work stress, mental illness and heart conditions, may vary (Sheppard, 1993).

All these are potentially significant issues and point to the relevance of precise research findings on these conditions to practice in these particular areas. It remains the case, however, given its wide significance, that social support provides an important dimension for situational assessment and intervention in care management.

PRACTICE

Systems analysis, social network and social support, although not covering exactly the same ground, are nonetheless closely related, and, indeed, complement each other. All three focus on what might broadly be called the individual's social environment and hence transcend the focus purely directed on to the individual. This is most clearly stated for practice in relation to systems analysis. The focus could remain on *individuals* (in a group context if appropriate) but the process of analysis and intervention would not be *individualistic* (Garbarino, 1983). Meyer (1973) argued that the anchor concept was still person-in-situation (hence consistent with care management). However, the systems framework provided the conceptual tools to make real the use of both sides of the hyphens instead of concentrating primarily on the person.

The same may be said for social network and social support. The complementary nature of these approaches is evident in the emphasis placed on each. Systems analysis is concerned centrally with processes; how energy (metaphorically) passes from one agent or group to another. Social network is concerned with structure; the positioning of different network members in relation to each other. Social support is concerned with function; that is what it is that the network, or its individual members, do for each other.

An ecological perspective goes some way to bringing these together. Germain's (1979) classification of the social environment distinguishes three layers of social organisation. The most immediate is the social network of family friends, neighbours and workmates. It includes natural helper, mutual aid systems and self help groups. Beyond this lies the layer of organisations and institutions designed to provide services and resources such as systems of welfare, education and housing. Further still lies the societal layer which includes the cultural value system, political and economic structure, law, statutes and policies. This third area is, as has been demonstrated, beyond the remit of social worker *qua* care manager. The other two approximate to a distinction, used in social support literature, between formal and informal social support. Informal support is that provided by natural support providers, such as friends and relatives. Formal supports are those arising from organised groups and institutions: these include the health and welfare organisations and their personnel, voluntary organisations and voluntary helpers attached to these organisations. This distinction helps focus intervention in a direction which takes account of the social environment

SYSTEMS AND NETWORKS

Social network concepts provide means both for the analysis (assessment) and intervention in the consumer's social environment. Network analysis helps place the consumer in their social situation and indicates their degree of social integration (Seed, 1990). In this respect, it can indicate the degree of stability in their social relations, their degree of isolation or involvement with others and the extent to which, in principle, others are available for social contact. These can be formally analysed by listing the individuals in the consumer's social network and examining in relation to each, the strength of ties. The size of the social network is indicated by the number of network members. The durability of each relationship can be indicated by the amount of time the consumer has known each network member. The intensity of the relationship can be indicated by the strength of feeling the consumer has for each network member (are they an acquaintance, friend, relative or lover?) and its reciprocity, by the extent to which this feeling is reciprocated. Reachability can be indicated by geographical proximity or frequency of contacts.

These concepts provide a rigorous means for establishing the place of the consumer in the (informal) social environment. It indicates the solidity of the network and strength of ties, both of which frequently provide an invaluable backdrop to understanding the nature of consumer needs and the intervention that may take place. Where, to take a simple example, a single parent suffering depression has some quite durable relationships characterised by considerable intensity we might expect the network to be of considerable help. However, reachability might be a problem. These relations may be kin relations: the consumer may live in Southampton and the kin live in York. The two alternatives available would seem to emphasise either making these relations more reachable (by for example moving to York) or to develop new relationships which will fit the bill. There appears, therefore, two types of questions arising from network analysis: what are the characteristics of the consumer's network? and to what extent is this satisfactory for the consumer? These questions may be asked in relation to each of the main dimensions: size, durability, intensity, reciprocity, density and reachability .

Diagrammatic representations of the consumer's social situation, which includes formal as well as informal relations is provided by ecomaps (Anderson, 1988; Hartman, 1979; Hartman and Laird, 1983). In the jargon of the ecological perspective, an ecomap 'is a drawing that diagrammatically depicts the person's ecological context and the boundaries of his or her life space'. At the centre is Ego (the consumer) and his relationship to others is depicted via a series of 'coded' lines.

Links between the consumer and individuals and institutions in his or her social environment can be shown diagrammatically as follows.

```
_____Strong link of needs and resources
-------------------------Tenuous or weak link
-------------------------->One directional
< ---------------------->Two directional
------------ • ------------Blocked
-----------✗ -----------Destructive/stressful.
```

This might be of a single adult referred to social services. The following diagram excludes, for convenience, the nuclear family although the same diagrammatic representations may be used for its members. A consumer may have a respiratory problem, and be referred for a needs assessment. The care manager may be concerned to establish what is currently available to them. This ecomap shows strong links of needs and resources to the welfare system, which is however unidirectional (from welfare to the consumer). It shows a tenuous link with health services (which may be because the consumer has poor relations with their family doctor). Links are blocked to work, destructive or stressful with

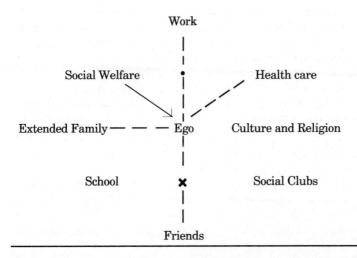

friends, tenuous with the extended family and non existent with social clubs, culture or religion and school (the latter because they have no children and do not attend). This is a picture of a socially isolated adult with poor relations with friends, no other informal outlet and a degree of reliance on the welfare system. This representation gives a clear indication, where social isolation is a consideration, of the areas upon which the social worker may focus to reduce this isolation: repairing the friendship relationships, linking the consumer with social clubs, and, if appropriate religious or cultural activities. It provides a clear way of linking client needs with their specific social circumstances. Most important it shows the need to improve links with health care services, by, perhaps, liaising with the doctor or changing to another doctor.

Pincus and Minahan (1973) classify the key element for intervention using a systems approach. They distinguish four systems upon which intervention may be built: client (consumer) system, change agent system, target system and action system. The client system is the individual, family or group seeking help, in this case the individual consumer. The change agent system is the system facilitating change: in this case the care manager and social services department. The target system are the people or organisation from whom change is sought by the change agent. Here, the care manager would be targeting the relevant medical practitioners, friends social clubs and so on. The action system are people with whom the change agent seeks to work to achieve the aims. The care manager may seek to work, for example with the family practitioners committee to find a new doctor or social club committees in order to obtain membership.

It is possible, furthermore, to classify strategies focusing on the social environment, rather then the individual consumer. Froland et al (1981) identifies a number of strategies of which four are consistent with the nature and limits of care management.

• Personal network strategy: here care managers consult, support and assist the informal helping efforts of family friends and neighbours of the consumer.
• Volunteer link strategy: involves matching lay helpers and consumers where existing sources of social support are limited.
• Mutual aid strategy: involves bringing together individuals with common problems for the purpose of sharing resources and reducing social isolation.
• Neighbourhood helping strategy: involves consulting with natural helpers - ie those already informally helping - to support those patterns of help, and if possible, avoid the need for formal professional services.

All this is fairly straightforward, and designed to show how systems and network analysis and intervention can provide a theoretical basis for practice. It can do so in more complex circumstances, and allows the practitioner to focus on formal and informal systems of care. This is important for two reasons. First, it provides a systematic means for examining the whole range of potential support systems in the community. It does not limit the care manager to existing welfare resources. In so doing it aids a more imaginative response to consumer need. Second, it provides a means by which formal and informal systems may be integrated to provide a total package of care. In order to maintain an elderly disabled person in the community it may be possible to link formal systems (home care, day care) with informal support (neighbours and family). Finally, where care managers possess a limited budget, it provides a means for maximising resource use in meeting need.

SOCIAL SUPPORT: LINKING RESOURCES TO NEEDS

A central element in care management is the requirement that resources be linked to needs. That is, where care managers are concerned with needs led assessments, those needs should determine, or at least significantly influence, the choice of resources. That which the consumer receives should not arise through a 'mind set' limited to existing resources. However, matters, even at this general level, are not that simple. The existence of a particular need does not dictate the most appropriate resource requirement. A simple example might be where a single mother, clinically depressed, is finding it hard (perfectly understandably) to cope with young children. A decision might be made to provide relief care, which might be provided by a nursery, childminder or friend or relative. The need is the same, but the resource response is different. These alternatives are presented in relation to one area of need. As the number of defined needs and range of resources required increases, so choice of resources - the package of care - becomes more complex. Different packages may fit the bill.

Clearly there is an intermediate dimension, between needs and resources, which links the two and help determine the choice of most appropriate resources. This is the area of social support. In our example, the need is the same, and each of the alternatives have a common characteristic: the capacity to provide practical support and care for the children. This is a form of social support. Hence, a proper care management assessment is at least a three stage process: assessment of needs, identification of support requirement to alleviate that need, and identification of resources which might provide that support. Social support, therefore, is not simply a concept which incorporates the consumer's wider social circumstances into assessment and intervention, it is a crucial variable in clear care management assessments.

Beyond the approaches of systems and network analysis, social support provides a linking concept between needs and resources which both allows needs to be linked with resources and for this to be done imaginatively. Any care management assessment requires the following:

- Identification of consumer needs.
- Identification of supports required to alleviate those needs.
- Identification of the types of support provided by available resources, formal and informal.
- Determination of whether supports required are provided by available resources.
- What supports are not provided by available resources, and

what kinds of resources should be developed to provide that support.

Identification of whether the resources on offer are adequate to meet need, and hence which new resources should be developed to meet need (both on an individual case basis and a community wide basis) requires, therefore, a clear understanding of what is on offer from resources, and this is the type of support available. Second, in order to be clear about the support available, a clear typology of the range of support should be developed. Hence, a proper needs led assessment requires a clear statement of types of support as well as types of need.

The main dimensions of social support, through which a taxonomy of support can be developed, are usefully presented by Vieil (1985). Vieil developed a framework over two dimensions, type of support and relational context. Type of support is broadly divided into two. The first area, psychological support, comprises transactions aimed at changing 'intra psychic parameters' such as mood, attitude and cognitive processing. Within this emotional support may be distinguished from the more cognitive aspects of psychological support. Thus coping with stress may be undertaken by some form of cognitive work to change perceptions, or through emotional support which helps lift mood, or cope better with that mood.

Instrumental support involves transactions designed to help the individual's overt performance directly. This may be further divided into practical support and informational support. The former is the provision of direct practical help, such as helping a disabled person with their shopping. Informational support is the provision of information which will help in relation to a particular task, such as providing information on DSS benefits enabling the person to obtain extra financial support. The second dimension is relational context: the role relationship between the supporter and provider of support. Informal supports are natural support providers, such as relatives, friends and workmates. The second source of supports is formal support providers, institutional, professional or voluntary providers whose purpose is the provision of support. These include social workers, doctors, nurses or voluntary befrienders.

It is important that a practical as well as conceptual, distinction is made between these two dimensions. It is the distinction between the kind of support offered or given and who, or what, it is that is providing the support. To state that an individual requires a family aide is not to state what it is that the family aide is offering that is relevant to this particular case. We can only know this precisely if we identify the type of support on offer from the family aide. Furthermore, the family aide may offer certain types of support, but might this be provided better from other sources, such as family centre workers? Without clearly indicating need in any particular case, and once need is identified, the supports required and the support on offer we are unable to link needs to resources or choose the best alternative between a range of resources.

Systematic analysis of resource requirements and resource provision requires, in the first instance the examination of a number of elements. These are consumer need, supports required (whether psychological or instrumental) to alleviate that need, facilities (formal or informal) which may provide this support and supports required which are not otherwise available and the kinds of resources which might provide this support. This can be set up through a form, in the light of a case example. A woman with three children, aged 2, 3 and 6, assessed as depressed, is having problems coping with the children. The six year old has behavioural problems, and in general she feels she is unable to care for them. She has a poor relationship with her spouse, who takes little part in the child care. She has very little confidence, considers herself a poor mother and has little hope that her relationship will improve or that she is capable of being a better mother. Her poor confidence has also led to a reduction in contact with, and reliance on, relatives and friends. This is reinforced by her spouse who accuses her of being a poor mother. This might be assessed as shown on the following pages (pp 250-251).

This schedule sets out systematically and clearly the fairly complex issues involved in making a systematic and clear care management assessment. It is complex because it requires clear delineation of the nature of the need(s), precise identification of the supports required, and a clear indication of how the resources used fit those need and support requirements. It is also clear that more than one care package might provide the resources and supports required in relation to the consumer's need. For example, it is possible to respond to all need requirements by the use of the two alternatives following:

- Specialist mental health worker, family centre, child care social worker, care manager, spouse, and voluntary car.

NEEDS LED ASSESSMENT
Incorporating social support.

NEEDS OR PROBLEMS.
(a)   Six year old' behavioural problems.
(b)   Marital difficulties/conflict with husband.
(c)   Destructive/esteem reducing comments by husband.
(d)   Poor child development.
(e)   A sense of generalised hopelessness./low confidence.
(f)   Difficulty in caring and controlling children

SUPPORTS REQUIRED
Support type corresponding to need area: Need:

Psychological:
(1)   A change of 'cognitive set' aiming to alter
      her sense of powerlessness and low confidence   (e)
(2)   A change of 'cognitive set' in the partner so that he
      stops the destructive comments reducing her confidence (b) (c)
(3)   A change in role assumptions, from one characterised
      by traditional role stereotyping to one involving
      sharing child care tasks and responsibilities.   (b) (c)
(4)   Development of problem solving or task
      achieving abilities in relation to child care.   (a) (f)

Emotional:
(5)   Esteem supporting comments designed to
      emphasise her achievements.   (e) (f)
(6)   Listening to the woman in her expression of distress.   (b) (e) (f)
(7)   Encouragement of the woman when
      attempting to resolve her problems.   (a to f)
(8)   Encouragement of the woman to rely
      more on support of her relatives   (a to f)

Informational:
(9)   Social skills training with child care.   (a) (d) (f)
(10) Information on the nature and origins of depression.   (e)
(11) Information on the range of resources
      available, including social clubs.   (a) (d) (f)
(12) Information on child development,
      including expected milestones.   (d)

Practical:
(13) Caring for children to give the woman a break.   (a) (d) (f)
(14) Behaviour alteration of child
(15) Provision of transport for child care.   (f)

This may not exhaust the range of support requirements, but provides an indication of what might be sought by the social worker.

RESOURCES

Resource: Support provided:

Formal

Resource	Support provided
Family centre	<1-3> (4) (5) <6- 8> (9)
Children home/resource unit	
Fostering	
Child psychology	(12) (15)
Health Visitor	(12)
Child care social worker	(12) (15)
Psychologist	(1) (10)
Specialist mental health worker	(1) (2) (3) (5-10)
Family aide	(4) <5> <6> (9)
Home help	
Relate counsellor/family conciliation	(1) (2) (3) <5-7>
Childminder	(13)
Playgroup	(13)
Care manager	(8) (11) (12)
Taxi, Voluntary car	(14)

Informal

Resource	Support provided
Spouse	(1-3) (5-8) (13)
Parents	(1) <4> (5-8) (13)
Sibs	(1) (5-8) (13)
Friends	(1) <5-8> (13)
Neighbours	<13>

POSSIBLE RESOURCES
Currently unavailable, to meet need (some examples).

Resource	Support provided
Depressed women's group	(1) (3) (5-8) (10)
Parents' child care skills group	(4) (9) (12)
Child guidance	(4-7) (9) (12) (15)
Creative activities workshop for unwaged mothers	<1> (5)

Note
Letters in brackets for each support required correspond to need areas identified in the section on need.
Numbers in brackets or arrows [<>] in the section on resources correspond to support areas identified in section on support.

Numbers in brackets in section on resources represent supports which may be primarily supplied by that resource, should it be used. Numbers in arrows in this section represent supports which may be secondarily provided by that resource, should it be used. For example a change of cognitive set aiming to alter the woman's sense of powerlessness and low self confidence might be primarily supplied by cognitive behavioural therapy. Hence this is indicated as a primary support or task of a psychologist, who has these skills. However, the family centre may also encourage the consumer in this respect without having the cognitive behaviour therapy skills. Their support is secondary because it is not necessary to the meeting of the relevant need and would not be sufficient on its own to meet it.

- Spouse, family aide, psychologist, care manager, child psychologist and taxi.

These are clearly not the only alternatives which are yielded by this example, but it is sufficient to illustrate the case. They enable the care manager clearly to identify the alternative care packages and the way in which each meets need.

Once the alternatives have been clearly identified, it is possible to choose a preferred care package. This would need to take into account two factors: the extent to which each care package is adequate or sufficient to meet identified need and the relative cost of each care package. The fact that a care package contains the resources which will provide the *necessary* support required by consumer need does not mean that this support would be *adequate* or *sufficient*. For example, the use of a psychologist to conduct cognitive behaviour therapy aimed at changing the woman's cognitive set may be necessary, but not quite sufficient to achieve its objective. It may be that enlisting the support of spouse, sibs and parents to reinforce the work of the psychologist is required in order that sufficient support is provided to meet need.

The issue of relative cost of care packages is fairly obvious. Where budgets are limited, it is incumbent on the care manager to make the best use of the money available. It may be, therefore, that they will be unable to opt for the care package which most adequately meets need. Instead they would opt for one which stayed within the available budget.

The care package, therefore should be that which is likely, in the view of the care manager (and consumer) to meet need most effectively within the constraints of the available budget.

All this, of course, is related to assessment and generation of the care package. It is, however, just as relevant for review and evaluation of the care package. Having been precise about the kinds of support which each resource is supplying to meet which particular need, it is possible to examine whether that resource has been adequate in the provision of support to meet that need. If it has not, then it is possible to re-examine the care package, identifying which alternative resources might more effectively meet need.

Systems analysis, social network and social support are closely related concepts and knowledge forms which are clearly highly relevant to the care management process. It is also clear that such assessments operate at a level, according to official guides, appropriate to social work, rather than a community care worker or assistant (Dept. of Health, 1991a). They require knowledge and skills which reflect and develop the knowledge base of social work, and make it highly relevant to the care management process. As such, it represents important competencies which help 'place' social work in the realm of care management.

These approaches are also important for their capacity to link formal and informal systems, network and support in the analysis of the consumer's situation. As a result care management can incorporate both spheres of a consumer's social life in a coherent and consistent care package. Indeed, the use of the concept of social support provides a means for linking needs with resources systematically and clearly, encouraging true needs led assessment. It furthermore allows these to be linked with budget in a manner which recognises the financial constraints inherent in care management. This is significant, furthermore, for a systematic analysis on which to base the care manager's brokering activities. Of course, there remains considerable scope for judgement, as is evident in the processes outlined.

Developing competence, therefore, in the kinds of skills outlined in this chapter, is an absolute requirement of basic social work courses. As such these approaches must be given a considerably higher profile in education and training. Obviously, systems and network analysis have a place on the social work training. However, they are given no greater importance than other approaches, such as crisis intervention and behaviour therapy. Given the fundamental importance of these skills to care management, considerably greater time should be spent in learning these approaches, and the capacity to use these skills should always be tested in practice placement, quite possibly in relation to all cases undertaken.

Chapter Thirteen

Care management and task centred practice

Social work generally tends to assume a variable capacity on the part of consumers for purposeful action. The most obvious limit to this is amongst those suffering severe learning difficulties or mental health problems. For most consumers, their capacity to act to some degree purposefully is part of the way social workers construct them as human beings. Task centred practice, however, *actively seeks* to mobilise and enhance the capacity of consumers to act in a purposeful manner. It is, furthermore, perhaps that area of practice most obviously and clearly related to the process of care management. Indeed, as Fisher (1992) has pointed out care management not only has much in common with task centred practice, but is, to a considerable degree, derived from it. Task centred practice's distinctive similarity to care management arises from the emphasis on precision in problem definition, development of plans, clear delineation of tasks, and review and evaluation of outcome. It is therefore possible for practice to be planned, precise and for outcomes to be clearly measured with this form of practice. These characteristics make training in task centred practice, despite its time limited nature, an excellent grounding for the rigorous conduct of care management.

Task centred practice is furthermore based on a value premise emphasising the primacy of the consumer's expressed request. What the consumer says they want - their conscious wishes - controls the helping effort of the practitioner, not the practitioners view or some other person's assessment of what the consumer needs. This is again consistent with the thrust of care management's proclaimed aims (though we should note the limitations on client self direction outlined earlier).

Task centred practice is form of brief intervention which aspires to develop consumers' problem solving abilities by the performance of tasks designed to alleviate identified and agreed (between consumer and practitioner) problem areas. It has a twofold strategy: to help the consumer alleviate problems that concern them and to provide a constructive problem solving experience that will strengthen their own problem solving capacities. It was developed in the early 1970s (Reid, 1972; Reid and Epstein, 1972). The model incorporated the time limited structural aspects of brief casework (Reid and Shyne, 1969) elements of Perlman's problem solving approach (Perlman, 1957), the concept of consumer tasks (Studt, 1968) and earlier work on the articulation of casework methods (Hollis, 1972). It was based, furthermore, on empirical work which consisted largely of the results of studies of the outcome of short and long term casework, counselling and psychotherapy.

There were three strands to the argument for brief intervention (Reid and Epstein, 1972, p 82-93). First, research on psychotherapy and casework showed most recipients failed to return after a few interviews. The number of interviews rarely exceeded six and few subsequently sought help elsewhere (Garfield, 1971; Fowler, 1967). Although this has sometimes been interpreted as indicating a lack of motivation on the part of the consumer, Reid and Epstein (1972, p 84) suggested that most expected improvements had been achieved in that relatively brief period of time. They supported this contention with further evidence that recipients of briefer intervention showed at least as much improvement and at times a better outcome than recipients of extended intervention (Reid and Shyne, 1969; Schlien, 1966). Studies of longer term intervention, furthermore, provided evidence that, if problems change in a positive direction, the bulk of the improvement comes relatively early in the intervention (Mertzoff and Kornreich, 1970). Reid and Epstein (1972) suggested that this was strong evidence for the efficacy of brief intervention, in view of the fact that the studies concerned contained, collectively, several thousand subjects. They suggested (p 90) that the function of social work involved 'stimulating, quickening and augmenting the kind of processes that naturally characterise problem change'

PURPOSEFUL ACTS AND TASK CENTRED PRACTICE

Underlying task centred practice are certain key assumptions about humans and their capacities. Task centred practice emphasises humans' capacities for self directed, purposeful and goal oriented actions, which is consistent in certain respects with the tradition outlined in the examination of interpersonal skills. The issues of intent and motive for actions emerge in this context. Hart and Honore (1985) point out that an action is intentional when it is purposeful and carried out by human agency. In this respect, the action is voluntary, that is the person is deemed to be the perpetrator of the action, rather than some outside causal factor. The person aims to bring about some particular end result in a certain manner: this is the essence of voluntary action.

Motivation, like intention provides the basis for understanding an action as voluntary. Weber (1947, p 98) defined a motive as a complex of subjective meanings which seem to the actor, or to the observer, to be an adequate ground for the conduct in question. The action is rational when a person's conduct involves the choice of the most effective means for the attainment of some particular end or objective. In his definition of motive, Weber refers to the idea of an agent regarding something as an adequate ground for the action in question. This indicates a significant element in many everyday explanations: the giving of reasons or grounds for what someone does: for example 'my reason for walking to work is that I think walking improves my blood circulation'. The general form of these explanations is 'my reason for doing Y was R', where R is some goal or other. In this respect, actions including intent and motivation (provided they are rational) are goal directed.

This goal directed nature of human action is not just central to task centred practice, but represents a major element of the conduct of human action in everyday life. In this respect, therefore, task centred practice is 'tapping in' to a central human capacity. Goal setting is central to the regulation of our activities in everyday life: self controlled behaviour is achieved in the service of some goal (Marcus and Whurf, 1987). In general, two types of factor appear to determine, either singly or jointly, goal selection. Expectation is a key factor: it relates to the perceptions of the probability that certain actions will achieve the desired outcome or indeed an individual's ability or willingness to carry out an action (Kirsch, 1985; Bandura, 1982). People generally - but not invariably - select goals which they have some expectation of being able to achieve, although they may also have fantasies about unachievable or low probability attainments. Self conception is a second factor postulated to influence goals. The person may select goals which represent not just achievements but enduring self definitions. The person whose goal is to write a novel may represent an individual who has an enduring concept of themselves as an artist, a great writer (Markus and Nurins, 1986; Little, 1983).

The pursuit of a goal requires also the capacity to choose between alternative strategies. The cognitive processes involved draw on the person's existing repertoire of strategies and their knowledge about which strategies will be useful in which situation and to meet which goals (Sternberg, 1984). This strategic knowledge can be used to plan actions or effective behaviour. In order to choose between strategies, the person must have an appropriate repertoire from which to choose. The repertoire of readily available strategies may be presented as some form of procedural knowledge that may be automatically executed in the appropriate situation. When no existing strategy is available or when the person is consciously trying to change their behaviour they may construct novel plans in the service of particular goals (interestingly, in this respect, similar to task centred work).

Goal directed action includes self monitoring. A cycle of self regulation typically includes monitoring behaviour, making a judgement about how well the behaviour is being executed and evaluating or reinforcing (if necessary) this behaviour. This involves attention to various aspects of their actions such as its quality or frequency. This is then judged against a criterion developed from the individual' own standards or that of significant others (Bandura, 1978). Carver and Scheier (1981) consider this self regulation involves three clear elements: attending to the self, including our own actions, comparing the self to some standard which the individual considers appropriate, and attempting to reduce the gap between the way the individual is acting and the way they wish to act.

Goals are implicated in an individual's interaction with others, where the focus is on how the person tries to shape a particular identity in the mind of his or her audience during an interaction, using a variety of strategies and tactics to fulfil one or more of several motives. An identity is an image of the self that an individual tries to convey to others. It exists both as a cognitive structure in the mind of the person trying to convey it and the audience themselves. A person might, for example, wish to convey to others that he or she is a caring person, or that they are decisive in decision making. This is an image they may have of themselves, but they may not be sure that others have this image of them also.

They would in those circumstances attempt to act in such a way that it creates a general acceptance of them as a caring or decisive person (Goffman, 1959). Depending on the goal and the audience the person may try to construct a different identity using one or more impression management technique. Although it may be conscious or unconscious, the effective use of conscious impression management may rely on the person's level of self awareness (Cheek and Hogan, 1983).

Reid, whose work was instrumental in developing task centred practice, himself recognises this link between human capabilities and the conduct of task centred practice, analysing a number of key concepts relating to the intent and actions of consumers (Reid, 1977). Reid stresses humans' autonomous problem solving capacities and the ability to initiate and carry through intelligent actions to obtain what they want. His emphasis, interestingly, is on wants rather than needs. This is consistent with an emphasis on the consumer themselves defining their problems and goals. People with wants are in a state of dissatisfaction: dissatisfied individuals want something they are not getting. A want, from a psychological perspective might be considered a cognitive-affective event consisting of an idea that something is desirable and a feeling of tension associated with not having it. There is a connection between wants and problems: when a want is experienced without a means of satisfaction at hand an individual has the sense of 'having a problem' (Goldman, 1970). Unsatisfied wants characterising problems consumers bring to social workers tend to be persistently occurrent, occupying a good deal of the consumer's attention much of the time and they occur with sufficient intensity to prompt them to seek social work help.

An emphasis on wants is deliberately designed to mobilise consumer motivation. Reid draws attention to the link between a person's motivation for change and their preparedness to act. Drawing on Ripple (1964) he identifies two key elements to wants: direction (what the person wants) and strength (how much he wants it). While motivation is significant, two further factors require consideration. The more difficult it is to resolve the problem the higher the motivation likely to be required. Also, other wants may conflict with problem solving actions: an addict wishing to kick the habit will find their craving in the way of problem resolution.

Wants are also closely connected to beliefs. Most wants of a social character, Reid thinks, have their origins in belief systems.

Beliefs are guides to action. An individual's actions are inevitably guided by specific beliefs about how the problem can best be solved. His or her beliefs may cause them to try various alternative actions of their own (their repertoire of strategies), to turn to others or to challenge the validity of the want itself. Thoughts about how to solve a particular problem are in turn influenced by beliefs about the importance of the problem and the possible consequences of various solutions.

Wants and beliefs influence the action that takes place. Reid (1977, p 59) links action specifically with intent 'For there to be an action there must be an agent with a purpose or intent'. The intent, in task centred practice, to alleviate a want, links intent with both wants and beliefs. Wants and beliefs may not directly produce action, but rather create intentions that, in turn, determine what a person does. These intentions may be thought of as plans, which are, in effect, a description of intent. Planning becomes an effective tool in shaping problem solving to the extent that it can take advantage of the human capacity for rational thought and foresight. Effective planning normally, according to Reid (1977; Reid and Epstein, 1972) normally takes into account a range of alternative problem solving actions and the possible consequences of each. Promising alternatives are 'thought through' to determine specific steps that may be required to carry them out. Contingencies that may arise are considered and ways of responding to them are devised. In task centred practice an important function of practitioners is to provide the consumer with structured opportunities for planning, and to contribute to the process through their own knowledge of psychosocial problems and of the particulars of the consumer's situation.

THE PRACTICE OF TASK CENTRED WORK

Task centred practice aims to be systematic and precise and is conducted through a number of stages. The practitioner seeks to help consumers identify specific problems which arise from unrealised wants and that are defined in terms of specific conditions to be changed. Work proceeds through the structure of contracts in which the consumer's problems, goals and the nature and duration of service are agreed on by both practitioner and client. In these respects there is a great similarity between task centred work and care management. Change is effected primarily through problem solving actions or task the consumers and practitioners undertake outside the interview. This reliance on tasks is the central and distinctive aspect of this form of practice. Task centred practice is appropriate where the practitioner can identify with the consumer a specific, acknowledged psychosocial problem that can be alleviated by the consumer through independent action, then task centred methods are appropriate. It can be a form of brief intervention in itself, or can be used within the context of longer term care arrangements (while itself being a brief episode). The interviews accompanying the problem solving tasks are normally expected to last one hour and the length of intervention is normally no greater than two to four months.

Problem Specification

The initial phase of contact involves problem specification and formation of the contract. In general it is expected that this would consist of between one and four interviews, although it is desirable to specify at least one problem and reach an initial contract by the end of the first interview. The purpose of problem specification is to enable the practitioner and consumer to achieve an understanding of the problem adequate for the development of tasks and for an analysis of obstacles to their accomplishment. It is essential that consumer and practitioner reach agreement on specified target problems before engaging in problem solving efforts.

Usually the first step in problem specification is to identify problem areas from which may be fashioned specific target problems that practitioner and consumer will work on. Where there is a specific request by the consumer for help the practitioner begins with the request and then engages in a process of clarification. The consumer is here termed an 'applicant'. This emerges either through the generation of a number of problems or, where problem specification is less clear, the practitioner may ask questions and probe possible areas until problem areas become apparent. Involvement of others in the consumers social network may occur if they are able to assist in the formulation of the consumer's problems. The consumer's definition of the problem are accepted unless there are specific grounds for its rejection (for example if it is unethical, illegal or not feasible). Where a consumer is referred with a problem attributed to them by others, but which they may not themselves accept, they are termed 'respondents'. Even though the consumer may not themselves favour referral (they may have no choice) the practitioner would help the consumer to come up with problems which they acknowledge and which they are prepared to work on. This may, indeed, involve attempts by the practitioner to bring about acknowledgement of the problem, although it all only be accepted as a problem and worked on if the consumer accepts it is a problem.

The second step in problem specification is detailed exploration of acknowledged problems. This is generally designed to obtain a picture of events leading up to, characterising and following the problem. From this the practitioner aims to construct a statement of the target problem and conditions to be changed. Problem specification requires a high degree of precision. For example a drinking problem needs to be defined in terms of how much alcohol is consumed during a specific period of time. Particular notice is taken of actions clients have already taken to alleviate the problem, noting the degree of success or failure attached to these problem solving methods. These can influence the construction of the problem solving tasks during intervention.

The next step is that of problem definition and explication. This is usually achieved through the practitioner formulating a problem statement and describing the conditions it refers to. Her formulation is an attempt to distil and reflect back the problem that the consumer has expressed. The definition of the problem needs to be made with some care since it will provide the direction for the collaborative efforts of practitioners and consumer. Both need to ensure they are not only aiming at the right problem but the same problem.

Where possible a baseline measure is taken against which any subsequent changes can be evaluated. This involves measuring the frequency and severity of a particular problem (or problem behaviour) over a stipulated period of time. Typically a seven day period is used, although the length of time used varies according to the frequency of the problem. The psychosocial focus for working on problems involves gaining information around a number of areas which will provide guidance as to the focus for problem solving tasks. These are consumers' wants, beliefs, action patterns and affective state; their physical condition and mental capacities; their identification with racial, ethnic and other reference groups; their performance and interactions with others in their social system; and their tangible resources and physical environment, such as income and housing.

Forming the Contract

Contracts have, in task centred practice, the essential purpose of providing an explicit agreement between consumer and practitioner on what is to be done and how. Contracts may be oral or written. Oral contracts are less time consuming, but unlike written contracts do not provide an enduring record of the actual agreement for future reference. The initial contract specifies at least one explicitly stated acknowledged problem that practitioners and consumers agree to work on. Where more than one target problem is identified the problems can be ranked in order of importance. Most contracts call for a specific number of interviews, usually between six and eight and within a range of two and four months.

Formulation of goals provide the second aspect of the contract. The purpose here is to make explicit exactly what the practitioner and consumer hope (and expect) to achieve through both their efforts. Goals represent the desired 'end state' for the consumer which they and the practitioner agree to work towards. Formulation of goals sets the stage for the development of tasks which then become the means for goal attainment. In general, precision and specificity in statements of goals are desirable, and where possible should characterise goal statements. This may not, however, always be possible: for example, while the consumer may be clear that they want a change they may not be clear about the kind or amount of change they wish to aim for. Like all parts of the initial contract, goal statements can be open to revision as work proceeds.

The contract, finally, incorporates an agreement about the expected amount and duration of service, usually expressed in terms of number of interviews over some specified period of time. The brief nature of this practice arose from a belief that the problems frequently suffered by consumers of social work services generally reflected temporary breakdowns in problem coping that set in motion forces for change, principally the consumer's own motivation to alleviate their distress. These forces for change were considered to operate rapidly in most cases to reduce the problem to a tolerable level. These beliefs suggest that consumers might be expected to benefit as much from short term as more extended forms of intervention.

Planning

The core of the intervention strategy consists of helping the consumer plan and execute problem solving actions. A plan is an inclusive concept which incorporates all tasks to be undertaken and whatever means of implementation that have been developed. Tasks are the central problem solving actions that the client and practitioner agree to carry out. They are at the heart of action plans. A task taken up by a consumer is a particular type of problem solving action. To qualify as a task, the action must be planned and agreed on by the practitioner and capable of being worked on by the consumer outside direct interviews with the practitioner.

Again, the starting point is with the consumer: consistent with the approach, practitioner and consumer may begin with whatever plan the consumer has begun to work on. While the plan may not be adequate to resolve the problem there may be elements of it that can be built upon. In some circumstances, furthermore, the nature of the problem may point to a particular course of action which can be developed. In others, alternative actions need to be considered and appraised, which can often be achieved through a process of brainstorming. Where a practitioner is well versed in task centred methods, many of the ideas generated may come from the practitioner because of her specialised knowledge about the kinds of tasks that generally work well for particular problems.

Regardless, however, of who suggests any task, it is critical that the consumer expresses a willingness to carry it out. This requires a task agreement. This involves agreement between consumer and practitioner on one or more actions to be undertaken. An agreement may be made after alternatives have been sorted out and the best selected, although at this stage it is a global agreement. The final agreement on tasks is made at the end of the planning process, after it is determined what the execution of the task will involve.

Once an alternative has been selected for consideration, the practitioner and client work on the plan for its execution. For a task plan to work, because of the central part played by the consumer in carrying out tasks, it is essential that they (the consumer) emerge with a clear notion of what they have to do. This is achieved by a process of planning which breaks tasks down into sequences of operations that may be required to carry it out . The tasks themselves may be individual, reciprocal or shared. An individual task is carried out independently by a single consumer. Reciprocal tasks are separate but interrelated tasks worked on by different individuals, usually members of the same family. They tend to assume a quid pro quo form. A shared task is a single task worked on together by two or more persons. Once the more precise process of task planning has been undertaken, the practitioner and client are expected to go over the plan in summary fashion, normally at the end of an interview (sometimes the first interview, if the planning stage has been reached).

Incentives and rationales for task performance are important elements of task centred practice. In order for the consumer to carry out the plan of action, it is assumed in task centred practice that the consumer would believe that its accomplishment will result in a benefit sufficient to make the effort worthwhile. The incentive refers to the gain the consumer anticipates in carrying out the task. Reid (1977) considers that a rationale, in the case of task centred practice is provided by the consumer's anticipation that the gain will provide adequate justification for completing the task. In some cases the extent to which the problem(s) will be alleviated by task performance will be clear in task planning, and this provides an important form of incentive. When matters are not this clear, the practitioner would usually be expected to clarify for the consumer the nature of the payoff they may be expected to gain from the execution of particular tasks. This might be indicated in particular where the consumer's motivation to work on the plan is questionable, when the connection between task achievement and problem alleviation is not clear and when the proposed action may have negative as well as positive consequences for the consumer.

Other kinds of incentives may include praise or approval from the practitioner, the sense of accomplishment or control over their lives the consumer may obtain from task achievement, praise or approval from others and so on. Incentives which take the form of rewards for task performance are also important. This can take the form of a particular 'treat' such as giving oneself permission to take a day out, or to have some food which is particularly liked but rarely eaten. Alternatively, a points system might be developed whereby points are accumulated for task performance, and later 'cashed in' for some indulgence which is particularly appreciated by the consumer. For children, a 'star' system may be used where achievement of a task is rewarded by the award of a star. Such tangible incentives, which can be built into the planning process, may be particularly indicated where the execution of tasks results in some immediate deprivation for the consumer, such as restricting the intake of alcohol (where, for example, they have a drink problem).

Task Strategies

There are a variety of strategies by which tasks may be carried out. Where, first of all, the tasks agreed with the consumer are difficult for them to perform, or in the first instance impossible for them to perform, an *incremental strategy* may be employed. This involves a series of tasks of progressive difficulty to help the consumer achieve their performance goal. A consumer with serious debts may first of all attempt to deal with particular debt problems before moving on to manage their income, spending and overall debts fully. Incentives and morale support from the practitioner may be particularly helpful in these circumstances. The difficulty of an incremental step may be lessened by placing an upper limit on the task. In this way the consumer may control anxiety and any impulse to do more than he or she is able, at that point, to cope with.

Concurrent task strategies involve circumstances where a number of different client and practitioner tasks are initiated more or less concurrently, once the problem has been formulated. The initial plan would set out a number of tasks representing a division of labour between the consumer and practitioner. Where, in even more complex circumstances, tasks are carried out by individuals other than the consumer or practitioner, these tasks are conceptualised as contractual arrangements between the practitioner and other individuals involved, who may be representatives of other agencies.

Simulation involves 'trying out' elements of the action plan under simulated conditions in the interview. These enable the consumer to carry out and perfect task behaviour under controlled and non (or less) threatening conditions. This is usually undertaken in the form of a role play: most frequently the consumer takes the part of themselves in relation to the tasks required by the action plan. The practitioner takes the role of some individual with whom the consumer will have to interact in order to carry out the required tasks. This kind of role play provides the opportunity for discussion and critical reflection of the consumer's performance from which lessons may be learned for when they carry out the task in reality.

Guided practice, finally, involves actual, as opposed to simulated work on tasks. For example, where the goal of a child is improvement in academic performance and the task is carrying out an (or many) academic assignment(s) they may be able to work on this task with the practitioner who can operate in a 'tutor' or adviser role. This is not a matter of rehearsing tasks but of actually carrying them out.

Practitioner and Independent Tasks

Practitioner tasks are undertaken outside direct interviews with clients, either to help the consumer achieve his or her own task or to bring about changes in problems independent of the consumer. Facilitating tasks are designed to enlist and structure the assistance of others in helping the consumer carry out their problem solving actions. These are, first, efforts to influence incentives that might positively affect consumers' efforts. This involves manipulating rewards and punishments provided by those in the consumer's social environment. This obviously depends on the kinds of incentives that may be under the control of those in the consumer's social system. Examples of these kinds of incentives for adults include approval and other reciprocal (quid pro quo) actions undertaken by others. For children such incentives may include food, gold stars, treats or presents.

Other facilitative tasks help the consumer in the actual execution of tasks. Again, the example of helping a child in their study provides a good example. Here the parents (the facilitator) may be asked to provide an adequate place for study for one hour per night. These kind of facilitative tasks may be of particular use for tasks the consumer is unable to perform properly on their own, or where obstacles exist to task performance and where individuals in the consumer's social environment may counteract these obstacles.

Independent practitioner tasks are designed to affect the target problem directly. They are intended to complement rather than assist consumer actions. For example, if a consumer's goal is to obtain employment, the practitioner's task might be to check out certain job opportunities, while the consumer looks into others. Independent tasks are called for where situations exist where the practitioner is in a better position to effect changes than the consumer. This most frequently occurs when the consumer lacks needed resources or is having difficulty dealing with organisations, which may present them with unfamiliar bureaucracies. The organisations may be more familiar to practitioners who work with them on a day to day basis.

Review, Ending and Evaluation

Review and evaluation of task performance in terms of the consumer's capacity to achieve their goals is embedded in task centred practice. This evaluation and review occurs both on a sessional basis and at the end of intervention.

Task review generally occurs at the beginning of each session with the consumer. It focuses on what the consumer (and practitioner) have achieved in their tasks between sessions. In general the consumer reports on what they have accomplished, records of task progress are examined and discussed and the practitioner may present any evidence she has received from colaterals or other sources. The consumer's progress is reported on a four point scale, and the practitioner is able to provide support and encouragement in giving them credit for their achievements in undertaking tasks.

Where the consumer has been unable to carry out agreed tasks, or has only partially completed them, two options are available. First, the task may be abandoned if it appears on review that it was inappropriate for the consumer in their particular situation. Alternatively, and more commonly, the reasons why the consumer was unable to complete tasks can be examined, obstacles may be identified and ways of overcoming these obstacles considered.

The continuous process of review characterising task centred practice is carried through to the end of intervention where a final review and evaluation of progress is made. As in any planned and time limited approach, the point of termination is set in advance as part of the treatment contract. In the final interview attention focuses on the main activities of termination. This first involves reviewing and assessing what was accomplished during intervention in relation to the consumer's problems. The final problem review is a systematic assessment of the status of the consumer's target problems, of other problems they may be facing and of their own perception of problem change. This review serves the twin purpose of helping the consumer see what they have accomplished and provides the practitioner with a basis for judging the effectiveness of intervention.

The target problems are assessed by a repeat of the process undertaken at the outset of intervention. Here, it will be recalled, certain target conditions were identified and the frequency of their occurrence was assessed during a retrospective baseline period, usually seven days preceding the interview. In the final review this assessment is repeated with frequency of occurrence obtained from a comparable period prior to the final interview. For example, the initial baseline may have measured frequency, duration and intensity of arguments during the week prior to the initial interview. In the final interview, data on the same aspects would be obtained for the week prior to that interview. Changes in other aspects of the consumer's life are also examined, with particular attention paid to areas that may have been positively or negatively affected by intervention. A second way of evaluating progress involves consumer's own views of matters. It is possible that the conditions of the problem may not have changed but the consumer is no longer troubled by it. A third method of evaluation is others' assessment of change. This part of the review is completed with colaterals who have first hand knowledge of change in the consumer's problems and who are briefly interviewed. Their assessment includes both target and other, ancillary problems.

A second activity of termination is 'post treatment planning'. This is about teaching and extending the problem solving process. The practitioner attempts to state clearly, and in jargon free language the process of problem solving the consumer had learned in the course of intervention. The key to this is helping the consumer to generalise from their experience so that they can gain some conceptual understanding of the approach that has been used and can apply it to future problems.

Finally limited extensions to intervention, or recontracting may occasionally be called for. Extensions would generally occur for the specific purpose of completing unfinished work. This is typically where it appears likely that some additional time would help the consumer make decisive progress on a target problem. For example, the practitioner and consumer may have hit upon an effective problem solving task late on in the intervention, or problem solving may be affected significantly by an event expected to occur in the near future. Recontracting may occur where, as termination approaches, the consumer is faced with a significant problem that they want help with but have not had the opportunity to work on. In these circumstances the consumer may be offered a second contract, although again this would be unusual.

CONCLUSION

Task centred practice is relevant in two respects for care management. It is, first, an effective method of brief intervention.

It therefore has considerable potential in relation to cases where intervention is not sufficiently great to justify bringing in the whole care management procedure, including divisions between purchaser and providers. The practitioner is able to undertake a considerable amount of work themselves in the knowledge that this will not drag on, without review or evaluation, over a long period of time. If intervention does become more extensive and longer term, then conventional care management procedures may be invoked, particularly in view of the similarity in many respects, between task centred practice and care management.

This leads to the second contribution of task centred practice. It has a great deal to offer the care manager, since it provides rigorous means for conducting processes which are similar in many respects to those required by care management. Task centred social work, in other words, provides a model of practice which may inform practitioners operating at the professional level of care management. To be sure, the nomenclature of care management at times differs from task centred practice: hence needs in the former have their equivalent in wants in the latter. However, the close relationship with the care management process is obvious from the very broadest of classifications provided in the Department of Health's practitioners' and managers' guides. Hence stages three to seven inclusive of the care management process involve assessing need (which in task centred language is called wants), care planning, implementing the care plan, monitoring and review. More precise examination of the care management process emphasises this relationship still more. Hence in the assessment stage of care management, the care manager is expected to negotiate the scope of assessment, clarify expectations, promote participation assess need, set priorities and agree objectives

Task centred practice has the advantage over care management in its more detailed examination of the process of intervention and the rigorous evaluation of practice. It is more specific in its definition and classification of practice actions. It is more detailed in its guidelines for the conduct of practice. Task Centred practice has been the subject of a number of evaluation studies which have shown it to be an effective form of intervention (Tolsen and Reid, 1994). However, there are differences. This is most apparent with consumers who are the subject of social work intervention or care management against their wishes. Although task centred practice can be undertaken with 'captive consumers' - those who do not wish for social work intervention - it is only in specific problem areas which the consumer themselves identify. Care management would in relation to any particular case, refer to the total process of managing intervention, including those areas where the consumer may be less than happy to be involved in.

The assumption underlying much care management that the consumer is often the best person to define their needs is one reflected in task centred practice. Task centred practice is, however, much more emphatic (and detailed) in recognising the role of the practitioner in helping the consumer decide exactly what their wants and problems are and the tasks required to alleviate those problems. It therefore tends to highlight to a greater degree the part of the practitioner in deciding what is the problem and what to do about it. It appears to assume that, while the practitioner builds upon the consumer's existing problem solving efforts, the practitioner can help them develop a more rigorous and effective method of problem solving.

Overall, however, both care management and task centred practice recognise the potential amongst humans for purposeful and rational actions to deal with their needs or problems. Task centred practice recognises the importance of intent and motivation in human actions. Both assume that humans can set goals and, even if they need help, develop rational ways of achieving these goals. Both, therefore, clearly aim to involve consumers in the resolution of problems and needs.

PART FIVE

CONCLUSION

Chapter Fourteen

Care management and the new social work

A central thrust of this book is that the advent of care management involves elements of both continuity and change. The change element, which is substantial, may be more evident than continuity to many observers. The purchaser-provider split, the notion of a market in social care, and the concern of care managers with the management of, rather than intervention in, the case all represent substantial changes from the past. This is underlined still more when we take note of the influence of ideas from the New Right on the development of social care. The scepticism about traditional virtues of public sector management, the advent of the New Managerialism and the implicit cost-benefit analysis in care management all reflect the influence of the New Right.

Yet it would be a mistake to dismiss the major elements of continuity. Social work may largely be understood as an arm of social policy, and as such what is considered to be social work is liable to undergo change with changes in social policy, particularly where changes are grounded on such deep ideological differences. In that sense the changes represent an aspect of the 'nature' of social work: that what constitutes social work is itself, to a considerable degree, subject to change. Even the profound changes arising from the ideology of the New Right have left in place core elements of social work. The interactionist dimension and the concern with the consumer as subject are implicit in official guidelines on care management. These, indeed, provide opportunities for social work, provided those responsible for practice, education and training can keep their eyes firmly on the prize: that of a place within the care managerial environment. The three core social work approaches identified: interpersonal skills, working with social networks and social supports and task centred practice are of the greatest relevance to the practice of care management. Furthermore, they provide a 'knowledge base' which allows for care management to be practised by social workers at the 'professional' level, as a result of the sophistication they lend to their care managerial activities. As important, however, is the analysis of the implications of these approaches. Together, they give a clear picture of significant aspects of social workers' understanding of consumers, and humans in general - that they are subjects, they are social beings and are capable of purposeful actions. These assumptions about humans are common to both care management and social work, and provide a strong link between the two.

Beyond this, however, it is important for social workers to recognise another key element of their knowledge: that theirs is a concern with a case focused emergent understanding of the situations of their consumers. This is about the manner in which assessments are carried out, rather than simply the application of some given knowledge which may be objectively applied to all situations. It requires a high level of analytic ability and a preparedness to look for factors which challenge their provisional constructions of what is going on. It requires additionally the widest possible range of constructs, categories and schemas with which to make sense of these situations. It also requires that the social worker is capable of critically assessing both the concepts and schemas they are using and the situations they are analysing. This is clearly a level of activity for which high levels of education and training are required. Indeed, this 'critical awareness' can only be developed where the critical functions of education as well as the applied function of training are brought together.

This chapter focuses on some central issues relating to the extent to which this formal knowledge, education and training can help social workers, in practice, develop a distinctive place within care management. It is about the potential for the transmission of these ideas into the real world of practice. This, first, involves an examination of the degree of technicality and indetermination in the conduct of practice which plays a significant part in the acceptance of the professional position and distinctive contribution of an occupation. Second, this involves exploring the extent to which the knowledge itself can provide the basis for a distinctive approach to care management, focusing particularly on the issues of content and 'boundary maintenance'. Finally, the possibility of intra-occupational divergence is examined, together with the importance of the orientation of members of the profession towards formal knowledge.

The work of Jamous and Peloille (1970) is illuminating in examining the place of social work in care management, since they focus on issues of relevance to the professional in an environment which increasingly emphasises the managerial and technical side of social care assessment, management and review. They distinguish between the technical aspects of a job - that which can be mastered and transmitted in terms of rules - and the indeterminate aspects of the job, which cannot. The ideas that indeterminate knowledge may be functional for a profession arises from the notion that they work within an area of uncertainty, which, because of the special skills of the professionals involved, can only be understood and assessed by those with the requisite skills and knowledge - those who are in the same profession. This encourages professional autonomy and limits, in the context of care management, managerial control. It may be possible to have consultation with a senior who is of the same profession, but those outside the profession will not have the competence to judge the appropriateness or otherwise of the practitioner's assessment and actions. Likewise, the degree of uncertainty is such that pre-defined forms assessing needs are likely to be inadequate for the task of identifying the real extent of need. This also reduces the degree of managerial control, since the forms themselves, as we have seen, exercise a control in terms of the way the consumer needs are defined. These forms represent a set of rules about what the practitioner may look for in order to define consumer need and also, frequently, the severity of that need.

While it is important for a job to have a degree of indeterminacy to maximise professional autonomy, this cannot take place, however, to the complete exclusion of technicality. If professional indeterminacy is viewed by others in a powerful position (such as politicians, relevant civil servants, managers and so on) to be too great, it is quite likely that deprofessionalising of that particular area of practice will occur. Once matters become very indeterminate, it becomes possible to suggest that knowledge in that area is not sufficiently generalisable, and hence provides no advantage over the knowledge possessed by the layperson. If each situation is unique, then how can someone with specialised knowledge claim they know more than the layperson? This is a problem which has dogged social work, where social workers have not been very convincing in claiming that they possessed knowledge not possessed by lay people. This was analysed in detail in chapter 4.

Jamous and Peloille (1970) suggest that successful professions strike the right balance between the degree of indetermination and degree of technicality which is presented as intrinsic to the job. This is the indetermination-technicality ratio. If there is insufficient indeterminacy, the occupation is likely to be perceived as a practical vocation. If, however, there is too much indeterminacy, the occupation concerned is liable to be subject to a managerial 'takeover' of the sort outlined in chapter 4. The appropriate indeterminacy-technicality ratio has been achieved by medicine. On the one hand, it has, through scientific evaluation and the media, been able to demonstrate to its public a high degree of effectiveness in areas regarded generally to be of great importance (health and illness). On the other hand, medicine has emphasised the virtualities of the practitioners concerned. Medicine values the qualities of individuals who practice (Freidson, 1970). 'Real medicine' is not a simple matter of academic learning, but is to be learned at the patient's bedside, through actual experience, which Atkinson (1977) refers to as the 'clinical gaze'.

The form filling, box ticking dimensions of care management seems to have little in common with the sophisticated analysis characteristic of reflexive eclecticism. They represent the deprofessionalising aspects of social care. The former emphasises the pre-designed nature of assessment, while the latter is characterised by the personal virtualities - the abilities and skills - possessed by the practitioner. The former appears to exercise greater control on the activities of the care manager, while the latter inevitably provides for greater independence. On a continuum, they appear to be at different ends.

This, in part, provides the answer. Social work is characterised, as we have seen, by uncertainty. It is difficult to predict outcomes, and it is not always clear that the practitioner has got their assessment right. The more straightforward the assessment, the easier to use the pre-designed forms. The less straightforward, the more difficult for these forms to provide adequate representations of the consumer's situation. Of course, most situations will possess some degree of complexity. However, this characterisation begins to indicate the 'space' that is appropriately filled by social work in care management. Social work is concerned with those situations where the complexity is such that they cannot be adequately represented by the pre-designed forms. These will usually be the most difficult of cases, and often those which are most dangerous (as with child protection assessments) or which carry the greatest responsibility for individual rights (such as those involving mental health, particularly compulsory admission assessments). It may be the case, as with compulsory admission assessments, that specific assessment schedules, which are complex and have been specifically and carefully developed, (Sheppard, 1990) may prove helpful. However, these are not managerial tools, but are complex instruments, developed out of research, and hence better defined as professional tools. In any case, they do not do away with the need for reflexive eclecticism.

The more, therefore, that the situations demand more complex analysis than can be provided by pre-defined forms, the more one moves into the terrain of social work. These forms may not become entirely redundant, but increasingly they are likely to become 'memory jogs' which are used in the context of the more qualitative analysis characteristic of reflexive eclecticism, rather than being the determinants of the way the assessment is conducted.

This also raises issues about the extent to which cost-benefit analysis inherent in care management can actually take place. The pre-defined forms represent not simply a potential deprofessionalising of the task, but also a tool by which such cost benefit analysis may take place. Tick the boxes, identify the severity of need, and have some idea about the overall budget available and it may be possible, in principle to develop a rational means for assessing the best care package, based on the benefits to the consumer and the cost of the package. However, social care is clearly far from being able to take such an apparently unproblematic approach to need assessment, even if computers are increasingly used in this process. Indeed, the more complex the case, the more difficult it is to undertake this kind of analysis. How accurately, for example, is anyone capable of working out the benefits of a particular programme for a young offender? apart from anything else, if there are any benefits they may not be seen for some considerable time. Given this, how can anyone assess the benefits of one package as against another?

The degree of uncertainty in outcome therefore, presents grave difficulties for carrying out a technicalist form of cost benefit analysis. This does not mean that some kind of analysis cannot take place. The more straightforward the case (again), the easier it is to identify needs, the easier it will be to undertake this kind of choice between alternative packages of care. However, such a choice does not go away simply because the case becomes more complex. There are generally at least two alternatives when considering a response to consumer need, and some kind of judgement is necessary to work out which alternative is likely to have the most beneficial effect. This again is a matter of focusing specifically on the case in hand, and analysing it to the best effect. It is, in other words, a matter of using the approach of reflexive eclecticism. While it may not be possible to develop general rules by which the practitioner may decide courses of actions in all cases of a particular type, an emphasis must be placed on the process of making a judgement in relation to each individual case. This is the essence of reflexive eclecticism.

The place of social work as a professional activity within the realm of care management is, therefore, best secured by a clear understanding and presentation of its particular knowledge forms. The processes involved in reflexive eclecticism represent the kind of virtualities which ought to be universally possessed by social workers. It both emphasises their particular competencies while underlining the case focused nature of assessment. Likewise, interpersonal skills, social support and network analysis and task centred practice represent aspects of practice which can be clearly demonstrated to have an applied knowledge base. As suggested earlier these are not the only areas of knowledge which social workers require, knowledge of the Law and welfare rights being obvious additional examples. They are, however, crucial to the presentation of social work as having a distinctive and professional contribution to make to care management.

PROFESSIONAL KNOWLEDGE AND PROFESSIONAL TRAINING

The kinds of abilities identified as central to social workers as care managers are not straightforward or easily learned. The implication is that their performance requires some kind of professional education and training. This training would represent the clearest indication of the existence and maintenance of social work in the professional area of care management. Certain issues remain, however. How confident can we be that this training will exercise a formative influence on the ways in which social workers conduct their activities? how far will they be committed to the kinds of values which underlie their practice (such as the capacity to conduct high levels of assessment characterised by reflexive eclecticism)? and how far is it likely to engender an approach to care management which is distinctive? could not other professions with different training possess the same abilities and competencies as social workers? These questions require us to look at certain key aspects of the process of training: the content of the training in terms of the curriculum, the impact of that curriculum on the characteristic way in which the profession acts in and views the world, and the relationship between these and the role and standards of the practitioner.

OCCUPATIONAL CULTURE

A central element in the link between the actions and beliefs of occupational members and the education and training programme which its members have undertaken is occupational culture. For social workers to make use of the areas of knowledge which have been outlined, two key characteristics must be present: a knowledge of and capacity to use these approaches and a belief in their efficacy, ie valuing these approaches. These, it should be emphasised do not constitute the only elements of occupational culture. However, they must be embedded in the occupational culture of the profession. For their approach to be distinctive, their occupational culture must itself possess some distinctiveness, from other professionals and those without professional education and training.

Where a group of people share the same understanding of reality and the social world, they may be said to have shared meaning. Shared meaning is a significant dimension of culture in general and occupational culture in particular. Weber (1949) defines culture as follows:

> Culture is the endowment of a finite segment of the meaningless infinity of events in the world with meaning and significance from the standpoint of human beings.

This conception of culture as a form of shared meaning is useful as a way of drawing attention to perspectives distinctively and generally held by members of an occupation. Being a member of an occupational group involves, according to Geertz (1983) a sense of identity and personal commitment, a 'way of being in the world' a matter of taking on a cultural frame of reference that defines a great part of one's life.

The means by which an occupational culture is acquired is through the process of occupational socialisation. Merton (1957, p 287) indicates what is involved: it is 'the process by which people selectively acquire the values and attitudes, the interests, skills and knowledge - in short the culture - current in the groups to which they are, or seek to become, a member. It refers to the learning of social roles'. These social roles are the roles of the occupation, which constitutes the reference group for the individual being trained for the occupation. As a reference group, the occupation provides aspiring members with perspectives that they use to deal with a range of situations, problems and demands. In the broadest sense, the group's perspectives may be used to structure the way in which individual members interact with the world around them.

Pavalko (1988) identified theory as a significant aspect of training and professional socialisation. Theory refers to the extent to which there is a systematic and esoteric body of abstract knowledge on which professional work is based. The body of knowledge is the basis of the profession's claim to expertise. Formal knowledge may have a major impact on the shared meanings, and hence culture, of an occupation. It is, according to Atkinson (1983) in a sense arbitrary. There is no pre-given corpus of knowledge which presents itself as a 'curriculum', and which is inherently endowed with order, sequential organisation and so on. The curriculum is a device whereby knowledge is classified and combined. It is, at least to some degree, a cultural imposition. However, this has a profound impact on the manner of thinking which takes place in a particular discipline. Atkinson (1983) goes on to state:

> Educational knowledge separates what is thinkable from what is unthinkable; it identifies what is deemed important and attempts to distinguish it from what is deemed trivial; it marks out what is introductory from what is considered specialised and advanced; it may construct an essential 'core' as opposed to the peripheral or optional.

In a real sense, therefore, the curriculum presents a way of viewing reality, at least in so far as it effects the professional practice of the individual members of the profession. It is not simply about what is included in the curriculum, but also what is left out; it is also about the priority given to certain facets over others.

In social work, however, the curriculum content is not 'subject defined' in the way that sociology, history or physics are defined. At one level, this is quite obvious. CCETSW (the Central Council for Education and Training in Social Work) is the governing body of social work training which, to a considerable degree, determines the content of social work training, and monitors the training process. Indeed, CCETSW has taken an increasingly directive line in relation to the content of training in recent years. Hence statements about essential knowledge, values, skills and so on exercise a considerable influence, not simply on the general direction of education and training, but, to some degree, on its detailed content. The emphasis, furthermore, on areas of competence, underlines the extent to which CCETSW (and through CCETSW, the government) wish to influence the 'product' of social work training. It is about training for a role.

The key, then, lies in the construction, as stated earlier, of a practice paradigm, which brings together the curriculum involved in training with the structural constraints on the practice of social workers, particularly as represented by the roles they are expected to undertake. These constraints are organisational, in terms of agency function and the roles, within agency function, that social workers are expected to fulfil. They are also definitional, or at the level of meaning. It is about accepting child abuse as child abuse, young offending as juvenile delinquency and so on. This is crucial, for these terms - social definitions - define the areas of social work concerns, as shown in chapter 3. The considerable concern (one might say at times, obsession) with competence, arises within this context. The knowledge learned is not 'knowledge for its own sake' but knowledge for practice. It is about being able to carry out competently the requirements of the social work role with individuals who have been socially defined. Of course, the issue of what constitutes competent practice is itself problematic, and much of this book has been devoted to identifying the kinds of qualities which might justify social work's place within care management.

CCETSW, therefore, through its control of the processes of education and training, exercises a formal institutional link between the content of the curriculum and the construction of the job of the social worker. It is in this context that the requirements of the role of the social worker come together with the at times indeterminate, and frequently conflicting approaches of social science which continue to have a major place in the curriculum of social work training. If social work training is about preparation for a particular kind of role, or set of roles, then the knowledge and skills acquired would be expected to facilitate the performance of those roles. In this sense, the competencies (which are in a sense outcome measures) represent the key to the kinds of formal knowledge acquired. The social sciences, while playing an important part in this respect do not lend themselves easily to this process, because of the conflicting approaches. The actual curriculum, therefore, may well 'fit' the needs of practice to a greater or lesser extent, depending on which subject discipline is involved. It is this which led to calls for the abandonment of more radical forms of sociology from the curriculum (Davies, 1981, 1986) and which led CCETSW increasingly to emphasise the importance of the practice, as opposed to academic constituency, in formulating plans for social work training culminating in the Diploma in Social Work (Sibeon, 1991). Yet, the emphasis on the subject and an interactional focus characteristic of social work makes the social sciences the logical home for much of social work training.

OCCUPATIONAL TRAINING AND THE CURRICULUM

The meanings, therefore, that social workers may take on from the curriculum, reflect (and are intended so to do), in certain respects, the constraints of the job. The understandable importance of the social sciences in the curriculum involves a degree of tension between some approaches and these constraints. Some of the curriculum influenced ways in which social workers are likely to 'make sense' of their professional world is bound to reflect themes derived from the social sciences which constitute parts of the curriculum. Hence, it is necessary first to identify that which is distinctive to social work, and second the sources of unity and divergence contained within the formal knowledge of social work.

These shared meanings may be presented in terms of the common ways a group possesses of categorising and interpreting (through common schema) the world, which was discussed at length in chapter 9. It is in this respect that the curriculum can influence the extent to which members of a profession have a common way of understanding situations with which they are confronted in their everyday professional life. The curriculum helps provide the academic equivalent of categories and schema - concepts and theories. The curriculum represents the means by which we may define, classify and structure the reality confronted in everyday life. Where this curriculum is (largely) common to professional courses, to the extent that the curriculum is successful in classifying and defining reality, the members of the profession may be said to have shared meanings.

In relation to Higher Education, this point is emphasised by Becher (1989). He suggests that 'we may appropriately conceive of disciplines as having recognisable identities and particular cultural attributes' (pp 22). This difference is emphasised by the 'greats' (such as Durkheim in Sociology and Einstein in Theoretical Physics) who provide a focus for the discipline. It may be difficult to regard social work as being an academic discipline in the sense that psychology, sociology, physics or mathematics are disciplines. Social work does not cohere around a commonly defined and accepted subject matter, but is concerned with socially defined individuals, and the 'subject matter' of social work may change from time to time. Furthermore, CCETSW requirements involve a number of subject disciplines in the construction of the social work curriculum. However, there are some boundaries to the social work curriculum, with its emphasis on the understanding of social phenomena, and these become evident when social work is compared with another occupation, such as community psychiatric nurses (CPNs) (Sheppard, 1991).

This may be further examined in terms of Bernstein's (1971, 1975) concepts of classification and boundary maintenance. Classification refers to the organisation of knowledge into curricula, or the various domains of educational activity. Basically this means that the areas of concern, or subject matter, of say, physics are different from, say sociology. This is because there is some degree of selection and separation between areas of knowledge, and that which is selected for the discipline of sociology constitutes the curriculum of sociology. Without such selection and separation between subject disciplines the curriculum would be coterminous with the entire universe of possible knowledge and experience. Becher (1987, 1989) similarly argues on the importance of selection and separation between academic disciplines. He uses a geographical metaphor for this. Where discussing adjoining disciplines, he comments, it is natural enough to think of knowledge in terms of landscapes and 'to saturate epistemological discussions with spatial metaphors: fields and frontiers; pioneering, exploration and false trails; charts and landmarks' (Becher, 1989, p 36). Disciplinary boundaries are relatively easy to identify: Economics is said to have common frontiers with Mathematics and Political Science; some 'trade relations' with History and Sociology, and a lesser measure of shared ground with psychology, philosophy and law.

Bernstein's (and Becher's) view of the curriculum, therefore is one of selection (of areas of knowledge) and combination, which together constitute the subject matter of the discipline. There are two key elements of curriculum structure. The first is about the external boundaries to the discipline. This involves the way in which the curriculum of the subject is to be distinguished from any other subject domain, and involves the issue of what is to be counted in and what is to be counted out of the discipline. The second involves the issue of internal differentiation: what are the nature of the 'study units'? what are their boundaries? and how do they relate to each other? Together, these elements of selection and differentiation involve the classification of the discipline(s). Classification is thus a matter of boundary, the definition, maintenance and validation of domains of knowledge (Atkinson, 1985).

Both curriculum content and knowledge boundaries, therefore, are of particular importance in social work (as with other disciplines). If content and boundaries of knowledge can exercise such an influence in the ways social workers make sense and act, then this clearly has major implications both for their practice and their practice distinctiveness. That which is set out as core to social work knowledge can exercise a major influence on the way in which practice is conducted. In this respect, the emphasis on interpersonal skills, social supports and networks and task centred practice has considerable implications for the distinctiveness of social work practice. The same goes for the use of social science in the assessment of cases.

There are reasons, furthermore, specific to social work, for believing that the content and boundaries of social work knowledge do have an impact on practice. This is evident from one study (the only one of which I am aware) designed to examine the implications of these knowledge boundaries for practice. In an earlier study (Sheppard, 1991) I examined the extent to which the broad domains of 'theory' were reflected in practice by comparing the work of social workers with community psychiatric nurses. Seven broad areas of discourse were identified: knowledge orientation, practice orientation, defining the client, context of intervention, contexts specific to mental health, direction and duration of work with clients. There was some overlap. The uncertainty of social work's social science foundations was reflected in CPNs mental health models. Both borrowed knowledge from other disciplines, although unlike CPNs social workers have also generated their own knowledge. Both also claim an interest in the psychosocial (although CPNs also claim an interest in the 'bio'). Both professions, furthermore, recognise limits to formal knowledge and ascribe importance to judgement. However, there were notable differences also. Phenomena were defined by CPNs primarily through mental health models, while social work emphasised its social science knowledge base. CPNs were more individualistic and social work more developed in relation to its theoretical treatment of the social environment.

In the area of interpersonal skills, and unlike nursing, for social work these skills are considered fundamental. Compared with social work, nursing examined skills in a fragmentary way, sometimes relatively simplistically. There is an expectation of a greater degree of mastery of these skills in social work, and of their being learned rather than innate. There is also a more consistent attempt, within social work, to operationalise them in a detailed way.

These differences were largely reflected in practice. Social workers defined their client's problems more frequently as social rather than mental health. They worked more widely in a community context. They tackled practical and emotional and relationship problems far more than CPNs whose approach was far more individualistic. Furthermore, social workers seemed to have a more definable 'philosophy of practice'. They undertook more long term work, their work was of greater intensity and there was a strong emphasis on psychodynamic and emotional support work. Furthermore, with both brief and extended intervention, social work clients identified more skills, made fewer criticisms about misused or unused skills, and less frequently suggested that intervention made no difference. With brief intervention social work clients more frequently identified listening, empathetic acceptance and advice skills. With extended work, they also identified analytic processes, releasing feelings and increasing self understanding.

Although conducted before the advent of care management, the cumulative effects of this study are clear. Although there was some degree of overlap between occupations, there were quite distinctive aspects to social work practice, and these broadly reflected the 'theoretical base' of the occupation. This suggested, in other words, that the content of the curriculum was significant for the conduct of practice, and there was a good deal of boundary maintenance between the occupations which reflected the thrust of their theory base. This is all the more remarkable because the two groups of practitioners worked alongside each other, providing the opportunity for 'knowledge seepage' between them, and because of the often emphasised importance of life experience rather than formal knowledge for the conduct of practice. Indeed, some of the information has particular importance for care management. Where interpersonal skills are of such importance, social workers' capacity to demonstrate them both suggests their suitability for care management and that they are not straightforward and hence at the professional end of the conduct of care management. Likewise, social workers' capacity to intervene in the environment again indicates an area where social workers have particular competence relevant for care management.

Becher, however identifies a second aspect of differentiation between disciplines. It sometimes happens that subject disciplines lay claim to the same intellectual territory. These distinctions may be of three types: a distinction in style or emphasis, a division of labour, or a difference in conceptual framework. A difference of emphasis is evident between history and philosophy. Megill (1987) contends that 'philosophers in their writing are apt to consider at great length matters which historians will pass over quickly and vice versa'. An example Becher gives of a division of labour involves Physics, Chemistry and Biology. Problems not amenable to Physics may be passed on to the Chemist, who in turn, if such problems are not amenable to them, may pass them on to the Biologist. This reflects the dominant approaches of the disciplines: deductive for Physics, inductive for Chemistry and phenomenological for Biology. Becher draws on Yates (1985) view of Sociology and Anthropology as an example of distinctions in conceptual frameworks. His distinction - between Sociology which seeks a methodology which is external and technical, related to the possibility of objective knowledge, and Anthropology, which emphasises the internal apprehension of relationships and their transformation through cultural meanings - is almost certainly overdrawn. Nonetheless, it is certainly true that different disciplines are characterised by methodological and epistemological differences: compare, for example, the dominant experimental tradition of psychology with the more qualitative tradition of some areas of sociology. Such differences become clearer when comparing social psychology with areas of micro sociology. The difference of central emphasis, between social problem definitions of social workers and mental health definitions of CPNs is a case in point (Sheppard, 1991).

The particular emphasis which may define a distinctive social work approach is that involved in emergent understanding: the approach of reflexive eclecticism. It may be that other groups are interested in areas similar to those of social workers. For example, the community psychiatric nurse may be interested in some aspects of mental health, or the paediatrician or health visitor in some areas of child protection. Their focus may, then, be similar to social work. Their approach, however, may not. Reflexive eclecticism suits the analysis of complex and sometimes dangerous situations, where the practitioner wishes to make an interpretation of those situations which, given the alternatives, is that which is least likely to be wrong. It suits the case based nature of social work and the uncertain status of much social science knowledge, while allowing the social workers to use that knowledge. It is consistent with the interactional focus of social work and its concern with consumers' subject status. It allows for the use of formal knowledge as well as categories and schema used in 'everyday life'. Its emphasis on rigour and falsification, furthermore, provides a means for going beyond the confirmation bias characterising much common sense approaches to the process of understanding. In all these respects, reflexive eclecticism engenders an approach which transcends common sense understanding and hence provides for a distinctive approach even in areas which are the 'common ground' of a number of occupations or professions.

These results, then, suggested both a considerable degree of 'boundary maintenance' between the disciplines, and that this boundary maintenance would be reflected in practice. Bernstein has made a further distinction of importance for this issue. Bernstein (1971) distinguishes between what he calls a collection code and an integration code (see Harker and May, 1993; Jacobson, 1981). A collection code consists of strongly classified and bounded domains. Each subject area has clearly separated contents: a 'science package might involve Maths, Physics and Chemistry; a social science package, Sociology, Psychology and Politics; and a humanities package, English, History and French. Each area is strongly differentiated and distinguished from each other. Integration (in integration code) refers to the subordination of previously insulated subjects to some relational idea which blurs the boundaries between the subjects. Integration can be within or between subjects (Bernstein, 1971, p 53). The kind of relational idea might be, for example, some concept or category which brings together some disparate areas of interest. An obvious example, from transfer of learning in social work, is that of loss, as indeed is that of social network.

In certain respects, it may appear that social work would benefit from a collection code. Its emphasis on strongly bounded domains of knowledge would, it appears, be likely to engender an exclusive area of knowledge and practice, distinctive to social work, and hence provide some justification for their place within care management. However, it is in the combination of the two that social work is liable to benefit most. If social work is to be served by reflexive eclecticism, then it has to incorporate, to some extent at least, an integration code. While, there is some emphasis on the principle of convergence, reflexive eclecticism encourages the use of concepts and ideas which may be used across different areas of practice. Knowledge is limited, understanding is often uncertain. Social work will at times have to use categories derived from everyday life and concepts from social science which are generic rather than convergent with the particular practice area with which they are concerned. These concept and categories will inevitably serve an integrating function. The process of conducting reflexive eclecticism will also be generic: it is applicable in principle to all areas of practice. Interestingly, although integrative (within the discipline of social work) this approach also, as we have seen, serves to underline boundary maintenance with other disciplines. This reflects in part Becher's view of differences of emphasis in the same 'territory'.

There is a sense in which a collection code is also being pursued. An emphasis on particular areas of knowledge, while encouraging integrating elements within social work, also serves to distinguish social work from the formal knowledge possessed by other occupations. It seeks to identify what is distinctive about social work. It is interesting, in this respect, that there was a considerable degree of boundary maintenance between social workers and CPNs in my earlier study (Sheppard, 1991). Of course, within the social work curriculum there may be elements of a collection code. This is most obviously the case with the Law, where discrete elements of the law generally relate to discrete areas of practice, As was stated earlier, the law remains an important area of social work's formal knowledge although it has not been discussed in detail in this book.

SOURCES OF DIVERSITY WITHIN SOCIAL WORK

While, of course, it is important to recognise the curriculum based sources of distinctiveness and consistency, it would be naive not to recognise the potential for some degree of diversity. The key issue, however, lies in the extent to which this diversity is to be contained within the overall unity and distinctiveness of social work. There are a number of ways, conceptually of understanding this.

Bucher and Strauss (1961) drew attention to the possibility of cultural and practice divergence within an occupation: with medicine they identified a heterogeneous set of groupings derived from the specialisms (paediatrics, surgery, obstetrics etc). They refer to these groupings as 'segments', which can have interests which diverge widely. They develop a process model, which emphasises the constantly negotiated and changing relationships between these groupings and the changing nature of the segments over time. Occupations, therefore are portrayed as loose amalgamations or segments pursuing different objectives in a different manner, more or less delicately held together under a common name and at a particular point in history.

Gouldner (1957) considered the orientation of professions can affect the degree of unity or segmentation within it. He distinguished between cosmopolitans and locals. A 'local' orientation is characterised by group loyalty which is focused on the organisation in which the individual works where the reference group against which the individual judges their performance lies within the organisation. A 'cosmopolitan' orientation involves the profession as a whole (not just the organisation) as the reference group. This is particularly interesting in multi-disciplinary settings, such as community mental health centres, where an orientation to one's local fellow professionals would indicate a 'local' orientation, and an orientation to one's specific social work contribution, to a 'cosmopolitan' orientation. Ruscio (1987) suggests either-or scenarios are not helpful. He suggests we should examine disciplines in terms of their unifying or segmenting *tendencies*. Using a biological analogy, he distinguishes between genotype and phenotype. The genotype represents a fundamental instruction to the organism and its potential for survival and growth. The phenotype represents the actual manifestation of that potential in a particular physical setting. His study of Higher Education showed phenotypical variations across institutions to be substantial but that genotypical cultures endemic to each discipline could be identified.

Becher (1989) distinguishes between more or less convergent or divergent disciplines. Convergent disciplinary configurations are those which are tightly knit, characterised by a high degree of consensus in terms of fundamental ideologies, common values, shared judgement of quality and awareness of belonging to a unique tradition. They are, he thinks, likely to occupy intellectual territories with well defined external boundaries. Divergent groups are loosely knit configurations. They lack a clear sense of cohesion and identity. There is no consensus on fundamental ideologies, limited shared values, no shared judgement of quality and a variety of traditions within the discipline boundaries. In some contexts this divergence is so wide that it is more meaningful to speak of identifiable and coherent properties of subsidiary areas within one disciplinary area or another. Once this occurs, it becomes possible or recognise between subspecialisms certain pattern of similarity and difference which cut right across disciplinary boundaries (Becher, 1989, p 43-44). Such might be the case (potentially) between community work and some radical forms of social work, or mental health social work and clinical psychology or community psychiatric nursing. Becher presented the convergent-divergent distinction along a spectrum in which disciplines may be more or less convergent or divergent.

The key to the degree of convergence or divergence, unity or segmentation, in social work, can be presented in terms of the orientation to knowledge characteristic of its practitioners. In this we can present social work orientations in three dimensions: an orientation towards formal knowledge based practice versus experience; an orientation towards the academic versus practice settings as the 'seat' of knowledge; and an orientation towards radical versus traditional approaches in both theory and practice. Of course, like Becher, it is best to present each of these orientations as a spectrum, with extremes at either end. In this respect, the important issue is the attitude of practitioners to the acquisition and use of formal knowledge. It would be of no use, for example, for social work to possess the most advanced formal knowledge for practice if practitioners, for whatever reasons, preferred experience to knowledge. In social work, as shown in chapter 8, the potential for this emphasis on experience is very great. Hence we are distinguishing here between the actual validity and use of the knowledge available, and the attitudes towards and beliefs about that knowledge characteristic of practitioners. If practitioners go too far in emphasising the experiential base for practice, it becomes increasingly difficult to justify their professional status, unique knowledge and professional training. This would, of course, have serious consequences for their place within care management.

Hence, the orientation of social workers to formal knowledge and its use, in terms of characteristic attitudes and beliefs, are as important as the actual formal knowledge available. It is, however, possible for a knowledge orientation to be developed which is consistent with the capacities of formal knowledge to provide a 'knowledge base' for social work. In terms of the three orientations, an emphasis on both experientialism and radical practice would be ill suited to social work's professional status within care management. The emphasis on reflexive eclecticism provides both a process of analysis appropriate to social work and allows the use of both experience an formal knowledge in practice. Likewise, interpersonal skills, task centred practice and social networks and supports provide a further knowledge base for practice. If social workers value these approaches and the knowledge contained within them, they will have gone a long way to possessing an orientation appropriate to the practice of social work. Likewise, the recognition of the reality of the social worker as state functionary (chapter 3) together with the adoption of the practice paradigm (chapter 10) would go a considerable way towards preventing inappropriately radical sentiments amongst practitioners. Taken together, these would also reduce the perceived gap between the academic and practice settings of student training, by making the two more convergent in their central concerns and foci.

Such convergence, it should be emphasised, does not necessarily entail complete uniformity. The phenotype-genotype distinction is helpful in this respect. We might expect some differences between social work professionals in terms of their specialist emphasis. We might expect that child care social workers would have specialist knowledge, interests and concerns, not characteristics, say, of mental health social workers. Inevitably there are aspects of child care practice which requires some form of specialised knowledge (for example welfare drift, or permanency). Likewise mental health social workers might be expected, generally, to know something of the significance of expressed emotion in practice with people suffering from schizophrenia. Different settings, furthermore, might create distinctions. The multi-disciplinary setting of the community mental health setting might lead to practice, and even ideological differences from district or area team settings. For example, on the whole practitioners in the former setting might give greater credence to biology as a factor in mental illness than those in the latter setting.

Such settings, furthermore, might provide the context for 'knowledge seepage'. This would be where the knowledge or approaches of one profession became characteristic of another profession occupying the same setting, as a result of day to day contact. Such contact would allow them to familiarise themselves with the approaches of the other profession, without these having been formally a part of their professional curriculum. The kind of work undertaken by social work might provide an auspicious basis for such knowledge seepage. The degree of uncertainty about outcome and the difficulties in the use of social science knowledge would suggest that 'on the job' experiential learning would be of some importance in the conduct of practice. In a multidisciplinary setting, this would include learning from other professions and professionals on the basis of day to day contact and joint working. Hence a genotypical variation of social workers based in a mental health setting might arise from their contact with other mental health professionals. While this is, in principle, possible, such evidence as exists (Sheppard, 1991) suggests that such knowledge seepage does not occur easily, and that there is a degree of boundary maintenance between professional disciplines.

CONCLUSION

This book has emphasised the context of care management for the pursuit of social work, as well as vice versa. Social work, as is clear from official documents, is not the only occupation which may be used for care management. However, the deprofessionalising elements of the New Managerialism, together with a poor public perception of the professional status of social work and uncertainty within social work about its knowledge foundations, potentially present threats to the position of social work within care management. It is, I think, possible to justify a special place for social work, and this is based on both its nature and the particular knowledge they can use in pursuit of care management.

This chapter has emphasised, however, three key elements to the uptake and use of this knowledge. The first is the technicality-indetermination ratio and where social work may be placed in relation to this. The second is the influence of the content of knowledge on the way members of the occupation characteristically view the situations with which they deal, and which particularly emphasises the boundaries to that knowledge. The third is the orientation of the members of the profession towards that knowledge, and the extent to which they are prepared to value and take seriously the formal knowledge which may be used for practice. It is clearly not enough to have the potential to offer a distinctive contribution to care management, which is nonotheless consistent with the main thrust of care management. It is important for social workers to reflect this potential in their actual conduct of practice.

If it ever had been the case that social work could rely on benign political support for its continued existence, regardless of its degree of effectiveness (I am not sure that this was ever the case), it is less likely that such support would any longer be forthcoming. Where care managers do not have to be social workers and with various occupations and community care workers carrying out care managerial tasks, it might be possible to conceive of a welfare system which does not require individuals qualified in the way formerly characterised by social work. It is this kind of situation which has led to a government requirement that CCETSW provide a model of training based on a clear analysis of its function (circa 1994). This book has attempted to provide a basis for a continued and distinctive contribution of social work to care management. In this, however, it is not sufficient to have the knowledge base which is suitable for a distinctive role. It is important that the practitioners value this formal knowledge, and are prepared to use it in practice. This, perhaps, presents the major challenge for social workers as they attempt to respond to the demand of the new environment of social care.

References

Abbott, P. (1992) *Rationalising The Skills Mix in Community Care for Disabled and Older People: A Report of Research in Cornwall*. Centre for Community Research, University of Plymouth.

Allais, M. (1979) The foundations of a positive theory of choice involving risk and a criticism of the postulates and axioms of the American School. In Allais, M. and Hagen, O. (ed) *Expected Utility Hypotheses and the Allais Paradox*. Dordecht. Reidl.

Anderson, J. (1984) Toward generic practice: the interactional approach. *Social Casework*, 65, 323-29.

Anderson, J. (1988) *Foundations of Social Work Practice*. New York. Springer.

Arrow, K.J. (1974) Gifts and exchanges. *Philosophy and Public Affairs*, 1, 343-362.

Atkinson, P. (1977) The reproduction of professional knowledge. In Dingwall, R., Heath, C., Reid, M. and Stacey, M. (ed) *Health Care and Health Knowledge*. London. Croom Helm.

Atkinson, P. (1980) *Writing Ethnography*. Mimeo.

Atkinson, P. (1983) The reproduction of the professional community. In Dingwall, R. and Lewis, P. (eds) *The Sociology of professions: Lawyers, Doctors and Others*. London. Macmillan.

Atkinson, P. (1985) *Language, Structure and Reproduction*. Methuen. London.

Bacharach, P. and Baratz, M. (1970) *Power and Poverty*. Oxford. Oxford University Press.

Badger, D. (1985) A comment on 'Learning for transfer' by Derek Gardiner. *Issues in Social Work Education*, 5, 1, 63-6.

Badminter, E. (1980) *Mother love, Myth and Reality*. New York. Macmillan.

Bailey, R. and Brake, M. (1975) *Radical Social Work*. London. Edward Arnold.

Bandura, A. (1978) The self system as reciprocal determinism. *American Psychologist*, 37, 344-58.

Bandura, A. (1982) Self efficacy mechanisms in human agency. *American Psychologist*, 37, 122-147.

Banham, J. (1988) *Redrawing the Frontier in the Public Sector*. London. Royal Institute of Public Administration.

Barclay, P. (1982) *Social Workers: Their Role and Tasks*. London. Bedford Square Press.

Barnes, D. and Todd, F. (1977) *Communication and Learning in Small Groups*. London. Routledge and Kegan Paul.

Barry, B. (1965) *Political Argument*. London. Routledge.

Bartlett, H. (1970) *The Common Base of Social Work Practice*. New York. National Association of Social Workers.

BASW (British Association of Social Workers) (1973) *The inalienable elements of social work*. Discussion Paper Number 3. Birmingham. BASW.

BASW (British Association of Social Workers) (1975) *A Code of Ethics for Social Workers*. Birmingham. BASW.

Becher, T. (1987) Disciplinary discourse. *Studies in Higher Education*, 12, 3, 261-274.

References

Becher, T. (1989) *Academic Tribes and Territories*. Buckingham. Open University Press.

Bee, H. and Mitchell, S. (1984) *The Developing Person: A Life Span Approach*. Second Edition. Cambridge. Harper and Rowe.

Bell, D. (1960) *The End of Ideology*. Chicago. The Free Press.

Bell, D. (1974) *The Coming of Post Industrial Society*. London. Heinemann.

Benn, S.I. (1967) Freedom and persuasion. *Australasian Journal of Philosophy*, 45, 259-75.

Benn, S.I. and Peters, R.S. (1959) *Social Principles and the Democratic State*. London. Allen and Unwin.

Berger, P. (1977) *Pyramids of Sacrifice*. Penguin.

Berlin, I. (1969) Two Concepts of Liberty. In *Four Essays on Liberty*. Oxford. Oxford University Press.

Bernstein, B. (1971) On the classification and framing of educational knowledge. In M.F.D. Young (ed) *Knowledge and Control*. London. Collier Macmillan.

Bernstein, B. (1975) *Class, Codes and Control, Vol 3: Towards a Theory of Educational Transmissions*. London. Routledge and Kegan Paul.

Berkowitz, L. (1986) *A Survey of Social Psychology*. London. CBS Publishing.

Bernstein, R.J. (1983) *Beyond Objectivism and Relativism.: Science, Hermaneutics and Praxis*. Oxford. Basil Blackwell.

Best, J. (1987) Rhetoric in claims making: constructing the missing children problem. *Social Problems*, 34, 2, 101-21.

Betts, K. (1986) The conditions of action, power, and the problem of interests. *Sociological Review*, 34, 1, 39-64.

Bhaskar, R. (1978) *A Realist Theory of Science*. Hassocks. Harvester.

Bhaskar, R. (1979) *The Possibility of Naturalism*. Hassocks. Harvester.

Biestek, (1957) *The Casework Relationship*. London. George Allen and Unwin.

Blom-Cooper, L. (1985) *A Child in Trust*. London. Kingswood Press.

Bloor, M. (1978) On the routinised nature of work in people processing agencies. The case of acute tonsillectomey assessments in ENT out patients clinics. In Davis, A. (ed) *Relationships Between Doctors and Patients*. Farnborough. Saxon House.

Blyth, M.J. and Hugman, B. (1982) Social work education and probation. In Bailey, R. and Lee, P. (eds) *Theory and Practice in Social Work*. Oxford. Basil Blackwell.

Bolger, S., Corrigan, P., Docking, J. and Frost, N. (1981) *Towards Socialist Welfare Work*. London. Macmillan.

Borgh, J.A. and Thein, R.D. (1985) Individual constructs, accessability, person memory and the recall-judgement link: the case of information overload. *Journal of Personality and Social Psychology*, 49, 1129-1146.

Bosanquet, N. (1983) *After The New Right*. London. Heinemann.

Bradbury, G. (1984) Learning styles and CSS student supervision. *Social Work Education*, 4, 1, 35-36.

Bradshaw, J. (1972) The Concept of Social Need. *New Society*, 19, 496, 640-42.

Brandon, D. and Jordan, B. (ed) (1979) *Creative Social Work*. Oxford. Blackwell.

Braverman, H. (1974) *Labour and Monopoly Capitalism*. New York. Monthly Review Press.

Braybrooke, D. (1987) *Meeting Needs*. Princeton. Princeton University Press.

Brewer, C. and Lait, J. (1980) *Can Social Work Survive?*. London. Temple Smith.

Brewer, M.B. and Lui, L.L. (1989) The primacy of age and sex in the structure of person categories. *Social Cognition*, 7, 262-74.

Brewer, W.F. and Nakamura, G. (1984) The nature and function of schemas. In R.S. Wyer and T.K. Srull (ed) *Handbook of Social Cognition*. Vol 1. Hillside, NJ. Erlbaum.

Brown, G.W. and Harris, T.O. (1979) *Social Origins of Depression*. London. Tavistock.

Brown, G.W., Birley, J. and Wing, J. (1972) Influence of family life on the course of schizophrnic disorder: a replication. *British Journal of Psychiatry*, 121, 241-258.

Brown, R. (1973) Feedback in family interviewing. *Social Work*, 18, 5, 52-9.

Bruner, J. (1957) On perceptual readiness. *Psychological Review*, 64, 123-152.

Bruner, J. (1958) Social psychology and perception. In E.E. Maccoby, T.M. Newcomb and E.L. Hartley (ed) *Readings in Social Psychology*. Third Edition. New York. Holt, Rheinehart and Winston.

Bryant, C. (1985) *Positivism in Social Theory and Research*. London. Macmillan.

Bryman, A. (1988) *Quantity and Quality in Social Research*. London. Unwin Hyman.

Buchanan, J.M., Burton, J. and Wagner, R.E. (1978) *The Consequences of Mr Keynes*. Hobart Paper 78. London. Institute of Economic Affairs.

Bucher, R. and Strauss, A. (1961) Professions in process. *American Journal of Sociology*, 66, 325-34.

Buckley, W. (ed) (1968) *Modern Systems Research for the Behavioural Scientist*. Chicago. Aldine.

Budgen, R.P. (1982) *A Critical Examination of the Principle of Self Determination in Social Work*. Ph.D. Thesis. University of East Anglia.

Bulmer, M. (1979) Concepts in the analysis of qualitative data. *Sociological Review*, 27, 4, 651-77

Bulmer, M. (1986) The value of qualitative methods. In Bulmer, M. (ed) *Social Science and Social Policy*. London. Allen and Unwin.

Burgess, H. (1992) *Problem Led Learning for Social Work Education: The Enquiry and Action Learning Approach*. London. Whiting and Birch.

Burgess, H. and Jackson, S. (1990) Enquiry and action learning: a new approach to social work education. *Social Work Education*, 9, 3, 3-18.

Burgess, R. (1984) *In the Field*. London. George Allen and Unwin.

Burrell, G. and Morgan, G. (1979) *Sociological Paradigms and Organisational Analysis*. London. Heinemann.

Busfield, J. (1986) *Managing Madness*. London. Unwin Hyman.

Buss, A.R. (1978) Causes and reasons in attribution theory: a conceptual critique. *Journal of Personality and Social Psychology*, 36, 1311-21.

Butler, E. (1983) *Hayek*. Temple Smith. London.

Butrym, Z. (1976) *The Nature of Social Work*. London. Macmillan.

Carew, R. (1979) The place of knowledge in social work activity. *British Journal of Social Work*, 9, 349-64.

Carver, C.S. and Scheier, M.F. (1982) Control theory: a useful conceptual framework for personality, social, clinical and health psychology. *Psychological Bulletin*, 111-35.

CCETSW. (1985) *Policies for Qualifying Training in Social Work: The Council's Propositions*. London. CCETSW.

Cheek, J. and Hogan, R. (1983) Self concepts, self presentation and moral judgements. In J. Suls and A.G. Greenwald (ed) *Psychological Perspectives on the Self*. Vol 2. Hillside, New Jersey. Erlbaum.

Cheetham, J. (1992) Evaluating the effectiveness of social work: its contribution to the development of knowledge base. *Issues in Social Work Education*, 12, 1, 52-68.

Child. S. (1969) *British Management Thought*. London.

Clark, C. and Asquith, S. (1985) *Social Work and Social Philosophy*. London. Routledge and Kegan Paul.

Clegg, S. (1979) *The Theory of Power and Organisation*. London. Routledge and Kegan Paul.

Cochrane, R. (1983) *The Social Creation of Mental Illness*. Hong Kong. Longman.

Cohen, C.E. (1981) Person categories and social perceptions: testing some boundaries of the processing effects of prior knowledge. *Journal of Personality and Social Psychology*, 40, 445-52.

References

Cohen, S. and Syme, S.L. (1985) Issues in the study and application of social support. In S. Cohen and S.L. Syme (ed) *Social Support and Health*. London. Academic Press.

Cole, G.D.H. (1947) *A Guide to the Elements of Socialism*. London. Labour Party.

Collins, J. and Collins, M. (1981) *Achieving Change in Social Work*. London. Heinemann..

Compton, B. and Galloway, B. (1979) *Social Work Processes*. Homewood, Illinois. The Dorsey Press.

Compton, B. and Galloway, B. (1989) *Social Work Processes*. Fourth Edition. London. Wadsworth.

Conrad, P. and Schneider, J. (1980) *Deviance and Medicalisation: From Badness to Sickness*. St. Louis. C.V. Mosby.

Corby, B. (1982) Theory and practice in long term social work. *British Journal of Social Work*, 12, 6.

Corden, J. and Preston-Shoot, M. (1987) *Contracts in Social Work*. Alderhot. Gower.

Corob, A. (1987) *Working With Depressed Women*. Aldershot. Gower.

Corrigan, P. and Leonard, P. (1978) *Social Work Practice Under Capitalism: A Marxist Approach*. London. Macmillan.

Coser, L. (1956) *The Functions of Social Conflict*. London. Routledge and Kegan Paul.

Coulter, J. (1973) *Approaches to Insanity*. London. Martin Robertson.

Culyer, A.J. (1976) *Need and the National Health Service*. Oxford. Martin Robertson.

Cupitt, D. (1985) *The Sea of Faith*. London. British Broadcasting Corporation

Curnock, K. and Hardiker, P. (1979) *Towards Practice Theory*. London. Rouledge and Kegan Paul.

Darley, J. and Gross, P. (1983) A hypothesis confirming bias in labelling effects. *Journal of Personality and Social Psychology*, 44, 20-33.

Davis, A.G. and Strong, P.M. (1976) Aren't children wonderful. In M. Stacey (ed) *The Sociology of the NHS*. Sociological Review Monograph No. 22

Davies, M. (1977) *Support Systems In Social Work*. London. Routledge and Kegan Paul.

Davies, M. (1981) Social work, the state and the university. *British Journal of Social Work*, 11, 275-88.

Davies, M. (1984) Training: what we think of it now. *Social Work Today*, 24th January, 12-17.

Davies, M. (1986) *The Essential Social Worker: A Guide to Positive Practice*. Aldershot. Gower.

Davies, M. (1991) *Sociology and Social Work*. Aldershot. Gower.

Davis, A.G. and Strong, P.M. (1976) Aren't children wonderful? In Stacey, M. (ed) *The Sociology of the NHS*. Sociological Review Monograph, No 22.

de Muralt, S. (1974) *The Idea of Phenomenology*. Evanston. Ill. Northwestern University Press.

Denzin, N. (1978) *The Research Act in Sociology*. Second Edition. London. Butterworth.

Department of health (1989) *An Introduction to the Children Act*, 1989. London. HMSO.

Department of Health (1991a) *Care Management and Assessment: Managers' Guide*. London. HMSO.

Department of Health (1991b) *Care Management and Assessment: Practitioners' Guide*. London. HMSO.

Department of Health (Neill, J.) (1991c) *Getting The Message Across*. London. HMSO for NISW.

Department of Health (1991d) *Implementing Community Care: Purchaser, Commissioner and Provider Roles*. London. HMSO.

Department of Health (1991e) *Purchase of Service*. London. HMSO.

Devlin, P. (1965) *The Enforcement of Morals*. Oxford. Oxford University Press.

Dingwall, R. (1989) Some problems about predicting child abuse and neglect. In Stevenson, O. (ed) *Child Abuse: Public Policy and Professional Practice*. London. Harvester Wheatsheaf.

DHSS (1984) *Report of the Commission of Enquiry into the Care and Supervision provided in relation to Maria Colwell*. London. HMSO.

Dominelli, L. and Mcleod, E. (1989) *Feminist Social Work*. London. Macmillan.

Doyal, L. and Gough, I. (1991) *A Theory of Human Need*. London. Macmillan.

Doyal, L. and Harris, R. (1986) *Empiricism, Explanation and Rationality*. London. Routledge and Kegan Paul.

Downie, R. and Telfer, E. (1969) *Respect For Persons*. London. Allen and Unwin.

Downie, R. and Telfer, E. (1978) Aim, Skill and Role in Social Work. In N. Timms and D.Watson (ed) *Philosophy in Social Work*. London. Routledge.

Dunsire, A. (1978) *Control in a Bureaucracy*. Oxford. Martin Robertson.

Durkheim, E. (1897) *Suicide: Studies in Sociology*. Paris. Felix Alcan.

Durkheim, E. (1947) *The Division of Labour in Society*. Glencoe, Illinois. The Free Press.

Durkheim, E. (1967) *Socialism*. New York.

Durkheim, E. (1953) *Sociology and Philosophy*. London. Cohen and West.

Durkheim, E. (1966) *The Rules of Sociological Method*. New York. Free Press.

Eber, R. and Fiske, S.T. (1984) Outcome dependency and attention to inconsistent information. *Journal of Personality and Social Psychology*, 47, 709-26.

Eckstein, O. (1958) *Water Resource Development*. Cambridge Massachusetts. Harvard University Press.

Edwards, R.E. (1982) Mental health and rational autonomy. In R.E. Edwards (ed) *Psychiatry and Ethics*. Buffalo, New York. Prometheus Books.

Emmet, D. (1966) *Rules, Roles and Relations*. London. Macmillan.

Emmet, D. and MacIntyre, A. (1970) *Sociological Theory and Philosophical Analysis*. London. Macmillan.

England, H. (1986) *Social Work as Art*. London. Allen and Unwin.

Entwistle, N. and Ramsden, P. (1983) *Understanding Student Learning*. London. Croom Helm.

Epstein, L. (1985) *Talking and Listening*. St. Louis. Times/Mirror/Mosby College Publishing.

Ernstbrunner, M. (1987) *The assessment of prospective foster parents. A study of intuitive practice*. M.Phil thesis. Cranfield Institute of Technology.

Evans, D. (1987) The centrality of practice in social work education. *Issues in Social Work Education*, 7, 2, 83-101.

Etzioni, A. (1969) *The Semi Professions and their Organisation*. London. Collier Macmillan.

Faiers, M. (1987) The importance of being relevant. *Community Care*, 16th April, 20-21.

Fay, B. (1975) *Social Theory and Political Practice*. London. George Allen and Unwin.

Feinberg, J. (1973) *Social Philosophy*. Englewood Cliffs, N.J. Prentice Hall.

Feinberg, J. (1977) Harm and self interest. In Hacker, P.M.S. and Raz, J. (ed) *Law, Morality and Society. Essays in Honour of H.L.A.Hart*. Oxford. Oxford University Press.

Feyerbend, P. (1978) *Science in a Free Society*. London. New Left Books.

Fischer, J. (1976) *The Effectiveness of Social Casework*. Illinois. Springfield.

Fishburn, P. (1983) Transative measurable utility. *Journal of Economic Theory*, 31, 293-317.

Fiske, S.T. and Taylor, S. (1991) *Social Cognition*. London. McGraw Hill.

Fisher, M. (1992) Defining the practice content of care management. *Social Work and Social Sciences Review* ,2, 3, 204-230.

References

Fisher, M., Newton, C. and Sainsbury, E. (1984) *Mental Health Social Work Observed*. London. George Allen and Unwin.

Fletcher, G. (1984) Psychology and common sense. *American Psychologist*, 39, 203-11.

Ford, J.L. (1983) *Choice, Expectation and Uncertainty*. Oxford. Basil Blackwell.

Ford, J.L. (1989) *Economic Choice Under Uncertainty*. Aldershot. Edward Elgar.

Forder, A. (1974) *Concepts in Social Administration*. London. Routledge and Kegan Paul.

Fowler, I. A. (1967) Family agency characteristics and client continuation. *Social Casework*, 48, 271-77.

Fox-Harding, L. (1991) *Perspectives in Child Care Policy*. London. Longman.

Freden, M. (1991) *Rights*. Buckingham. Open University Press.

Freidson. E. (1970) *The Profession of Medicine*. New York. Harper and Row.

Friedman, A. (1977) *Industry and Labour: Class Struggle at Work and Monopoly Capitalism*. London.

Friere, P. (1972) *Pedagogy of the Oppressed*. London. Sheed and Ward.

Froland, C., Panacost, D.L., Chapman, N.J. and Kimboko, P.J. (1981) *Helping Networks and Human Services*. Beveley Hills California.

Funch, D.P. and Mettlin, C. (1982) The role of social support in relation to recovery from breast surgery. *Social Science and Medicine*, 16, 1, 91-98.

Gadlin, H. and Dizard, J. E. (1984) Family life and the market place. Diversity and change in the American Family. In K.J. Gergen and M.M. Gergen (ed) *Historical Social Psychology*. Hillside. New Jersey. Erlbaum.

Gaertner, S. L. and McLaughlin, J.P. (1983) Racial stereotypes: associations and ascriptions of positive and negative characteristics. *Social Psychology Quarterly*, 46, 23-40.

Galper, J. (1975) *The Politics of Social Service*. New York. Prentice Hall.

Garbarino, J. (1983) Social support networks: RX for the helping professions. In J.K. Whittaker and J. Garbarino (ed) *Social Support Networks: Informal Helping in the Human Services*. New York. Aldine.

Gardiner, D. (1984) Social work education and the transfer of learning - a comment. *Issues in Social Work Education*, 4, 1, 55-57.

Gardiner, D. (1984a) Learning for transfer. *Issues in Social Work Education*, 4, 2, 95-105.

Gardiner, D. (1987) Debate. *Issues in Social Work Education*, 7, 1, 53-55.

Gardiner, D. (1988) Improving student learning setting: an agenda for quality in the 1990s. *Issues in Social Work Education*, 8, 1, 3-10.

Gardiner, D. (1989) *The Anatomy of Supervision*. London. Falmer.

Garfield, S.L. (1971) Research on client variables in psychotherapy. In A.E. Bergin and S.L. Garfield (ed) *Handbook of Psychotherapy and Behaviour Change: An Empirical Analysis*. New York. Wiley.

Geertz, C. (1983) *Local Knowledge*. New York. Basic Books.

Germain, C.B. (1979) *Social Work Practice: People and Environments - An Ecological Perspective*. New York. Columbia University Press.

Germain, C. and Gitterman, A. (1980) *The Life Model of Social Work Practice*. New York.

Giddens, A. (1974) *Positivism and Sociology*. London. Heinemann.

Giddens, A. (1993) *New Rules of Sociological Method*. Second Edition. London. Polity Press.

Gil, D. (1975) Unravelling child abuse. *American Journal of Orthopsychiatry*, 45, 346-54.

Gilbert, D.T., Krull, D.S., and Malone, P.S. (1990) Unbelieving the unbelievable: some problems in the rejection of fake information. *Journal of Personality and Social Psychology*, 59, 601-13.

Glaser, B. and Strauss, A.L. (1967) The Discovery of Grounded Theory. Chicago. Aldine.

Goffman, I. (1959) *The Presentation of Self in Everyday Life*. New York. Doubleday.

Goldberg, E.M. and Wharburton, W. (1979) *Ends and Means in Social Work*. London. George Allen and Unwin.

Goldman, A.I. (1970) *A Theory of Human Action*. Englewood Cliff, New Jersey. Prentice Hall.

Goldstein, H. (1973) *Social Work Practice: A Unitary Approach*. Columbia, South Carolina. University of South Carolina Press.

Goldstein, H. (1981) *Social Learning and Change*. London. Tavistock.

Gouldner, A. (1957) Cosmopolitans and locals - towards an analysis of latent social roles. *Administrative Science Quarterly*, 2, 231-300.

Graham. H. (1991) Feminism and social work education. *Issues in Social Work Education*, 11, 2, 48-64.

Green, T.H. (1991) Liberal legislation and freedom of contract.In Miller, D. (ed) *Liberty*. Oxford. Oxford University Press.

Greenwell, S. and Howard, B. (1986) An exercise in collaboration. *Issues in Social Work Education*, 6, 2, 129-36.

Greenwood, E. (1965) Attributes of a profession. in Zeal, M. (ed) *Social Welfare Institutions*. Wiley.

Grey, S., Corti, P. and Tate, A. (1988) External Relations. In R. Echlin (ed) *Community Mental Health Centres / Teams Information Pack*. London. Good Practices In Mental Health.

Griffin, J. (1986) *Well Being*. Milton Keynes. Open University Press.

Griffiths, Sir Roy (1988) *Community Care: Agenda For Action*. London. HMSO.

Gurin, A. (1972) *Community Organisation and Social Planning*. New York. John Wiley.

Gusfield, J.R. (1981) *The Culture of Public Problems*. Chicago. University of Chicago Press.

Gusfield, J. R. (1989) Constructing the ownership of social problems. *Social Problems*, 36, 5, 431-41.

Haines, J. (1981) *Skills and Methods in Social Work*. Revised edition. London. Constable.

Halfpenny, P. (1982) *Positivism and Sociology*. London. Allen and Unwin.

Halmos, P. (1978) *The Personal and the Political: Social Work and Political Action*. London. Hutchinson.

Hammersley, M. and Atkinson, P. (1983) *Ethnography: Principles in Practice*. London. Routledge.

Hamilton, G. (1941) The underlying philosophy of social casework, *Family*, 23, 139-48.

Hamilton, G. (1953) *Theory and Practice of Social Casework*. New York. Columbia University Press.

Hammersley, M. (1983) Reflexivity and Naturalism in Ethnography. In M. Hammersley (ed) *The Ethnography of Schooling*. Chester. Benrose Press.

Hammersley, M. (1992) *What's Wrong With Ethnography?* London. Routledge.

Hammersley, M. amd Atkinson, P. (1983) *Ethnography: Principles in Practice*. London. Tavistock.

Hanson, N. (1958) *Patterns of Discovery*. Cambridge Cambridge University Press.

Harbert, W. (1985) Status professionalism. *Community Care*, 10th October, 14-15.

Hardiker, P. (1981) Heart and Head - the function and role of knowledge in social work. *Issues in Social Work Education*, 1, 85-111.

Harker, R. and May, S. (1993) Code and habitus: comparing the accounts of Bernstein and Bourdieu. *British Journal of Sociology of Education*, 14, 2, 169-79.

Harris, R. (1983) Social work education and the transfer of learning. *Issues in Social Work Education*, 3, 2, 103-17.

References

Hart, H.L.A. (1960) *The Concept of Law*. London. Oxford University Press.

Hart, H.L.A. (1963) *Law, Liberty and Morality*. Oxford. Oxford University Press.

Hart, H.L.A. and Honore, T. (1985) *Causation and the Law*. Second Edition. Oxford. Clarendon.

Hartman, A. (1979) *Finding Families: An Ecological Approach to Family Assessment in Adoption*. Beverley Hills. Sage.

Hartman, A. and Laird, J. (1983) *Family Centred Social Work Practice*. New York Free Press.

Hayek, F.A. (1949) *Individualism and the Economic Order*. Chicago. Chicago University Press.

Hayek, F.A. (1960) *The Constitution of Liberty*. London. Routledge and Kegan Paul.

Hayek, F.A. (1978) *New Studies in Philosophy, Politics and the History of Ideas*. London. Routledge and Kegan Paul.

Hayek, F.A. (1979) *Law, Legislation and Liberty, Vol 3. The Political Order of Free People*. London. Routledge.

Hazlerigg, L.E. (1986) Is there a choice between constructionism and objectivism? *Social Problems*, 33, 6, 1-13.

Heald, D. (1987) *Public Expenditure*. Oxford. Basil Blackwell.

Hearn, J. (1982) The problem of theory and practice in social work and social work education. *Issues in Social Work Education*, 2, 2, 95-118.

Henderson, A.S. (1977) The social network, support and neurosis: the function of attachment in adult life. *British Journal of Psychiatry*, 131, 185-91.

Henderson, A.S. (1984) Interpreting the evidence on social support. *Social Psychiatry*, 19, 49-52.

Heraud, B. (1981) *Training for Uncertainty: A Sociological Approach to Social Work Education*. London. Routledge and Kegan Paul.

Heritage, J. (1978) Aspects of the flexibility of language use. *Sociology*, 12, 79-103.

Hestletine, M. (1980) Ministers and management in Whitehall. *Management Services in Government*, 35.

Hey, J.D. (1979) *Uncertainty in Microeconomics*. Oxford. Martin Robinson.

Higgins, E.T. and King, G.A. (1981) Accessability of social constructs: information processing consequences of individual and contextual variables. In N. Cantor and J.F. Kihlstrom (eds) *Personality, Cognition and Social Interaction*. Hillside, New Jersey. Erlbaum.

Hinde, R. (1982) Attachment: some conceptual and biological issues. In G. Murray Parkes and J. Stevenson Hinde (ed) *The Place of Attachment in Human Behaviour*. London. Tavistock.

Hirtschi, T. (1969) *Causes of Delinquency*. California. California University Press.

Hoghughi, M. (1980) *Assessing Problem Children*. London. Sage.

Hoghughi, M. (1980a). Social work in a bind: which way welfare? *Community Care*, April 3, 17-23.

Hoghughi, M. (1980b) Social work in a bind - the nature of the task. *Community Care*, April 10, 27-32.

Hoghughi, M. (1980c) Social work in a bind: a way out. *Community Care*, April 17, 22-27.

Holdsworth, L. (1991) *Empowerment Social Work With Physically Disabled People*. Norwich. Social Work Monographs.

Hollis, F. (1972) *Casework. A Psychosocial Therapy*. Second Edition. New York. Random House.

Holme, A. and Maizels, J. (1978) *Social Workers and Volunteers*. London. Allen and Unwin.

Homans, G.C. (1951) *The Human Condition*. Routledge and Kegan Paul.

Homans, G. (1973) Bringing men back in. In Ryan, A. (ed) *The Philosophy of Social Explanation*. London. Oxford University Press.

Horne, M. (1987) *Values in Social Work*. Aldershot. Gower.

House, S. (1981) *Work Stress and Social Support*. Reading Mass. Addison Wesley.

Howe, D. (1979) Agency function and social work principles. *British Journal of Social Work*, 9, 1, 29-49.

Howe, D. (1980) Inflated states and empty theories in social work. *British Journal of Social Work*, 10, 3, 317-40.

Howe, D. (1986) *Social Workers and their Practice in Welfare Bureaucracies*. Aldershot. Gower.

Howe, D. (1988) *An Introduction to Social Work Theory*. Aldershot. Wildwood House.

Hudson, A. (1985) Feminism and social work: resistance or dialogue? *British Journal of Social Work*, 15, 6, 635-55.

Hudson, B. and Macdonald, G. (1986) *Behavioural Social Work: An Introduction*. London. Macmillan.

Hughes, E. (1958) *Men and their Work*. New York. Free Press.

Hughes, E. (1971) *The Sociological Eye: Selected Papers*. Chicago. Aldine Atherton.

Hughes, J. (1990) *The Philosophy of Social Research*. Second Ed. London. Longmans.

Hugman, R. (1991) *Power in the Caring Professions*. Basingstoke. Macmillan.

Hume, D. (1875) *An Enquiry Concerning Human Understanding*. London. Longman.

Huntington, J. (1981) *Social Work and General Medical Practice: Collaboration or Conflict?* London. Allewn and Unwin.

Hughes, J. (1990) *The Philosophy of Social Research*. Longman. London.

Hull, C.L. (1943) *Principles of Behaviour*. New York. Appleton.

Huxley, T. (1902) *Collected Essays*. London. Methuen.

Jacobson, B. (1981) Collection type and integration type curricula in systems of higher education. An empirical and theoretical study. *Acta Sociologica*, 24, 1-2, 25-41.

Jamous, H. and Peloille, B. (1970) Professions or self perpetuating systems? Changes in the French University Hospital System. In Jackson, J.A. (ed) *Professions and Socialization*. Cambridge. Cambridge University Press.

Jevons, W. (1970) *The Theory of Political Economy*. Middlesex. Penguin.

Johnson, R.E. (1979) *Juvenile Delinquency and its Origins*. Cambridge. Cambridge University Press.

Jones, C. (1983) *State Social Work and The Working Class*. London. Macmillan.

Jones, R. (1982) A comment on 'through experience towards theory: a pychodynamic contribution to social work education' by Mary Barker. *Issues in Social Work Education*, 2, 2, 149-52.

Jordan, W. (1979) *Helping in Social Work*. London. Routledge and Kegan Paul.

Kadushin, A, (1983) *The Social Work Interview*. New York. Columbia University Press.

Kauffman, H. (1981) Fear of bureaucracy: a raging pandemic. *Public Administration Review*, 41, 1, 1-9.

Kauffman, W. (1957) (ed) *Existentialism From Dostoevsky to Satre*. London. Thames and Hudson.

Keat, R. and Urry, J. (1982) *Social Theory as Science*. London. Routledge and Kegan Paul.

Keith-Lucas, A. (1963) A critique of the principle of self determination. *Social Work*, 8, 3, 66-71.

Keith-Lucas, A. (1972) *Giving and Taking Help*. Chapel Hill N C. University of North Carolina Press.

Kirsch, I. (1985) Self efficacy and expectancy: old wines in new labels. *Journal of Personality and Social Psychology*, 49, 824-30.

Kolb, D.A. (1974) On management and the learning process. In D.A. Kolb, I.M. Rubin and J.M. McIntyre (ed) *Organisational Psychology: A Book of Readings*. Englewood Cliffs, New Jersey. Prentice Hall.

References

Kruglanski, A. and Freund, T. (1983) The freezing and unfreezing of lay inferences: effects on impressional primacy, ethnic stereotyping and numerical anchoring. *Journal of Experimental Psychology*, 19, 448-64.

Kuhn, T.S. (1970) *The Structure of Scientific Revolutions*. Chicago. University of Chicago Press.

Laswell, H. (1952) The threat to privacy. In Mciver, R. (ed) *Conflict and Loyalties*. New York. Harper and Row.

Langan, M. and Lee, P. (ed) (1989) *Radical Social Work Today*. London. Unwin Hyman.

Layder, D. (1990) *New Strategies in Social Research*.Cambridge. Polity Press.

Lealman, G.T., Haigh, D., Phillips, J.M., and Ord-Smith, C. (1983) Prediction and prevention in child abuse - an empty hope? *The Lancet*, 25th June, 1423-4.

Lee, D. (1959) *Freedom and Culture*. New York. Prentice Hall.

Lefcourt, W.E., Martin, R.A. and Selak, W.E. (1984) Locus of control and social support: interactive moderators of stress. *Journal of Personality and Social Psychology*, 47, 378-389.

Leff, J. and Vaughn, C. (1984) *Expressed Emotion in Families*. London. The Guildford Press.

Le Grand, J. (1990) Quasi markets and social policy. *The Economic Journal*, 101, 1256-67.

Le Grand, J. (1993) *Quasi Markets and Community Care*. Bristol. SAUS Publications.

Leonard, P. (1965) Social control and class values in social work practice. *Social Work*, 22, 4.

Leonard, P. (1975) Towards a paradigm for radical practice. In R. Bailey and M. Brake (ed) *Radical Social Work*.

Leonard, P. (1975b) Explanation and Education in Social Work. *British Journal of Social Work*, 5, 3, 325-34.

Lerghinger, L. (1978) Professionalisation and social work education: substance and structure. *Journal for Social Work Education*, 183-213.

Lilienfield, R. (1975) Systems theory as an ideology. *Social Research*, 42, 637-60.

Lindesmith, A.R. (1968) *Addiction and Opiates*. New York. Aldine.

Lipsky, M. (1990) *Street Level Bureaucracy*. New York. Russel Sage Foundation.

Little, B.R. (1983) Personal projects: a rationale and method for investigation. *Environmental Behaviour*, 15, 273-309.

Littler, C.R. (1978) Understanding Taylorism. *British Journal of Sociology*, 29, 2, 185-202.

Lord, C., Lepper, M. and Ross, L. (1979) Biased assimilation and attitude polarisation: the effects of prior theories and subsequently considered evidence. *Journal of Personality and Social Psychology*, 37, 2098-2110.

Lukes, S. (1974) *Power: A Radical View*. London. Macmillan.

Lutz, C. (1982) The domain of emotion words in Ifaluk. *American Ethnologist*, 9, 113-128.

Macdonald, G., Sheldon, B. and Gillespie, J. (1992) Contemporary studies of the effectiveness of social work. *British Journal of Social Work*, 22, 6, 615-47.

MacIntyre, A (1967) *A Short History of Ethics*. London. Macmillan.

Marcelesson, F., Winnubst, A., Buunk, B. and de Wolff, C. (1988) Social support and occupational stress. *Social Science and Medicine*, 26, 3, 365-73.

March, J.G. and Simon, H.A. (1970) Decision Making Theory. In Grisky, O. and Miller, C.A. (ed) *The Sociology of Organisations*. New York. Free Press.

Marcus, H. and Nurins, P. (1986) Possible selves. *American Psychologist*, 51, 954-69.

Marcus, H. and Whurf, E. (1987) The dynamic self concept. *Annual Review of Psychiatry*, 38, 299-337.

Marcuse, H. (1964) *One Dimensional Man*. London. Routledge and Kegan Paul.

Margolis, H. (1982) *Selfishness, Altruism and Rationality*. Cambridge. Cambridge University Press.

Marsh, C. (1982) *The Survey Method: The Contribution of Surveys to Sociological Explanation*. London. Allen and Unwin.

Marshall, A. (1947) *Principles of Economics*. London. Macmillan.

Marshall, T.H. (1963) *Sociology at the Crossroads*. Heinemann.

Maslow, A.H. (1954) *Motivation and Personality*. Second Edition. New York. Harper and Row.

Mayo, E. (1933) *The Human Problems of an Industrial Civilization*. New York. Macmillan.

McKean, R. (1958) *Efficiency in Government Through Systems Analysis*. Wiley. New York.

McClosky, H.J. (1985) Respect for human moral rights versus maximising good. In Frey, R.G. (ed) *Utility and Rights*. Oxford. Basil Blackwell.

McClosky, H. and Schaar, J.H. (1965) Psychological dimensions of anomie. *American Sociological Review*, 30, 14-40.

McGuire, A., Henderson, J. and Mooney, G. (1988) *The Economics of Health Care*. London. Routledge and Kegan Paul.

McIver, R. (1950) *The Ramparts We Guard*. New York. Macmillan.

Mechanic, D. (1962) Sources of power of lower participants in complex organisations. *Administrative Science Quarterly*, 7, 2, 349-64.

Medawar, P. (1979) *Advice to a Young Scientist*. New York. Harper and Row.

Megill, A. (1987) Provocation on belief, part four. *Social Epistemology*, 1, 1, pp 106-108.

Meir, D.L. and Bell, W. (1959) Anomie and differential access to life goals. *American Sociological Review*, 24, 189-202.

Melden, A.I. (1959) *Rights and Right Conduct*. Oxford. Basil Blackwell.

Merton, R. (et al) (1957) *The Student Physician*. Camb. Mass. Harvard University Press.

Merton, R.K. (1967) *Social Theory and Social Structure*. New York. The Free Press.

Mertzoff, J. and Kornreich, M. (1970) *Research in Psychotherapy*. New York. Atherton Press.

Meyer, C. (1973) Direct services in new and old contexts. In A.J. Kahn (ed) *Shaping the New Social Work*. New York. Columbia University Press.

Middleman, R. and Goldberg, G. (1974) *Social Service Delivery: A Structural Approach to Social Work Practice*. London. Columbia University Press.

Midgely, M. (1984) On being terrestrial. In S.C. Brown (ed) *Objectivity and Cultural Divergence*. London. University of Cambridge Press.

Mill, J.S. (1909) *Principles of Political Economy*. London. Longman Green and Co.

Mill, J.S. (1972) *Utilitarianism. Liberty. Representative Government*. London. J.M. Dent.

Miller, C., Crosbie, D., Vickery, A. (1991) *Everyday Community Care. A Manual for Managers*. London. NISW.

Miller, D. (1976) *Social Justice*. Oxford. Clarendon.

Miller, P.M. and Ingham, J.G. (1976) Friends, confidants and symptoms. *Social Psychiatry*, 11, 51-58.

Miller, W. and Neususs, C. (1978) The welfare state illusion and the contradictions between labour and capital. In J. Holloway and S. Picotto (ed) *State and Capital*. London. Edward Arnold.

Milne, A.J. (1968) *Freedom and Rights*. London. Allen and Unwin.

Miles, I. (1985) *Social Indicators For Human Development*. London. Francis Pinter.

Mishan, E.J. (1988) *Cost Benefit Analysis*. London. Allen and Unwin.

Mitchell, B. (1967) *Law, Morality and Religion in a Secular Society*. Oxford. Oxford

Mitchell, J.C. (1969) The concept and use of social networks. In Mitchell, J.C. (ed) *Social Networks in Urban Situations*. Manchester. Manchester University Press.

References

Moffett, J. (1968) *Concepts in Casework Treatment*. London. Routledge and Kegan Paul.

Morgan, G. (1990) *Organisation and Society*. London. Macmillan.

Morgan, M., Calnon, M. and Manning, N. (1985) *Sociological Approaches to Health and Illness*. London. Croom Helm.

Morgan, P. (1980) The state as mediator: alcohol problem management in the postwar world. *Contemporary Drug Problems*, 9, 107-30.

Morns, C. (1975) *Literature and the Social Worker*. London. Library Association.

Myrdal, G. (1961) Value loaded concepts. In Hegeland, H. (ed) *Money Growth and Methodology*. Gleerup.

Neill, J., Sinclair, I., Gorbach, P. and Williams, J. (1988) *A Need For Care? Elderly Applicants For Local Authority Homes*. Aldershot. Avebury.

Niskanen, W.A. (1971) *Bureaucracy and Representative Government*. Chicago. Aldine.

Niskanen, W.A. (1978) Competition among government bureaus. In J.M. Buchanan (ed) *The Economics of Politics*. I.E.A. Reading 18. Institute of Economic Affairs.

Norbeck, J.S. and Tildon, V.P. (1983) Life stress, social support and emotional disequilibrium in complications of pregnancy. *Journal of Health and Social Behaviour*, 24, 30-46.

Nuckols, K.B., Kassel, J., Kaplan, B. H. (1972) Psychosocial assets, life crises and the prognosis of pregnancy. *American Journal of Epidemiology*, 95, 431-41.

O'Connor, G. (1988) Case management: system and practice. *Social Casework*, 69, 2, 97-106.

Offe, C. (1976) *Industry and Inequality*. London. Edward Arnold.

Orme, J. and Glastonbury, B. (1993) *Care Management: Tasks and Workloads*. London. Macmillan.

Outhwaite, W. (1987) *New Philosophies of Social Science*. London. Macmillan.

Packman, J. (1981) *The Child's Generation*. Oxford. Blackwell.

Paley, J. (1987) Social work and the sociology of knowledge. *British Journal of Social Work*, 17, 169-86.

Parsons, T. (1949) *The Structure of Social Action*. New York. Free Press.

Parton, N. (1979) The natural history of child abuse: a study in social problem management. *British Journal of Social Work*, 9, 4, 431-53.

Parton, N. (1985) *The Politics of Child Abuse*. Basingstoke. Macmillan.

Parkin, M. (1990) *Economics*. Wokingham. Addison Wesley.

Paton, H. J. (1949) *The Moral Law*. London. Hutchinson.

Pavalko, R.M. (1988) *Sociology of Occupations and Professions*. Second Edition. Itasca Illinois. F.E. Peacock.

Payne, G., Dingwall, R., Payne, J. and Carter, M. (1981) *Sociology and Social Research*. London. Routledge and Kegan Paul.

Peacock, A.T. (1980) On the anatomy of collective failure. *Public Finance*, 35, 33-43.

Pearce, D. (1983) *Cost Benefit Analysis*. Second Edition. London. Macmillan.

Pearson, G. (1975) *The Deviant Imagination*. London. Macmillan.

Peck, D. ands Whitlow, D. (1975) *Approaches to Personality Theory*. London. Methuen.

Penfold, P.S. and Walker, G. (1984) *Women and the Psychiatric Paradox*. Milton Keynes. Open University Press.

Penz, P (1986) *Consumer Sovereignty and Human Interest*. Cambridge. Cambridge University Press.

Perlman, H.H. (1957) *Social Casework. A Problem Solving Process*. Chicago. Chicago University Press.

Perlman, H.H. (1979) *Relationships. The Heart of Helping People*. Chicago. University of Chicago Press.

Perrow, C. (1979) *Complex Organisations: A Critical Essay*. Second edition. London. Scott Foreman and Co.

Peters, R.S. (1960) *The Concept of Motivation*. London Rouledge.

Pfohl, S. (1977) The 'discovery' of child abuse. *Social Problems*, 24, 310-24.

Pinker, R. (1971) *Social Theory and Social Policy*. London. Heinemann.

Pippin, J. (1980) *Developing Casework Skills*. London. Sage.

Perlman, H.H. (1979) *Relationship: The Heart of Helping People*. Chicago.

Phelps, E. S. (1985) *Political Economy*. New York. W.W. Norton.

Philp, M. (1979) Notes on the form of knowledge in social work. *Sociological Review*, 27, 1, 83-111.

Picardie, M. (1980) Dreadful moments: existential thoughts on doing social work. *British Journal of Social Work*, 10, 483-490.

Pierce, G.R., Sarason, B.R. and Sarason, I.G. (1990) Integrating social support perspectives, working models personal relationships and situational factors. In S. Duck (ed) *Personal Relationships and Social Support*. London. Sage.

Pincus, A. and Minahan, A. (1973) *Social Work Practice: Model and Method*. Itasca Ill. Peacock.

Plant, R. (1970) *Social and Moral Theory in Casework*. London. Routledge and Kegan Paul.

Plant, R., Lesser, H. and Taylor-Gooby, P. (1982) *Political Philosophy and Social Welfare*. London. Croom Helm.

Platt, S. (1981) Social adjustment as a criterion for treatment success: just what are we measuring? *Psychiatry*, 44, 95-112.

Pollit, C. (1990) *Managerialism and the Public Services*. Oxford. Basil Blackwell.

Popkewitz, T.S. (1987) *Critical Studies in Teacher Education: Its Folklore, Theory and Practice*. London. Falmer.

Popper, K. (1959) *The Logic of Scientific Discovery*. London. Hutchinson.

Popper, K. (1963) *Conjectures and Refutations*. London. Routledge and Kegan Paul.

Popplestone, G. (1971) The ideology of professional community workers. *British Journal of Social Work*, 11, 143-58.

Porter, L. (1937) *Social Work as Cause and Function*. New York.Columbia University Press.

Pratt, J. and Grimshaw, R (1985) A study of social work agency: the occupational routines and working practices of the educational social work service. *Sociological Review*, 33, 1, 106-35.

Ragg, N. (1977) *People Not Cases*. London. Routledge and Kegan Paul.

Rawls, J. (1955) The two concepts of rules. *Philosophical Review*, 64, 9-11.

Rawls, J. (1972) *A Theory of Justice*. Oxford. Oxford University Press.

Reese, S. (1978) *Social Work Face to Face*. London. Routledge.

Reid, W. J. (1972) Target problems, time limits, task structures. *Journal of Education for Social Work*, 8, 2, 58-68.

Reid, W. (1978) *The Task Centred System*. New York. Columbia University Press.

Reid, W. and Epstein, L. (1972) *Task Centred Casework*. New York. Columbia University Press.

Reid, W.J. and Shyne, A. (1969) *Brief and Extended Casework*. New York. Columbia University Press.

Rein, M. and White, S.H. (1981) Knowledge for practice. *Social Service Review*, March, 1-14.

Rensholm, S. (1977) Human needs and political analysis: an examination of framework. In R. Fitzgerald (ed) *Human Needs and Politics*. New South Wales. Rashcutters By. Pergamon.

Rickman, H.P. (1967) *Understanding and the Human Sciences*. London. Heinemann.

Ripple, L. (1964) *Motivation, Capacity and Opportunity: Studies in Casework Theory and Practice*. Chicago. University of Chicago.

Rist, G. (1980) Basic questions about human need. In K. Lederer (ed) *Human Needs*. Camb. Mass. Olgeschelager, Gunn and Ham.

References

Rist, R.C. (1984) On the application of qualitative research to the policy process: an emergent linkage. In L. Barton and S. Walker (ed) *Social Crisis and Educational Research*. London. Croom Helm. p 153-70.

Roberts, R.J. (1981) Further notes on systems analysis of social work practice. *Contemporary Social Work Education*, 4, 3, 220-8.

Roberts, R. (1990) *Lessons From The Past. Issues For Social Work Theory*. London. Tavistock/Routledge.

Robinson, T. (1983) Lessons from elsewhere: the case for enriching the client studies tradition. In M. Fisher (ed) *Speaking of Clients*. Sheffield. JUSSR. University of Sheffield Press.

Robinson. T. (1978) *In Worlds Apart. Professionals and their Clients in the Welfare State*. London. Bedford Square Press.

Robinson, W.S. (1951) The logical structure of Analytic Induction. *American Sociological Review*, 16, 6, 812-8.

Rock, P. (1973) Phenominalism and Essentialism in the sociology of deviance. *Sociology*, 7, 1, 17-29.

Rock, P. (1979) Another commonsense conception of deviancy. *Sociology*, 33, 75-88.

Rogers, C. (1951) *Client Centred Therapy: Its Current Practice, Implications and Theory*. London. Constable.

Rogers, M. (1983) *Sociology, Ethnomthodology and Experience*. Cambridge. Cambridge University Press.

Rojek, C., Peacock, G. and Collins, S. (1988) *Social Work and Recieved Ideas*. London. Routledge.

Rosaldo, M. (1980) *Knowledge and Passion. Ilongot Notions of Self and Social Life*. Cambridge. Cambridge University Press.

Rose, H (1982) Making science feminist. In E. Whitlegge (ed) *The Changing Experience of Women*. Oxford. Martin Robertson.

Ross, L. and Anderson, C.A. (1982) Shortcomings in the attribution process: on the origins and maintenance of erroneous social assessment. In D. Kahneman, P. Slovic and A. Tversky (ed) *Judgement Under Uncertainty*. Cambridge, Cambridge University Press.

Rotenstreich, N. (1977) *Theory and Practice*. The Hague. Martinus Nijhoff.

Rotter, J.B. (1966) *Generalised Expectations For Internal Versus External Locus of Control of Reinforcement*. Psychological Monograph 80.

Runciman, W.G. (1972) *Relative Deprivation and Social Justice*. London. Routledge and Kegan Paul.

Ruscio, K.P. (1987) Many sectors, many professions. In B.R. Clark (ed) *The Academic Profession*. Berkeley. University of California Press.

Ryle, G. (1963) *The Concept of Mind*. Harmondsworth. Penguin Books.

Sainsbury, E. (1969) *Social Diagnosis in Casework*. London. Routledge and Kegan Paul.

Sampson, E.E. (1983) Deconstructing psychology's subject. *Journal of Mind and Behaviour*, 4, 135-64.

Samuelson and Nordhaus, W.D. (1989) *Economics*. Thirteenth edition. London. McGraw Hill.

Satre, J.P. (1948) *Existentialism and Humanism*. London. Methuen.

Sayer, A. (1985) *Method in Social Science: A Realist Approach*. London. Hutchinson.

Schacht, R. (1984) *Classical Modern Philosophers: Descartes to Kant*. London. Routledge and Kegan Paul.

Scheff, T. (1968) Negotiating reality: notes on power in the assessment of responsibility. *Social Problems*, 16, 3-17.

Scheffer, I. (1967) *Science and Subjectivity*. Indianapolis. Bobbs-Merrill.

Schlien, J.M. (1966) Comparison of results with different forms of psychotherapy. In G.E. Stollak, B.C. Guerney and M. Rothberg (ed) *Psychotherapy Research*. Chicago. Rand McNally.

Schoemaker, P. (1982) The expected utility model: its variants, purposes, evidence and limitations. *Journal of Economic Literature*, 20, 529-63.

Schotter, A. (1990) *Free Market Economics*. Oxford. Basil Blackwell.

Schumaker, E.F. (1973) *Small is Beautiful*. London. Bland.

Schur, E.M. (1973) *Radical Non-intervention: Rethinking the Delinquency Problem.* Englewood Cliffs, New Jersey. Prentice Hall.

Schutz, A. (1954) Concept and theory formation in the social sciences. *Journal of Philosophy*, 51, 257-73.

Schutz, A. (1967) *The Phenomenology of the Social World.* Evanston. Northwestern University Press.

Schwartz, W. (1977) Social groupwork: the interactional approach. In J.S. Turner (ed) *Encyclopedia of Social Work*. Vol II. New York. National Association of Social Workers.

Scott, J. (1991) *Social Network Analysis*. London. Sage.

Seed, P. (1990) *Introducing Network Analysis in Social Work*. London. Jessica Kingsley.

Sen, A. (1970) *Collective Choice and Social Welfare*. San Fransisco. Holden Day.

Sen, A. (1977) Rational fools: a critique of the behavioural foundations of economic theory. *Philosophy and Public Affairs*, 6, 317-44.

Sen, A. (1984) *Resources, Values and Development*. Oxford. Blackwell.

Shaw, I. (1975) Making use of research. In H. Jones (ed) *Towards a New Social Work*. London. Routledge.

Shaw, I. (1976) Consumer opinion and social policy: a research review. *Journal of Social Policy.*, 5, 1, 19-32.

Shaw, I. and Walton, R. (1978) What use is social work training? *Community Care*, 18th January, 22-3.

Shaw, I. (1984) Literature review: consumer evaluations of the personal social services. *British Journal of Social Work*, 14, 277-84.

Sheldon, B. (1978) Theory and practice in social work: a re-examination of a tenuous relationship. *British Journal of Social Work*. 8, 1, 1-21

Sheldon, B. (1983) The use of single case experimental designs in the evaluation of social work. *British Journal of Social Work*, 13, 477-499.

Sheldon, B. (1986) Social work effectiveness experiments: review and implications. *British Journal of Social Work*, 16, 223-42.

Sheldon, B. (1987) The psychology of incompetence. In Dept of Social Policy and Social Science, Royal Holloway and Bedford New College University of London (ed) *After Beckford*. Luton. Inprint.

Sheppard, M. (1984) Notes on the use of social explanation to social work. *Issues in Social Work Education*. 4, 1, 27-43.

Sheppard, M. (1985) Communication between general practitioners and a social services department. *British Journal of Social Work*, 15, 25-43.

Sheppard, M. (1987) Dominant images of social work: a British comparison of general practitioners with and without attachment schemes. *International Social Work*, 30, 1, 77-91

Sheppard, M. (1990) *Mental Health: The Role of the Approved Social Worker*. Sheffield. JUSSR. University of Sheffield Press.

Sheppard, M. (1991) *Mental Health Work in the Community: Theory and Practice in Social Work and Community Psychiatric Nursing*. London, Falmer Press.

Sheppard, M. (1992) Client satisfaction, brief intervention and interpersonal skills. *Social Work and Social Sciences Review*, 3, 2, 124-150.

Sheppard, M. (1993) Client satisfaction, extended intervention and interpersonal skills in community mental health. *Journal of Advanced Nursing*, 18, 246-259.

Sheppard, M. (1993) Maternal depression and child care: the significance for social work and social work research. *Adoption and Fostering*, 17, 2, 10-17.

References

Sheppard, M. (1993) The external context for social support: towards a theoretical formulation of social support, child care and maternal depression. *Social Work and Social Sciences Review*, 4, 1, 27-59.

Sheppard, M. (1993) Theory for approved social work: the use of the compulsory admissions assessment schedule. *British Journal of Social Work*, 23, 231-235.

Sheppard, M. (1994) Child Care, social support and maternal depression: a review and application of findings. *British Journal of Social Work.*, 24, 287-310

Sheppard, M. (1995) Social work, social science and practice wisdom. *British Journal of Social Work*. Forthcoming.

Strean, H.F. (1971) *Social Casework: Theories in Action*. Metuchin, NJ. Scarecrow Press.

Shulman, L. (1984) *The Skills of Helping*. Itasca, Illinois. F.E. Peacock.

Shulman, L. (1992) *The Skills of Helping*. Second Edition. Itaska, Illinois. Peacock.

Sibeon, R. (1982) Theory-practice symbolisation. A critical review of the Hardiker/Davies debate. *Issues in Social Work Education*, 2, 2, 119-47.

Sibeon, R. (1990) *Towards a New Sociology of Social Work*. Aldershot. Avebury.

Silverman (1985) *Qualitative Methodology and Sociology*. Aldershot. Gower.

Simpkin, M. (1979) *Trapped Within Welfare: Surviving Social Work*. London. Macmillan.

Simon, H.A. (1955) A behavioural model of rational choice. *Quarterly Journal of Economics*, 69, 174-83.

Sinclair, I., Parker, R., Leat, D. and Williams, J. (1990) *The Kaleidoscope of Care: A Review of Research on Welfare Provision For Elderly People*. London. HMSO for NISW.

Sinclair, I. (1992) Social work research: its relevance to social work and social work education. *Issues in Social Work Education*, 11, 2, 65-80.

Siporin, M (1975) *Introduction to Social Work Practice*. New York. Macmillan.

Smale, G., Tuson, G., Biehal, N. and Marsh, P./Department of Health (1993) *Empowerment, Assessment, Care Management and the Skilled Worker*. London. HMSO.

Smalley, R. (1967)*Theory for Social Work Practice*. New York. Columbia University Press.

Smith, D. (1978) K is mentally ill. *Sociology*, 12, 25-53.

Smith, E. (1984) Model of social inference process. *Psychological Review*, 91, 392-413.

Smith, E. (1989) Procedural efficiency: general and specific components and effects on social judgements. *Journal of Experimental Social Psychology*, 25, 500-523.

Smith, G. (1980) *Social Need*. London. Routledge and Kegan Paul.

Smith, J. (1980) Self as experience in Maori culture. In P. Heelas and A. Lock (eds) *Indigenous Psychologies*. London. Academic Press.

Snyder, M. (1984) When beliefs create reality. In L. Berkowitz (ed) *Advances in Experimental Social Psychology*. Vol 17. London. Academic Press.

Snyder, M. and Campbell, B. (1980) Testing hypotheses about other people: the role of hypothesis. *Personal and Social Psychology Bulletin*, 6, 421-26.

Snyder, M. and Swann, W. (1978) Hypothesis testing processes in social interaction. *Journal of Personality and Social Psychology*, 36, 1202-12.

Spector, M. and Kituse, J.I. (1977) *Constructing Social Problems*. London. Cummings.

Spicker, P. (1990) Mental handicap and citizenship. *Journal of Applied Philosophy*, 7, 2, 139-151.

Srole, L. (1956) Social integration and certain corolories: an exploratory analysis. *American Sociological Review*, 21, 709-16.

Strasser, H. (1976) *The Normative Base of Sociology*. London. Routledge and Kegan Paul.

Steier, F. (ed) (1991) *Research and Reflexivity*. London. Sage.

Sternberg, R.J. (1984) Toward a triarchic theory of human intelligence. *Behavioural Science*, 7, 269-315.

Stevenson, O. (1971) Knowledge for social work. *British Journal of Social Work*, 1, 2, 225-7.

Stevenson, O. and Parsloe, P. (1978) *Social Services Teams: The Practitioners' View*. London. HMSO.

Strauss, A., Fagerhaugh, S., Suczek, B. and Weiner, C. (1982) Sentimental work. *Sociology of Health and Illness*. 4, 3.

Sugden, R. (1986) New developments in the theory of choice under uncertainty. *Bulletin of Economic Research*, 38, 1, 1-24.

Sugden, R. and Williams, A. (1978) *The Principles of Cost Benefit Analysis*. London. Oxford.

Taylor, C. (1973) Neutrality in political science. In A. Ryan (ed) *The Philosophy of Social Explanation*. London. Oxford University Press.

Taylor, C. (1991) What's wrong with negative liberty. In Miller, D. (ed) *Liberty*. Oxford. Oxford University Press.

Taylor, I. (1993) Self directed learning and social work education: a critical analysis. *Issues in Social Work Education*, 13, 1, 3-24.

Taylor, I., Walton, P. and Young, J. (1973) *The New Criminology*. London. Routledge and Kegan Paul.

Taylor, S.E. and Crocker, J. (1981) Schematic bases of social information processing. In E.T. Higgfins, C.P. Herman and M.P. Zanna (ed) *Social Cognition: The Ontario Symposium*. Vol 1. Hillside, NJ. Erlbaum.

Thomas, D. (1983) *The Making of Community Work*. London. Allen and Unwin.

Thomas, W.I. and Thomas, D.S. (1982) *The Child in America*. New York. Knopf.

Thompson, G. (1987) *Needs*. Routledge.

Thorpe, D., Smith, D., Green, C. and Paley, J. (1980) *Out of Care: The Community Support of Juvenile Offenders*. London. Allen and Unwin.

Thyer, B. (1993) Social work theory and practice research: the approach of logical positivism. *Social Work and Social Science Review*, 4, 1, 5-26.

Timms, N. (1963) *Social Casework*. London. Routledge and Kegan Paul.

Timms, N. (1983) *Social Work Values: An Enquiry*. London. Routledge and Kegan Paul.

Tobin, J (1970) On limiting the domain of inequality. *Journal of Law and Economics*, 13, 263-77.

Tolsen, E.R. and Reid, W.J. (1994) *Generalist Practice: A Task Centred Approach*. New York. Columbia University Press.

Towle, C. (1969) Social work: cause and function. In H.H. Perlman (ed) *Helping: Charlotte Towle on Social Work and Social Casework*. Chicago. University of Chicago Press.

Trigg, R. (1982) The sociobiological view of man. In Brown, S.C. (ed) *Objectivity and Cultural Divergence*. Cambridge. The Press Syndicate of the University of Cambridge.

Truax, C. and Carkhuff, R. (1967) *Towards Effective Counselling and Psychotherapy*. Chicago. Aldine.

Tullock, G. (1976) *The Vote Motive*. London. Institute of Economic Affairs.

Valk, M. (1983) Imaginative literature and social work education. *Issues in Social Work Education*, 3, 1, 17-26.

Van Rossam, E., Deijkers, R. and Hamer, R. (1985) Students' learning conceptions and their interpretation of significant learning concepts. *Higher Education*, 14, 617-41.

Verhave, R. and Van Hoorn, W. (1984) The Temporalization of the Self. In K.J. Gergen and M.M. Gergen (ed) *Historical Social Psychology*. Hillside. New Jersey. Erlbaum.

Vieil, H.O. (1985) Dimensions of social support: a conceptual framework for research. *Social Psychiatry*, 20, 156-62.

References

Von Bertalanffy, L. (1973) *General Systems Theory*. Harmondsworth. Penguin Books.

Wallace, C. and Bruce, S. (1983) Accounting for action: defending the common sense heresy. *Sociology*, 17, 97-111.

Waltz, M., Badura, B., Pfaff, H. and Thomas, S. (1988) Marriage and psychological consequences of heart attack: a longitudinal study of adaptation to chronic illness. *Social Science and Medicine*, 27, 2, 149-58.

Warham, J. (1977) *An Open Case*. London. Routledge and Kegan Paul.

Warner, N. (1986) Social work: a cautionary tale. *Social Services Insight*, 1st March, 13-15.

Warner, W. L. and Lunt, P.S. (1941) *The Social Life of a Modern Community*. New Haven. Yale University Press.

Watson, D. (1978) Social services in a nutshell. In Timms, N. and Watson, D. (ed) *Philosophy in Social Work*. London. Routledge and Kegan Paul.

Watson, D. (1980) *Caring For Strangers*. London. Routledge and Kegan Paul.

Webb, D. (1981) Themes and continuities in radical and traditional social work. *British Journal of Social Work*, 11, 143-58.

Weber, M. (1946) *Essays in Sociology*. London. Oxford University Press.

Weber, M. (1949) *The Methodology of Social Sciences*. New York. Free Press.

Weber, M. (1969) *The Theory of Social and Economic Organisation*. Glencoe. Illinois. Free Press.

Weeks, D. (1980) Organisations and Decision Making. In Salaman, G. and Thompson, K. (ed) *Control and Ideology In Organisations*. Milton Keynes. Open University Press.

Weick, A. (1981) Issues of power in social work practice. In Weick, A. and S. Vandiver (ed) *Women, Power and Change. Selected Papers from Social Work Practice in a Sexist Society*. New York. National Association of Social Workers.

Weir, M. (1977) Are computer systems and humanised work compatible? In Otway, R.M. (ed) *Humanising the workplace*. London.

Weiss, R. S. (1974) The provisions of social relationships. In Rubin, Z. (ed) *Doing Unto Others*. Englewood Cliffs, New Jersey. Basic Books.

Weiss, R.S. (1978) Couple relationships. In M. Corbin (ed) *The Couple*. New York. Penguin.

Wexler, P. (1983) *Critical Social Psychology*. London. Routledge and Kegan Paul.

White Paper (1989) *Caring For People: Community Care in the Next Decade and Beyond*. Cmnd 849. London. HMSO.

Whitaker, J.K. and Garbarino, J. (1983) *Social Support Networks*. New York. Aldine.

Wilcox, B.L. and Vernberg, E.M. (1985) Conceptual and theoretical dilemmas facing social support research. In I.G. Sarason and B.R. Sarason (ed) *Social Support. Theory, Research and Applications*. Dordecht. The Netherlands. Martinus Nijhoff Publishers.

Wilding, P. (1982) *Professional Power and Social Welfare*. London. Routledge and Kegan Paul.

Wilkes, R. (1981) *Social Work and Undervalued Groups*. London. Tavistock.

Williams, A. in Culyer, A. (1974) *Needs and the National Health Service*. London. Martin Robertson.

Williams, A. (1990) *Health Economics, Priority Settings and Medical Ethics: Implications for Multiple Sclerosis*. University of York. Centre for Health Economics.

Williamson, O.E. (1975) *Markets and Hierarchies: Analysis and Anti Trust Implications*. New York. Free Press.

Wilson, T.P. (1974) Normative and interpretive paradigms in sociology. In J.D. Douglas (ed) *Understanding Everyday Life*. London. Routledge and Kegan Paul.

Winch, P. (1958) *The Idea of a Social Science and its Relationship to Philosophy*. London. Routledge and Kegan Paul.

Winch, P. (1964) Understanding a Primitive Society. *American Philosophical Quarterly*, 1, 307-24.

Wolf, C. (1979) A theory of non market failure: framework for implementation analysis. *Journal of Law and Economics*, 22, 107-39.

Wood, R. (1978) Casework effectiveness: a new look at the research evidence. *Social Work*, 23, 6, 437-59.

Woolgar, S. (1988) (ed) *Knowledge and Reflexivity*. London. Sage.

Woolgar, S. and Pawlich, D. (1985a) Ontological gerrymandering: the anatomy of social problem explanations. *Social Problems*, 32, 214-27.

Woolgar, S. and Pawlich, D. (1985b) How shall we move beyond constructivism? *Social Problems*, 33, 2, 159-162.

Wootton, B. (1959) *Social Science and Social Pathology*. London. George Allen and Unwin.

Wright Mills, C. (1960) *Images of Man: The Classic Tradition in Sociological Theory*. New York. George Braziller.

Yates, P.D. (1985) Science and sensibility. Mimeo. University of Sussex.

Younghusband, E. (1951) *Social Work in Britain. Supplementary Report*. Edinburgh. Constable.

Younghusband, E. (1971) *Social Work and Social Change*. London. Allen and Unwin.

Znaniecki, F. (1934) *The Method of Sociology*. New York. Rinehart.

Zola, I. (1972) Medicine as an institution of social control. *Sociological Review*, 20, 4.

Index